AMERICA IN
1900

AMERICA IN
1900

NOEL JACOB KENT

M.E. Sharpe
Armonk, New York
London, England

Library of Congress Cataloging-in-Publication Data

Kent, Noel J.
America in 1900 / Noel Jacob Kent.
p. cm.
Includes bibliographical references and index.
ISBN 0-7656-0595-3 (hardcover : alk. paper)
1. United States—History—1865–1921. 2. United States—Civilization—1865–1918.
3. Nineteen hundred, A.D. I. Title.

E711.K46 2000
973.8´8—dc21

99-089342

Printed in the United States of America

The paper used in this publication meets the minimum requirements of
American National Standard for Information Sciences
Permanence of Paper for Printed Library Materials,
ANSI Z 39.48-1984.

∞

BM (c)   10   9   8   7   6   5   4   3   2   1

For Chelsea and Daniel

And in memory of my father,
Alexander Kent

Table of Contents

Acknowledgments

The field work for this study was aided immeasurably by grants from the National Endowment for the Humanities and the University of Hawaii Manoa Research Relations Fund and Social Sciences Research Institute. My thanks to the staffs of the University of Hawaii at Manoa Library, the Library of Congress, the Smithsonian Institution, the Wisconsin State Historical Society, the Oregon State University Library, Portland State University Library, Honolulu and Seattle Public Libraries, the Hagley Museum, the University of Wisconsin–Madison Library, the University of Washington Library, and the Bancroft Library at the University of California Berkeley for their patient and gracious treatment of an often confused stranger who wandered into their midst. I owe special thanks to Norma Kent, Edie and Frank Mahlmann, Jonathan Okamura, William Chaloupka, Franklin Odo, Lynn Sasaki, Peter Manicas and Jeremy Bentley for their support at various times during the course of this project.

Introduction

This study is a looking glass into the United States circa 1900. It is concerned with understanding the nation's trajectory as the nineteenth century turned into the twentieth, the lives that different kinds of Americans were living, and how various perspectives and myths helped them to interpret and cope with the changes they were experiencing.

These changes were profound, indeed. What was locking into place, as the English historian Geoffrey Barraclough has written in *An Introduction to Contemporary History* (Pelican, N.Y., p. 16), were "the basic structural changes which have shaped the modern world." In the United States, a series of overlapping revolutions in business, technology, and communications and the movement of people out of rural areas to cities were altering the country's physical and psychological landscapes. The way Americans worked and played was being transformed. Convinced as they were that theirs was the country of the future, Americans still remained divided about what that future might look like and how to reach it. Massive labor unrest sparked by growing social inequalities and an epidemic of racial violence in both the North and South exposed some of the nation's faultlines. Doubts were appearing (even among those welcoming the United States' new role as a world power) about the wisdom of soldiers in blue fighting a protracted war in the remote Philippines.

This work is also about making connections between then and now, of utilizing the years around 1900 as a mirror for reflecting upon our own time. This might seem a curious venture. After all, looking back from 2000, the United States of a century ago seems enormously remote, framed in photogravure images of top-hatted gentlemen clad in Prince Albert frock coats and whalebone-corseted ladies carrying lace-trimmed parasols, John Philip Sousa marches, and houses bedecked with towers and cupolas.

And the twentieth century has, of course, witnessed phenomenal transformations. What then were sleepy, backwater towns are now sprawling metropolises. Far-flung suburbs, superhighways, airports, and satellite dishes dot our external landscape. Computers, CD players, televisions, and faxes are fixtures in our homes and offices. The rhythms of daily life have altered beyond recognition, as have the vocabulary and symbols we use to give meanings to things.

Nevertheless, one might wonder if a 1900 Bostonian or San Franciscan suddenly catapulted into the Massachussetts Avenue or Market Street of today would not be terribly surprised by the way things have turned out. Certainly, they would marvel at the range and sophistication of year 2000 machines and technologies, not to mention the abundance currently available to Americans. None of this, however, would be incomprehensible. After all, by the year "double-zero," the Industrial Revolution was already rolling along in high gear, Americans were becoming accustomed to adaptation as a way of life, and a consumer revolution was emergent on the horizon.

By no coincidence, it was also around the beginning of the twentieth century that the core dilemmas that confront us today were appearing more or less full-blown. Geoffrey Barraclough says it well: "Contemporarary history begins when the problems which are actual in the world today first take visible shape." In that sense, we are still living in the same epoch as the Americans of 1900 *(An Introduction to Contemporary History, p. 20)*.

Our travelers in time, in fact, scanning this morning's headlines or television news would find much that resonates. Charges of monopoly practices against Bill Gates and Microsoft might easily recall the bitter controversy during their own time surrounding the machinations of John D. Rockefeller's Standard Oil Company, or Henry Havemeyer's American Sugar. Mergers on the scale of Exxon and Mobil would sound quite familiar. Reports of U.S. military action in the Middle East or the Balkans might conjure up the war in the Philippines. News stories about technological breakthroughs, trade disputes with China and Europe, racial problems and violence in Chicago or Texas, high levels of crime and frequent shootings, rising income gaps between rich and poor, volatile stock market prices, homelessness in the cities, the dangers of immigration, the controlling role of special interest money in elections and on Capitol Hill—all would have something déjà vu about them.

So for all the water that has flowed under the national bridge during the last century, a core of 1900's most complex and difficult issues remain salient unto our own day. If this has a logic of sorts, it is that, contrary to Henry Ford, history is not "bunk," and that the United States as it entered the twenty-first century was still being shaped by what had both happened and not happened as it entered the twentieth.

Here we are reminded of the mysterious and deep-reaching presence of the past in the present—how the deeds and omissions of forgotten ancestors continue to reverberate among us today. Ironically, much of what our time travelers are viewing is none other than the legacy bequeathed by their own generation of Americans to the current one. What was the nature of that legacy and what lessons can we in 2000 learn from it?

AMERICA IN
1900

Part I

In the Year Double-Zero

Chapter 1

New Year's Day 1900

> We step upon the threshold of 1900 which leads to the new
> century facing a still brighter dawn of civilization.
>
> —*New York Times*, December 31, 1899

> The annals of the world afford no parallel to the moral and
> physical advancement which has come to the United States in
> the rounded century which has passed since the death of the
> first president.
>
> —*Lesley's Illustrated Weekly*, January 6, 1900

> We're a gr-reat people. We are that. An' th' best ov it is, we
> know we are're.
>
> —"Mr. Dooley," Peter Finley Dunne, 1898

The first morning of 1900 arrived in Washington, D.C., crisp and cold, accompanied by a night's fall of fresh snow. While some 2,000 citizens queued patiently for admission to the White House and the traditional New Year's presidential handshake, inside the mansion's lavishly furnished Blue Parlor room Mr. William McKinley and his frail wife received multitudes of diplomats, Supreme Court justices, congressmen, and other notables. A Marine band in full-dress red uniforms provided musical embellishment.

The night before, a nation of 75 million had found innumerable ways of celebrating the coming of the new year. Americans had thrown open houses and parties, gathered together and sung such popular ditties as "There'll Be a Hot Time in the Old Town Tonight" and "I'd Leave My Happy Home for You," and at midnight touched off fireworks, blew whistles, rung bells, and fired their Winchesters into the air. In New Orleans, boisterous crowds along Canal Street hailed carriages carrying flamboyantly attired women holding Roman candles. People also prayed, attended church socials, sat rocking on farmhouse porches, or did more or less what they did on any Sunday evening.

Despite the layer of snow covering much of the nation, New Year's Day was actively celebrated. Winnebago Indians gathered at their chief's house in Chicago to do war dances. In Greeley, Colorado, the Odd Fellows held a ball at the Armory Hall, while on Denver's Fifteenth Street, five hundred hungry people had turkey dinners served to them by volunteers. Cincinnati's Queen City Club luncheon featured a two-foot-high cake shaped in the form of a wheelbarrow. Eggnog and cigars were freely dispensed. The streets of fashionable neighborhoods in Houston were crowded with carriages as people exchanged visits. The members of a Boston bicycle club, the Metropolitan Wheelmen, celebrated by mounting their iron steeds and journeying over to the quaint seaboard town of Newburyport.

In the nation's largest city, clusters of people promenaded along Eighth Avenue and lined up for popular Broadway shows like *Sherlock Holmes* and Ben Hur, or to see ragtime singer May Irwin in the title role of *Sister Mary* at the Bijou. Along Fifth Avenue carriages carried men in top hats and women in fur coats to venues like the Holland House and Murray Hill, where hotel chefs were artistically fashioning table scenes depicting Neptune, Venus, and Mephisto. Up in the Bronx's Van Cortlandt Park rink, ice skaters were out in force, while in lower Manhattan the homeless slept on cellar gratings on Twenty-third Street, a tenement fire put a dozen families out on the street, and laughing boys threw snowballs and sledded in Tompkins Square Park.

The world was not particularly peaceful this January 1, perhaps a harbinger of what the coming century would bring. In the Philippines, three U.S. Army columns were beginning a coordinated drive across the island of Luzon aimed at rooting the "rebel" commander Emiliano Aguinaldo and his troops out of populated areas and destroying their capacity for combat. Two battalions of the Thirty-ninth Infantry occupied Cabuyan at the cost of twenty-four Filipino and two American lives. Heavy fighting occurred on the road to the town of Santa Rosa, while elsewhere, U.S. gunboats bombarded Filipino positions.

Encircled British soldiers at Mafeking and Ladysmith in South Africa were making sorties against the Boers, whose fighting prowess had won the Americans' admiration. The British General John French was announcing the imminent capture of Boer-held Colesburg. Meanwhile, January 1 had been chosen by Wilhelm, the mercurial German kaiser, for an ominous, saber-rattling speech saluting the German army as "the embodiment of our history" and proclaiming his intention to double the size of Germany's navy in order to secure his nation's "place in the sun."[1]

But these were specks on the distant horizon and generally ignored amid New Year's Day celebrations.

What also was passed over in the media and elsewhere was any meaningful attempt at assessing the tumultuous decade just ending. The late nineteenth century had been an era of massive, pulverizing change, and the Gay Nineties had brought its epic conflicts and contradictions to a head. Quite suddenly, the expansive vistas of an earlier America seemed to have vanished: "Now the nation seemed filled. The cities huge and choked, corporations omnipresent and overpowering, the frontier closed, immigrants everywhere."[2]

Life was culturally ajar and dislocated. Throughout the nineties, tensions and conflicts were being thrown up faster than the capacity of existing institutions to cope with them. If the United States had entered the modern industrial age, then the emotional loyalties of Americans still seemed rooted in an earlier era. Big corporations had not yet gained widespread legitimacy. Many citizens, such as skilled artisans making a last-ditch defense of their old autonomy, found they could no longer protect cherished lifestyles. The ending of the great spree of railroad building seemed to leave the nation without an engine to drive economic expansion.

Not only was the United States still in the midst of a transition from a small town–rural commercial and agriculture economy to an urban industrial one, but the genteel middle-class mores of the Victorian Age were giving way to a popular culture exemplified by rowdy popular music like ragtime and dances such as the cakewalk.[3]

Particularly unsettling was the realization that the free, open western frontier had passed. "And now four hundred years from the discovery of America, after a hundred years of life under the Constitution," the University of Wisconsin's Frederick Jackson Turner had intoned in 1893, "the frontier has gone, and with its going has closed the first period of American history."[4]

What Turner had done rather brilliantly was to recreate the frontier as a mythic story of national self-creation and loss. He argued that the process of conquering and civilizing the continent had been decisive for shaping the American national character, and inspiring citizens with the love for freedom and autonomy. So if "the West was another name for opportunity," a channel for national energy and talent, and a safety valve for the frustrated, then its demise as a frontier amounted to a catastrophe. To the pessmistic

Turner, nothing less than the future of American democracy was at risk.[5]

So Frederick Jackson Turner's analysis of the frontier as the crucial element in their history both nourished Americans' sense of a heroic past and unleashed fears of what a frontierless future might bring. If his analysis was evasive of the willful brutality, greed, and violence (amounting to genocide) found along various American frontiers, it was an evasion the people of his generation were happy enough with. Turner's story seemed compelling and scary enough—especially to a group of influential political, media, and military figures, led by Theodore Roosevelt, Senator Henry Cabot Lodge, Henry Adams, Josiah Strong, and Admiral Alfred Mahan, dedicated to making the United States an imperial power.[6]

Deeply anxious about the chaos in American life, the imperial party was convinced that internal tensions might be relieved and national confidence restored through overseas expansion. War and conquest represented an escape from the historic dead end they perceived the country to be in, the means of overcoming an intolerable *fin de siècle* blues. And no one epitomized this mood better than the talented, inexhaustibly exhuberant Roosevelt, in 1898 strategically situated as assistant secretary of the navy.[7]

The program they advocated mixed up elements of idealism, commercial selfishness, racism, and the "strategic innocence" Americans habitually bring to foreign affairs. It was vastly ambitious: Build a world-class navy and overseas bases to anchor it, establish hegemony in the Caribbean and a U.S.-controlled isthmian canal, annex Hawaii, and gain access for American goods to Asian markets. If this was accomplished through war, so much the better. The warrior qualities of the Anglo-Saxon were threatened by the decadence of modern life and needed rekindling.

The mid-nineties were defined by hard times. Americans throughout the nineteenth century had experienced divisions along shifting lines of class, race, ethnicity, section, gender, and religion. Now economic distress intensified these cleavages.

Agricultural prices had been in decline since the eighties. Out there in the hinterland of wheat, corn, cotton, and tobacco were the same pioneers who had listened only too well to Horace Greeley's injunction to "Go west" and sought fortune and economic freedom along the new frontier. But they were being savaged by dismal crop prices, peonage to the railroads and banks, and, having trekked into semi-arid lands, drought.

A fierce hue and cry arose across the southwest and trans-Mississippi Valley and grew in intensity through the nineties. Farmers alliances sponsored an intricate network of cooperative and educational associations and, in the form of the People's party, or Populists, put governors, senators, and state legislatures in office pledged to curb the "Big Money Power" of eastern capital.[8]

8

They denounced the concentration of wealth in the hands of a few thousand families (the 1890 census revealed that the richest 1 percent of Americans had more total income than the poorest 50 percent) and indicted both major parties as creatures of business and enemies of farmers, workers, and the jobless.

People's party supporters wanted the government on their side, trusts reined in, railroads regulated, a scandalously corrupt and inefficent political system reformed, and "reasonable work and fair reward" made available. A social order become antihuman needed fixing. The eloquent writer and attorney Henry Demarest Lloyd defined the Populist goal as "a fuller, nobler, richer, kinder life for every man, woman and child in the ranks of humanity."[9]

Most Populists had no quarrel with dominant American values built around aspirations for individual business and financial success. They carried a mystique about the solidarity of "producers" and were much given to seeking out conspiracies to explain their ills. Yet, the creation of a just social order and a more cooperative path of economic modernization were central to their mission. What they had launched was a heavily evangelical and spiritual crusade, combining religious and political elements, to democratize political and economic life, temper economic ruthlessness, and make the quality of life of ordinary folk the measure of progress. At its boldest and most visionary, populism posed an alternative line of national development to "the sky's the limit/anything goes" mode of late nineteenth-century capitalism.[10]

After huge electoral gains in 1892, the Populists claimed the loyalties of a sizable group of voters in a score of states. But to emerge as an authentic national force, they would have to extend their constituency from southern and western agrarians to midwestern farmers and eastern workers, a formidable, if not impossible, task.

Nothing really had prepared the country for the full-blown depression that arrived in 1893, the nation's most catastrophic to date. Goods could not find markets. Agricultural exports to Europe crashed, imports soared, and gold poured out of the country; 15,000 factories and 550 banks closed their doors. Railroads were heaped on the bankruptcy courts like pickup sticks. Three million were jobless and wage cutting was widespread. The market prices of grains and cotton nose-dived and Great Plains farmers by the thousands lost their holdings. Real income declined 18 percent from 1892 to 1894. "The country began to be overrun with tramps," ran one contemporary account. "Men out of work and stopping to beg a meal and permission to sleep in barns . . . began to be seen daily. . . . "[11]

It seemed to at least some within the nation's elite that unless prosperity could be restored, the country might lurch out of control. In New York financial circles, men talked of the imminence of "revolution," and armories were fitted out in major cities. Newspapers speculated on the implications of "the forming of military organizations by the unemployed."[12]

When a few hundred of Jacob Coxey's comic-opera "army" arrived in front of the Capitol after a march from Ohio (Coxey called it "a petition to Washington with boots on") to demand federal public works and support for the jobless, they were brusquely dispersed by troops. President Cleveland was advised by businessmen to vastly increase the army. His secretary of state, Walter Gresham, a man acutely sensitive to the inequalities and chaos of the new industrial order, wrote to a friend: "What is transpiring in Pennsylvania, Ohio, Indiana, Illinois and in regions west of there, may fairly be viewed as symptoms of revolution."[13]

These were years when businessmen and their political allies routinely used hard-knuckled repression. Indictments were issued against union organizers and striking workers for fabricated criminal conspiracies. Chicago railwaymen and Idaho miners were imprisoned or shot. The July 1894 Pullman strike, which immobilized vast stretches of the nation's railways, petered out when thousands of federal troops were deployed by U.S. Attorney General Richard Olney against strikers, and union leaders like Eugene Debs were jailed. In 1897, the same Pennsylvania state militia that had previously broken the Homestead strike suppressed a major strike in the coalfields.

Certainly much of the ferocity of the nineties derived from, as Alan Trachtenberg argues, its being "a period of trauma, of change so swift and thorough that many Americans seemed unable to fathom the extent of the upheaval." Farmers and workers were shaken by the decline of abundance, the dashing of both established routines and future possibilities, the "loss of individual mastery."[14]

In such a context, nativism and scapegoating of "others" inevitably thrived. Anti–Roman Catholic feeling ran high, its main vehicle the American Protective Association (APA). Founded in 1887 by one Henry F. Bowers, the son of a German officer, the APA's basic message was that Jesuitic conspiracies were threatening the nation. The 1893–1894 economic collapse drove a surge in both APA membership and the political clout it wielded. It (and similar organizations flourishing during the mid-nineties) tapped a strain of paranoid nativism seeking out internal enemies to explain American dreams gone sour.[15]

Recent immigrants came under assault as both undigestible and undesirable. Prominent intellectuals argued that the immigration tide theatened the nation's "Anglo-Saxon" heritage and was overwhelming its carrying capacity. A popular movement to restrict immigration gathered force, moving the U.S. Congress in 1896 to legislate unprecedented restrictions on those seeking to enter. Acts of violence included the lynching of eleven Italians in New

Orleans. Asians living in California were singled out for discriminatory legislation. Those discontented with federal gold policy castigated Jewish international financers for causing the nation's troubles.[16]

The nineties also witnessed the finale to post–Civil War black hopes for equality. In the former Confederate states, conservative Bourbon economic elites, deeply disturbed by Populist class agitation against them, had entered alliances with poor whites. African Americans were the designated scapegoats, their civil and human rights sacrificed to consummate this reconciliation. In 1896 came the Supreme Court's watershed *Plessy* v. *Ferguson* decision, upholding the legality of segregation. New state constitutions disenfranchised black voters en masse, while white supremacy was fortified by frequent acts of vigilante violence and lynch law.

The historian Richard Hofstadter has argued that the debacles of the nineties brought on a "psychic crisis" among some Americans and a demand for outlets to both vent frustrations and express genuinely humanistic impulses. Such an environment made the imperial party's vision of the United States as a global power and world leader tremendously appealing.[17]

Thus came the outpouring of popular support for a buildup of the U.S. Navy, and the wildly toughest-kid-on-the-block jingoism that dominated U.S. foreign policy after 1895. Rumblings of war with Germany, then Chile, and finally Great Britain were heard, and there were moments when a visceral, evangelical American nationalism seemed anxious to take on anybody or everybody. Immense pressures on the stolid, cautious William McKinley led him to rebuff fairly major Spanish concessions on Cuba following the February 1898 destruction of the U.S. battleship *Maine*. Washington would dictate the island's future or there would be war. When war did indeed come and the U.S. bumbled to victory over a moribund Spain, rhetoric about defending the human rights and aspirations of the Cubans quickly gave way to a far different, far more imperial vision.[18]

Ultimately, the New Industrial Order handily survived the challenges of the nineties. A turning point was the decisive triumph of Republican William McKinley over William Jennings Bryan's free silver crusade in the 1896 presidential election. The huge Republican advantage in funding and press support, fears that free coinage of silver would lead to the ruin of modest savers, and the adroit handling of the candidate by national campaign manager Marcus Alonzo Hanna all contributed to the outcome.

But it was also a victory forged from popular belief in the return of good times and the country's unlimited potential. Crucial voting blocs like midwestern farmers and eastern workers were attracted by slogans heralding McKinley as "the advance agent of prosperity."

At the outset of the election campaign, the populist People's party, desperate to break out of its regional isolation and appeal to a national audience, and swept up in the Bryan euphoria, had endorsed the Democratic presidential nominee. Following McKinley's decisive victory, the party's always fragile unity broke on the issues of war and intense divisions over continued alliance with Democrats. With the party's passing withered the vision Populists had offered of the "cooperative commonwealth."

Yet, the Sturm and Drang of the middle nineties had in some way rent the sublime sense of American faith, optimism, and harmony. Things that simply were not supposed to happen in the land of perpetual progress had indeed occurred. And the undercurrent of anxiety people felt was accentuated by an unprecedented pace of economic and social change that showed no prospect of slowing down.

The modern world was a place, thought pioneer feminist Olive Schreiner, ". . . where nothing is as it was, and all things are assuming new shapes and relations." The new economic and social order was forcing Americans to make painful accommodations, a relentless economic revolution reorganizing lives and identities across the continent. The "losers" were legion. Rural youth found good farm land harder to get and more expensive. New divisions of labor into specialized tasks separated workers from the products they made. A wide spectrum of citizens felt a definite lack of control over the larger changes occurring in their lives and were left wondering about the meaning of the vaunted American "democracy."[19]

Among native-stock Americans there was a pervasive sense of having irrevocably lost something of value— thus the turn-of-the-century popularity of Booth Tarkington and Joel Chandler Harris, two authors whose forte was evoking a wistful nostalgia for an earlier, simpler, and mythically harmonious America. Additional evidence of a lingering crisis of confidence is found in reports by European travelers in the United States of constantly being interrogated as to "what do you think of America" and told point-blank that this was the "finest nation on God Almighty's Earth."[20]

There were also the loudly publicized fears of affluent younger white men that American ("Anglo-Saxon") manhood was being endangered by soft urban living and bureaucratic jobs. For a generation bred on fathers' and uncles' tales of Gettysburg and Antietam, the taste for action was palpable. President McKinley had called for 125,000 volunteers to fight Spain and a million men had rushed to enlist. The quick end of the war had left many of these fellows still groping for "manly" new adventures. "For a million dollars you cannot lawfully kill a buffalo," wrote one critic. "There is no West. Our young men long for one more such country. America is . . . a country with mission still unfulfilled, yet certain of fulfillment."[21]

Yet, on this January 1, the relative peace and domestic prosperity of the last eighteen months seemed to have vanquished other realities. Given the national talent for historical amnesia, the rough upheavals of the nineties were whisked aside as only a temporary glitch in the program. Dominant cultural assumptions were not under challenge; relatively few people were questioning why so much sacrifice was being exacted in the name of the march of "progress." If such silence signified denial, it also meant that as the United States entered 1900, it appeared to be on a great and irresistible roll.

The "splendid little war" with Spain had accomplished everything its promoters had hoped for and more. Clear-cut victory on both Caribbean and Pacific fronts brought a new role for the United States in the global arena. The first conflict since the Civil War thirty years before, it had been a powerful stimulus for reconciliation between North and South. Military parades of returning soldiers and a stream of newspaper and magazine articles kept the victory-at-arms vividly before the public. The United States now held dominion over the Philippines, Puerto Rico, Hawaii, Guam, and Cuba, the Caribbean was an American lake, and the Pacific well on its way to becoming so. Mounting the world stage as a new world power had swollen the national "brag."

In fact, in late September 1899, Admiral George Dewey, whose victory at Manila Bay had made him a national cult figure, sailed into New York harbor to a reception unprecedented in United States history. Dewey means "heroic achievement," editorialized *Harper's Weekly*. "He stands for what we think we are . . . a manly discharge of our duty to civilization in the Asian archipelago." Impeccable in his naval blues and epaulettes, the white mustached, sixty-two-year-old admiral (like a conquering proconsul of ancient Rome) reviewed an immense parade flowing under a seventy-foot triumphal arch built for the occasion on Fifth Avenue. Two million people watched and cheered. Throughout that fall, Dewey made a grand tour across the continent, stopping in various cities for similar parades of homage.[22]

Economic recovery accompanied military triumph. In late 1898, the economy had gone into boomtime. The discovery of new sources of gold in Alaska and South Africa relieved an obstacle to commercial expansion. Reviving European economies began buying huge quantities of U.S. products. Farm prices moved to levels unseen in decades. New revolutionary technologies in energy, transportation, communications, and manufacturing drove production forward, generating employment. The return of prosperity in the aftermath of a successful war guaranteed that the country would continue on its existing trajectory of national development.

Americans circa 1900 were not unaware that the turning of the century

13

was coming at a watershed moment in their country's history: The United States was simultaneously coming to economic maturity and making its debut as a major international player. "It was," writes David Traxel in an important recent study, "an uncertain time when anything seemed possible." Yet this also meant unprecedented challenges as new issues arose and older ones were recast into new molds. Americans would engage a trio of provocative questions:[23]

• How should the nation address the logic of markets in concentrating increasing wealth and economic power in corporate elites and big business, while marginalizing vast numbers of working and poor people? In brief, could the society be democratized to provide opportunity for the majority of Americans?

• Would Americans accept and draw strength from what they really were—a great experiment in ethnic/racial diversity—and create pluralistic ideas and institutions, or hunker down and seek to remain a "White Man's Country"?

• How was the United States to fulfill its new role as a world power and balance its moral and economic objectives abroad?

Each issue posed the quandry of how deliverance, American-style, and balance and national cohesion might be achieved. All were intermeshed. The responses that citizens were to make would be framed by two overshadowing national realities: the emergence of a powerhouse economic engine uniquely capable of generating just about anything asked of it, and the unchallenged dominance of the American dream ideology over national thought.

Chapter 2

The Invincible Economy

We have entered upon an era of unprecedented prosperity and
expansion seems to be the order of the day.

—A Seattle financier, December 1899

It may be said without exaggerating that there is scarcely a
corner of the world which does not feel the impulse of
American energy and push.

—Frederick Emory, U.S. Department of State, January 1900

Today is better than yesterday and tomorrow
will be better than today.

—Collis B. Huntington, industrialist, 1900

An American who was middle-aged in 1900 was living in a different country
from the one he had grown up in. True, in rural stores men in faded work
overalls still sat around potbellied stoves, munching on soda crackers from
the ubiquitous cracker barrel, and talking crops, weather, and politics. On
autumn days their wives stored away preserved peaches, plums, berries, sweet
potatoes, and apples in cellars. But over the last generation, the United States,
in the throes of an unparalleled wave of industrialization, had undergone
monumental changes—railroads, the outriders of a new era, spanning the

15

continent, the new open-hearth steel furnaces coming on line, steamships replacing sail, the telegraph and telephone zipping messages across the continent in seconds. By century's end, Nebraskan agricultural produce, meat packed in Chicago by Armour and Swift, cases of Cincinnati-made Ivory ("99 and 44/100% pure") soap, and Atlanta-made Coca-Cola rolled down the rails to a national market stretching from Boston to California.

The science/technology axis that would define the coming century was coming to maturity. The incandescent lamp and electric power stations, together with petroleum and the new inventions of the chemical industries, were driving the changeover to continuous-process manufacturing. Harvester-thresher combines had transformed the horizonless spaces of the Great Plains into the world's primary breadbasket. Electric street cars were altering the configuration of urban living.

Quantity and size had become all-important—productivity assuming the status of a new deity. The Singer Sewing Machine Company manufactured a million sewing machines annually. One of Buck Duke's Bosnack machines rolled out 120,000 cigarettes each year. In 1899, the American Bicycle Company finished a thousand bikes each working day. At Great Lakes ports, grain elevators operated by steam-engine-driven belts off-loaded 180,000 bushels of wheat each hour into mammoth terminals. On dry docks from the Puget Sound to Newport News, great caches of timber and steel were being turned into modern steamships. High-speed cranes transported 150–ton train locomotives between construction bays.[1]

At the helm of the economic transformation was the American corporation itself, continuously shaped and reshaped by revolutions in communications and production technology. Big-business organizations were being revamped to accommodate the requirements of national markets and the presence of the telephone, the new rapid-delivery post office, and sophisticated machinery.

General office command systems had been established, with top management and professional managers controlling operations. Centralized corporate bureaucracies coordinated the production activities of newly designed multifunctional factories employing thousands of workers, and established sales and marketing divisions to exploit the new techniques in marketing and distribution.[2]

In some industries, the economics of production and marketing pushed the creation of corporations of unprecedented size. The Singer Sewing Machine Company had 20,000 production employees and a sales force triple that. Carnegie Steel and Baldwin Locomotive built multi-unit production plants designed to accommodate 10,000 workers operating high-speed continual-process machinery.[3]

The instability of business conditions during the nineties meant a corporate focus on greater efficiencies and reducing costs. Companies that could mobilize financial resources, make innovations in technology, marketing, and distribution, and secure political protection not only overcame their rivals, but might metamorphose into the legendary corporate "trusts," to be celebrated and damned.[4]

What bedazzled foreign observers of the American scene wasn't simply the size of these new corporate juggernauts, or even the astounding rate in the increase in national wealth (now reckoned at $100 billion). Rather it was the *sheer dynamism and velocity of the American economic scene*, the crackling nervous energy animating commercial life.

The dense crowds hurrying through the streets of the great cities, the breakneck pace of workers in Pittsburgh feeding the massive blast furnaces at the Edgar Thompson Steel Works or bottling fifty-seven varieties of ketchup at the Heinz factory, Great Northern locomotives running a hundred miles an hour full throttle across the prairies carrying settlers into North Dakota and Montana, the turbines churning at Niagara Falls, the chaotic hurly-burly at the stock exchanges—all seemed to spell the coming of a qualitatively different civilization, open to imagination and defiant of limits.

Even the nation's starch-collared, frock-coated president, William McKinley, a rather portly cigar chain-smoker, seemed, on his vigorous, arms-swinging, 9:30 A.M. constitutional along Pennsylvania Avenue, to have caught the pace of American life.

Americans would do what others lacked the resources or will to do; thus, the formation shortly before New Year's Day of a new Panama Canal Company dedicated to finishing the isthmian canal begun by the French. An obscure and quite eccentric thirty-seven-year-old with a touch of mechanical genius, Henry Ford, had left the Edison Company a few months before and was constructing a new gas-powered automobile in his Michigan garage. There was a young Wisconsin-born architect with a growing reputation, Frank Lloyd Wright, who was designing suburban Chicago homes in radically innovative new ways.

The country's big cities, whose glitter and opportunities were attracting huge numbers of inmigrants from rural America and overseas, were definitely the nerve center of the new economy. Four of ten Americans now lived in urban places. Industries were highly concentrated spatially and gathered large numbers of factories and workers in close proximity. Older commercial cities like Chicago (whose population reached 1.7 million by 1900), Philadelphia (1.3 million), St. Louis (575,000), and Cleveland (381,000) were being transformed into industrial metropolises overflowing their boundaries and annexing surrounding rural areas.

But New York remained unchallenged as the premier American city. Home to three and a half million people, the Wall Street financial complex, numerous corporate headquarters, the mile-long Brooklyn Bridge, Central Park, palace-like homes and hotels, and a unique ethnic mosaic, it was displacing London as the paramount city of business and culture in the Western world. Here, change was relentless: Beneath the streets of Manhattan Island, a twenty-one-mile train system utilizing state-of-the-art construction technology and design was on the eve of construction.

Manhattan's universally acknowledged symbol of power was the skyscraper, ingenious end product of modern engineering and architectural design, the magical coalescing of thousands of tons of steel girders, electric lighting, and new high-speed elevators. The 29–story, 950–room Park Row was the skyline's most impressive recent addition (and the world's tallest building). Dug seventy feet down into granite rock and visible across the Hudson in New Jersey, it was inhabited workdays by 4,000 people and contained electric elevators, marble staircases, restaurants, bars, shops, telephones, stock exchange offices, telegraph services, and waterworks plants.[5]

But if Europeans admired the Yankee dynamism, it also had begun to unsettle them. Throughout the nineteenth century, Englishmen, Frenchmen, and Germans had complacently viewed the United States as a colossus in the making whose emergence lay safely in some distant future. The way American visitors in London, Paris, and Rome behaved, their gaucheries and overtipping and irritating declamations on the United States's greatness, encouraged Europeans to see America as an adolescent nation dedicated to harmless excess.

Recently, however, the ease with which American forces had demolished Spanish fleets and armies had given reason for alarm, and now there was a sudden, grudging recognition that this upstart was surpassing Great Britain as a world economic power. The United States, shedding its traditional status as a debtor nation, had become the place Europeans came to borrow money.

The most glaring evidence of the passing of industrial leadership from Old to New World was in the startling shift in trade relations. Agricultural exports were nothing new—American farmers had for years been exporting much of their cotton and wheat. Before 1897, however, U.S. manufacturers had been content to dump surpluses abroad. But now, U.S. industry was producing a third of the world's manufactured goods and exporting iron and steel goods, leather boots, machine tools, bicycles, and electrical supplies. Singer controlled three-quarters of the world's sales of sewing machines and utilized direct sales from its offices in Britain, Germany, and Russia. Standard Oil's blue cans were familiar throughout Europe and beyond all the way to China, while Buck Duke's tobacco monopoly exported tens of millions of cigarettes annually. General Electric and Westinghouse were emerging as leading exporters of electrical goods.[6]

In the emerging global economy of 1900, U.S. producers had crucial advantages, not the least being access to cheaper raw materials like coking coal and iron ore. Manufacturers of locomotives, steel rails, lighting oil, and sewing machines had already mastered high-volume/low-cost production processes and established overseas marketing networks. Firms like General Electric (whose laboratory scientists were working on creating a tungsten filament) were world leaders in scientific and technological research. All of this led businessmen and government officials to casually assume that the national destiny was global leadership in industry and trade. In January 1900, a high-level U.S. State Department official trumpeted "the growing popularity of American goods everywhere."[7]

Indeed, no market seemed safe from Yankee invasion. Made-in-U.S.A. watches were bought by Swiss, and silk by French buyers. England, incubator of the Industrial Revolution, was purchasing pig iron, steel rails, and billets from Carnegie's phenomenally efficient mills, and train locomotives from East Coast plants. European farmers were using McCormick harvesters. A hundred ships a week left San Francisco carrying beans, flour, pianos, and wine to China, and printing machinery, whiskey, tools, and paper to Japan. Remington typewriters were showing up in British army tents in South Africa, California canned goods and flour were in markets in Siberian towns, and American steel was girding bridges in Russia and Africa.[8]

Massive, well-financed U.S. corporations, operating out of continental bastions, seemed intent on seizing every overseas market in sight. Directly investing in European plants, they were reorganizing production and marketing structures according to their needs. This made retaliation inevitable. A concerned Kaiser Wilhelm put out feelers for a European economic union; the German government slapped restrictions on American products and subsidized its own manufacturers. Austrian Foreign Minister Agenor Goluchowski denounced "the disastrous war of competition" being waged from across the Atlantic. Frequent allusions to the "American peril" reflected not only a growing apprehension about U.S. business, but also the subversive impacts of American culture, ideology, and business methods on conservative European societies.[9]

Americans never quite understood this hostility. Trade with the United States and the spread of American ideas, they reasoned, could only advance the material prosperity and freedom of others. Didn't U.S success in overseas markets only prove the superiority of their home-grown model of economic development based on private enterprise, free trade of information and culture, and a pro-business government? It followed that *all* societies that wished to develop had better do it the American way.

The export boom was only one element of what made 1899 an economically stunning year. The speculative bulls on Wall Street ran wild through the fall, the dollar value of securities climbing by hundreds of millions. Standard Oil directors Henry H. Rogers and William Rockefeller, in combination with the stone-faced National City Bank honcho James Stillman, secretly bought the Anaconda Copper Company for $39 million, renamed it Amalgamated Copper, and resold it to the public for $75 million. Business was running at flood tide: *Harper's Weekly* noted "the prosperity wave which is now sweeping the country." Construction boomed: The downtown business districts of large and small urban areas were recast in the image of reinforced concrete and structural steel. New industries emerged based upon products patented in the nineties. The railroads were operating above capacity, taking in record profits and laying miles of additional track. There is "still greater room for further increase . . . our country being hardly opened west of Minot," wrote Western railroad magnate James Hill to a business associate. "I think it is reasonably safe for us to expect that our net income will reach $20 million within the next five years."[10]

With prices of pig iron doubling during 1900 and steel rail prices rising by five times, new iron ore mines and blast furnaces were hurriedly brought on line. Cotton, wheat, corn, beef, and pork prices climbed to their highest in years, providing growers with a cash bonanza and swollen bank accounts. Travelers to Kansas, Nebraska, and Oklahoma remarked on the presence of pianos, new furniture, and lace curtains in farmhouse parlors, spanking new buggies parked outside, and freshly painted bright red barns.[11]

In Atlanta, capital of the "New South," prosperity was visible in the melange of new office buildings transforming the downtown skyline. From Seattle, a base for mining, the Alaska gold rush, and export of lumber overseas, came reports of "a record breaking production in nearly all lines of business and industry. The demand has been such that manufacturers can hardly keep pace." In other cities, too, companies had long backlogs. Personal debt and business inventories were at their lowest levels in years. Money was cheap (interest rates at 1 percent) and new business startups were legion.[12]

And jobs seemed plentiful enough. Arizona copper mines, Carolina textile mills, and Massachussets shoe factories were all hiring. Some manufacturers even noted a lack of skilled employees, and railroads complained of a dearth of workers to help maintain and expand their facilities. During harvest season, farmers in Kansas and Oregon were paying an unheard-of three or four dollars per day for scarce agricultural labor.

Just before Christmas 1899, a spree of holiday buying seemed to validate President McKinley's claim that "unusual prosperity" was the rule of the day. The brightly lit and artistic plate-glass windows of great downtown department stores like Macy's and Altman's in New York, Boston's Jordan Marsh, Wanamaker's in Philadelphia, Chicago's Marshall Field drew animated crowds, while inside the stores' opera house-like interiors, shoppers clogged the aisles and jostled each other at bargain counters. To meet the holiday demand, stores hired temporary workers—Jordan Marsh's usual complement of 3,000 employees swelling by a thousand or more.[13]

What was occurring that Christmas signaled something beyond simply lavish holiday gift buying. Rather, this was symptomatic of a gathering transformation in the consciousness and life habits of Americans, the embryo of a mass-consumption revolution and the ongoing transformation of North American cities into marketplaces where human interaction would become ever more commodified. Already, the names of companies like Nabisco, Singer, and Kodak and their intensely advertised products were being assimilated into the patterns of popular speech and thought.[14]

The upper class in the United States had long adopted certain distinctive modes of consumption as integral to their status and way of life. This lifestyle was, in turn, faithfully mimicked by the better off in the middle classes. The notion of what passed for the art of fine living, however, had been dramatically altered by the fantastic new wealth produced throughout the last quarter-century. Now the recently arrived American industrial-financial aristocracy a la the Vanderbilts, Harrimans, and Huntingtons made the signature of their class Fifth Avenue castles, Newport mansions, 100–foot yachts, private railroad cars, and European expeditions.

Undaunted, middle-class folk plunged ahead with their own consumption revolution, largely driven by the explosion in mass-produced consumer goods filling store shelves and by the advent of installment plans, which made buying without ready cash easier. Susan Strasser has called this "a culture in the making, a culture founded on new technologies and structured by new personal habits and new economic forms." The rising half-billion-dollar-a-year advertising industry was teaching Americans to want and need far more things than their parents before them. Advertising professionals had discovered how lucrative playing to the vulnerabilities of men and women in an era of traumatic change could be. Campaigns promoted consumerism as therapy to a population anxious about powerlessness and seeking self-realization and reassurance. Legendary ad men like John Lee Mahin studied how to make products more appealing to the status-anxious middle classes, targeting married women with servants at home and the leisure, money, and ennui to define themselves through shopping. American society would attempt to absorb the still unresolved crises of the nineties into a new mass production/mass consumption order.[15]

21

So Christmas 1899 was promoted galore through newspapers, magazines, and billboards. Shoppers with sufficient incomes had, according to *Harper's Bazaar*, "a bewildering number of goods" available. There were black silk dresses at 85 cents, ladies' jackets lined with silk for $7.75, men's overcoats priced $16 to $20, golf shirts at a dollar, men's bathing suits costing 45 cents, corsets at $2.75, and ladies' silkwaists ranging from $4 to $7 dollars a piece. Hart, Schaffner & Marx suits were priced at $10 to $30, and ladies' hose, 17 cents a pair. For the twelve-year-old girl, silk, wool, and cashmere riding suits were in fashion; women preferred fine lingerie and rich silver-gray gauze dresses and furs.

There were bicycles to be had in the price range of $40 to $75. For an outlay of $10 to $17 you might "Take a Kodak Home for Christmas." The futuristic-looking "talking machine," an Edison concert phonograph, could be obtained for $75. Automobiles powered by electricity or gas were available, and 4,000 would be sold during 1900. Motorcycles were being introduced from France.

For domestic tasks, a host of new appliances such as Hoover vacuum cleaners, Detroit gas ranges, and washing machines and porcelain bathtubs were in the stores. The candy shops had Whitman's chocolates and bonbons, the flower shops had orchids. There were Waterman's fountain pens, and F.A.O. Schwartz's toys. Diamonds sold particularly well. Smith and Wesson handguns ("Yours to command," read one of its advertisements. "The revolver is always ready") were popular.

Leisure-time activities were beginning to preoccupy the families of the growing professional class of lawyers, doctors, journalists, engineers, and managers. A distinctive leisure lifestyle of recreational clubs, summer vacations at the local hot springs hotel or Chatauqua, and fishing and hunting trips to the Wisconsin forests or the Adirondacks was emerging. As part of the end-of-the-century cult of the "strenuous life," activities such as mountain hiking and camping in the woods boomed.

Sports like golf and tennis were popular among those who could afford them, and college football was becoming a great passion. The Ivies were dominant (the highly ritualized Harvard–Yale game attracting large crowds), but Midwest powerhouses Wisconsin, Michigan, and Chicago were rising fast. Here, like everywhere else, professionalism/commercialism was intensifying. Before the 1900 season, the innovative Princeton football coach Langdon Lea was wooed away by the University of Michigan for the lofty seasonal salary of $3,500. Suddenly, professional golfers and baseball players had celebrity status. At $10,000 a year, a leading jockey earned considerably more than the president of the University of California. Automobile racing (at twenty miles an hour) between Philadelphia and New York, or across the flats of Long Island, developed a devoted following of enthusiasts who were demanding the construction of "speedways."[16]

Leisure travel had terrific and widening appeal. Thus the glossy advertisements appearing in popular magazines read by the more comfortably middle class: the Northern Pacific Railroad proposing the "Wonderland 1900" Northwest trip to the Columbia River and Mount Hood; the Atchison, Topeka, and Santa Fe Railway promoting California as "a land of sunshine, more delightful in the winter than the Mediterranean." The Burlington Railroad, whose gravure photo ads pictured snow capped peaks, ran passengers from Chicago and St. Louis to "your vacation in Colorado."

The upscale White Star Steamship Line made frequent passages to Southampton, while the Hamburg American Line was offering "A Cruise Around the World," and various lines took passengers to the Caribbean and "the battlefields of the Spanish-American War." Staterooms in the best ships were hard to come by during the summer of 1900 as tourists crossed the Atlantic to see the glitzy Paris Exposition on the banks of the Seine. At West Palm Beach and other spots along the Florida coast, Standard Oil partner Henry Flagler was opening luxury hotels and sparking the original Florida land boom.[17]

On the horizon were the mass vacation culture and tourism-inspired migrations of the next century. Northern Pacific Railroad ads were, in fact, starting to tease cold northerners with a momentous question: "Why endure disagreeable weather when California is reached by so quick and comfortable a journey?"

In recent years the consumption revolution had begun spreading beyond the urban middle classes to the more prosperous farm and small-town folk. The arrival at the local railroad station of brown-paper–wrapped Sears and Roebuck and Montgomery Ward packages literally embodied the promise of American abundance; the two Chicago mail order establishments were modern-day incarnations of the biblical storehouses of plenty. Indeed, in countless rural parlors, the well-thumbed 1,000-page Ward or Sears catalogue offering everything from books, glasses, cutlery, and coffeemakers to buggies, bicycles, wigs, eyebrow pencil, and cherry pitters had a place in family affections rivaling the Holy Bible.[18]

The mail-order business also brought turn-of-the-century Americans, always distrustful of doctors (and carrying a definite streak of hypochondria), access to a new range of quack practitioners and patent medicines. Among the many choices were Swamp Root sold for "weak kidneys caused by overwork, by lifting, or a strain," Beeman's original pepsin gum to "cure indigestion and sea sickness," and from Denver, Dr. M.A. McLaughlin's "electric belt" to "cure pain and nervous diseases." "Swift's Specific" proclaimed itself "as the only hope for cancer." The cures for syphilis, rupture, "lost manhood," and stomach difficulties were innumerable.

The passion for new goods was also trickling down into the town and city lower-middle and the skilled working classes, the "nickel customers." It came in the form of Swift's premium hams and bacon, "Schlitz, the beer that made Milwaukee famous," Wrigley chewing gum, and Bull Durham smoking tobacco. The families of bank clerks and machinists might breakfast on Grape Nuts ("Healthy Brains Move the World; Keep Them Healthy"), use packaged gelatin desserts, brush with Hood's tooth powder, and perhaps wash up with Sapollo soap. The considerable immigration from southern and eastern Europe meant the advent of new ethnic restaurants and dishes like spaghetti. "Ready to eat" foods and canned peas were appearing in grocery windows.

The identity of male skilled workers was increasingly tied to their ability as breadwinners. Their wives prized the heavy-laced curtains, overstuffed furniture, and bric-a-brac ornaments that were proof of respectability. Skilled Carolina mill town workmen prided themselves on the gilt clock cabinets in their parlors with gospel hymns and "God Bless Our Home" etched on the face, and rag carpets on the floors. On Sunday, attired in suits adorned with heavy watch chains, they attended the local Baptist church with its stiff dose of old-time religion and sin. Home ownership for the working and lower-middle classes, although still difficult, was possible in places like Chicago's Ashland Avenue, and in cities like St. Paul, Washington, D.C., and Detroit, where builders were erecting modest bungalows.[19]

It was the factory workers, secretaries, cashiers, and tradesmen lining up for music halls and vaudeville, porno penny arcades and burlesque shows, and the ethnic theaters of the immigrant ghettos, who were in the vanguard of the revolt against the late nineteenth-century American Victorian facade of genteel respectability and relentless moralizing. Couples danced sensuously in the noisy, smoky concert saloons.

On a summer weekend day, Brooklyn trolleys and boats from the Battery might carry (heavily immigrant) crowds of 150,000 and more to the spit of sand called Coney Island to bathe in the sea and enjoy the shooting galleries, ferris wheels, bowling alleys, variety theaters, the fantasy and escape of Steeplechase Park. Picking up dates for the day was a ritualized art form. Other ventures into the new modernistic mass culture—Cleveland's Euclid Beach, Chicago's Chettenham Beach, and Revere Beach in Boston—boasted amusement parks, pavilions, dance halls, and vaudeville shows. Fans hailed their favorite baseball players, Honus Wagner, Nap LaJoie, or Ohio farmboy turned great pitcher Cy Young, as they walked in full uniform from hotels to the ballparks. That such spectacles were urban helped speed the exodus out of the country.[20]

So as 1900 rolled around, there were simply more things to do and see and indulge in than ever before; more colors, diverse sounds, a galaxy of new images. Americans now had access to penny newspapers with their lurid murder stories, half-toned photographs, and Sunday color supplements, highly readable dime magazines like *Munsey's* and *McClure's*, and the titillating *Police Gazette*, whose plump chorus girl covers and sports stories made it so popular in barbershops and saloons. On Saturday afternoons "matinee girls,'" fixated on celebrity actors and actresses such as Henry Montague and Maude Adams, filled the theaters.[21]

New communications and media technologies gave national events a more instantaneous dimension. The advent of local and regional telephone systems joined midwestern farms and western ranches to the rest of the country and diminished the cruelty of rural isolation. In one of the innumerable small towns sprinkled across the hinterland, a speech by William Jennings Bryan or President McKinley evoked barbershop talk the following day. Locals lounging in town squares in upstate New York, or on Georgia courthouse porches far from the ballparks where Ned Hanlon's National League champion Brooklyn Superbas, or the fire-eating John McGraw's Baltimore Orioles were playing, could get a play-by-play from the local newspaper ticker. Championship prize fights between the massively built ex-boilermaker Jim Jeffries and the stylish master boxer James Corbett evoked intense excitement and huge betting around the country.[22]

Inevitably, the Americans of 1900 would seek to give meaning to and make the quickly changing panorama of experience sensible. What they would utilize was a cultural lens shaped by the national *mythomoteur*. The mythomoteur is that central engine of mythmaking and identity that makes traditions and symbols coherent. Indispensable to any culture, it produces the assortment of myths, stories, scripts, and ideals that gives a society self-legitimacy, binds its people to a common vision of a future worth struggling for, and exacts their commitment.[23]

It fell to the American mythomoteur to create a national mythology of original and awesome power. The term "American dream" would not be coined until three decades later, but certainly by 1900, American dreams were being manufactured in abundance. The dream has constituted Americans' very special mission and they have been attached to it as only a self-chosen people could be. It was the dream circa 1900, both in its marvelous strengths and appalling flaws, which marked the United States as a revolutionary civilization and foretold the triumphs and tragedies of the century to come.

Chapter 3

American Dreaming
The Power, the Glory, and the Chaos

The best time to be a boy the world has ever known is just this time—just at the start of a great, vigorous forceful, wisdom—loving century. And just the birthplace to be a boy is right here in the United States, the one point of the earth where a boy can grow up with a reasonable chance of making the most of himself.

—David Starr Jordan, President,
Stanford University, May 1900

Our great country is a land of promise, if not the Promised Land. It is a land flowing with the milk of opportunity and the honey of success.

—*Saturday Evening Post*, November 1900

Before there was a United States, there was an American dream. Its distant outlines may be traced back to that seventeenth-century New England notion of American "exceptionalism," the "shining city on the hill," where those who made the trans-Atlantic voyage might flourish free from the bondage of Europe's ungodly ills. Here, unlike there, as Abraham Lincoln said, a man did not have to "pull down the house of another to rise, he could build one

26

himself." The dream brought functioning unity to a fragmented polyglot of peoples, while a huge land mass, favored in resources and fertility, provided the material base.[1]

Always full of paradox, the dream speaks of tangible objects to be possessed, yet remains largely experienced in the realm of personal feelings about self-worth and self-fulfillment. It hints at a moment of "arrival," but creates an environment where even the "arrived" are sometimes convinced of their relative deprivation.

But if the American dream has been about *anything*, it is freedom, autonomy, and specialness: freedom from the petty (and not so petty) tyranny of local bosses, barons, kings, bishops, landlords, and grand inquisitors; even more, the freedom to use one's peculiar genius to find economic abundance, to be special and seek a kind of fulfillment scarcely imaginable in older worlds.

Americans have always regarded the American dream and democracy as one and inseparable, a linkage sanctified by the Declaration of Independence as "the pursuit of happiness." At its core runs an implicit social contract: *The country's vast resources and uniquely fluid social system would work toward rewarding the conscientious, thrifty individual who placed shoulder to the wheel and pushed sufficiently.* If not her or him, then surely their children. In Robert Weibe's phrase: "All citizens who cared could join the endless march upward."[2]

What legitimated the American Dream, then, was the promise of immediate, or at least, long-term (intergenerational) betterment: "Making it" justified going to extraordinary (and often extralegal) lengths. Possessing determination and ingenuity, the classic American hero would single-mindedly hack his way through enemies and wilderness of one sort or another to stand upon the summit of Success.

American civilization makes the grandly optimistic assumption that it can provide a setting where deserving people will gain some degree of specialness and power over their own lives. The modestly talented individual, through endeavor and luck, can hope to embark upon the upward ascent to material well being (and perhaps riches). Vertical mobility will push new people upward.

So Americans took it for granted that the nation would prove uniquely favorable to all kinds of endeavor. This quest helped to rationalize the harshly unequal outcomes. Anyway, the American dream has never been about social and economic equality. Rather, it was dedicated to equality of opportunity in making the Great Ascent. And to gauge how far you had come, it was always helpful to know where you had started from.

Every national mythomoteur seeks to provide some notion of the larger purpose for living. The American dream's uniqueness lies in its preoccupation with the *individual* destiny. The individual is unbound, writ larger than life, free to exploit any and every opportunity either to rise to full height, or fail. The enterprising New American Man was ballooned into dynamo and hero of the young civilization. "The meaning of life for most Americans is to become one's own person, almost to give birth to onseself," notes a recent study of U.S. cultural mores. No wonder that the specter of limits, of constraints on the possible, have always seemed so suffocating.[3]

By the early nineteenth century, foreign visitors like Alexis de Tocqueville were noting the existence of a unique American "restlessness of temper." The observant Frenchman noted the "strange unrest of so many happy men. . . forever brooding over advantages they do not possess. . . . "Everyone is in motion, some in quest of power, others of gain."[4]

The dream was interwoven into such a temperament both as motivator and love object. Economic expansion in the youthful republic always brought on a frenzied aura of buying, selling, and speculating, which escalated to outright hysteria during boom conditions along new frontiers. European visitors noted the incessant jockeying of entrepreneurs and speculators as they maneuvered for position. "The pursuit of wealth is nowhere so eager as in America," remarked an English visitor, adding, "The opportunities for acquiring it are nowhere so numerous."[5]

Who was to be the agent of the American dream? That role was assigned early on to the "self-made man" exemplified by Ben Franklin, the impoverished printer's apprentice turned Philadelphia man of commerce and international statesman. The conviction of Franklin and other Americans that they were an "exceptional" people was fortified by the inmigration of Germans, Irish, Englishmen, Scots, Welsh, and Scandinavians, who were flowing into Atlantic ports right up to the Civil War, drawn by cheap land, plentiful work, and the promise of autonomy.[6]

Americans had only to look at their pantheon of born-poor national heroes like Franklin and Andy Jackson to see the dream writ large: Abraham Lincoln, the legendary "railsplitter," whose career personified the possibility of transcending humble beginnings, always identified himself with the upwardly mobile aspirations of ambitious men like himself. By enriching himself, the industrialist, farmer, railroad manager, merchant, land speculator was sanctified as enriching the country, too. Individual interest and the national interest, private and public good, became indivisible. Earthly salvation lay in hard work and tenacious defense of one's turf.

By the mid-nineteenth century, the American persona had been privatized, individualized, and dedicated to the god of material progress. Property and liberty had become indistinguishable. The market had emerged as ultimate arbiter of value and values, "success" defined in terms of tangible goods.

Yet, the dream could not remain wholly an individual one, detached from the communities that inevitably caught up with every kind of frontier. National coherence, in fact, has been most at risk whenever individualism has run amok; and Americans (as Christopher Lasch observes) have never been "completely sold on the dream of progress and abundance without limits."[7]

Embedded within the dream was a tension between personal and civic/communal values. Convinced as the Puritans were of the godliness inherent in accumulating worldly things, they understood community as essential. The treasured "good life" has always been bound up with civic virtue, mutual help, and neighborliness, too. There is a muted tradition of defining liberty in terms of human solidarity transcending mere money making; a yearning for a shared and moral community in which responsibilities are equitably shared, bonds matter, the human person cherished—an ethos in which all moved together along the progress road.[8]

In the economically and emotionally depressed years between 1892 and 1897, the dream's dominant tradition of acquisitive individualism was vulnerable to communitarian challenges. Populist politics were one facet of a movement including community stores and gardens, labor exchanges, utopian communities, and schemes for combining self-help and cooperation. Beyond sheer survival and relief, many of those involved sought alternatives to capitalist society.

The defeat and disintegration of populism during the mid-nineties, and the limited appeal of socialism, by 1900 would undercut the political force of this tradition. But its strength remained in the communal, nonmonetary values of millions of Americans, in working-class notions of republican equality, the flourishing farmers cooperatives, and in the widespread animosity toward the "Money Power." In southern Illinois' Union County, for exmple, as in much of rural America, "an ethic of generalized reciprocity" prevailed, neighbors joining together to fill silos, husk corn, raise barns, and sell their products, help each other in times of illness and death, and make sure the poor got fed.[9]

The post–Civil War business expansion confirmed that the United States would be a business civilization, a nation devoted to the pursuit of wealth and property. "A way of life has evolved in America that turns exclusively upon . . . acquiring material goods, a fortune," contemptuously mused the visiting Norwegian writer Knut Hamsun in 1888. "Americans are so absorbed in the scramble for profit that all their faculties are devoted to it."[10]

Now, the Great Race was more shrill and consuming than ever before. The stakes had never been higher, the spoils more glorious and continental in scope. Wall Street created instant millionaires. Entrepreneurs swooped in swiftly to seize their share of this or that market, mobilizing techniques and capital and political muscle against the rivals snapping at their heels.

A handful climbed clear to the apex of business life—the Rockefellers, Goulds, Morgans, Harrimans—classic American men on the make, but cut from a harsher cloth and operating on a far grander scale than in the past. Steamrolling opposition, manipulating alliances, buying judges, legislatures, and senators like shares on the New York Stock Exchange, they built empires of unprecedented size in finance, steel, oil, meat packing, and railroads.

It was the heyday of the robber barons. John D. Rockefeller was lord and master of four of every five barrels of oil refined in the United States. Collis Huntington of Pacific Associates, the reigning economic-political-newspaper kingpins in California, cemented alliances with Eastern financiers from his Fifth Avenue chateau. Paramount among railroad tycoons were E.H. Harriman, nicknamed "the human dynamo," a power in Western railroads and Wall Street finance, of whom it was said, "he gave little quarter and expected none," and the burly, fierce-eyed James Hill, driving the Northern Pacific Railroad, like a man on a personal vendetta, across the prairie, up over the Rockies to the Pacific, absorbing any and all rivals.[11]

As the logic toward large-scale production intensified, as companies and factories grew larger and more mechanized, the hallowed Jeffersonian ideal of an independent, self-reliant citizenry faded, the promise that every family could be lord and master of its fate subverted by conglomerations of wealth and power. Artisans, sensing that the America of small enterprise was in extremis, staged strikes and built producers cooperatives during the 1880s and 1890s in a last-ditch stand to preserve their autonomy.

The deepest strength of the American dream has always been its marvelous fluidity. Around 1900, however, it was still volatile, still accommodating massive industrial and cultural changes, in *transition* from what lay just behind, the values of the free frontier and self-reliance, the nineteenth-century ethic of work as self-validation, and what lay just over the horizon—the emerging national affair with mass consumption and leisure.

But even in transition the dream continued to function as nothing less than an unofficial national religion. And what was remarkable in a nation increasingly citified, bureaucratized, and technologized was the *sheer staying power* of some of the core elements of the earlier rural, agricultural American dream.

The guiding premise remained what it had been since the advent of European settlement: the United States as the open, illimitable land of the future, where any (white) man with the "right stuff" could make his mark. Thus did Governor Theodore Roosevelt, in his Thanksgiving 1899 message to New Yorkers—"this great people in the first flush of its mighty manhood is going forth to meet its destiny"—catch this powerful spirit of optimism and mission.

The individual success ethic retained its hold on the American imagination, the English writer, H.G. Wells, noting "a huge preoccupation with dollar getting."[12] Little wonder, since every major source of information sustained it. As the young learned to read, for instance, they absorbed the wisdom of *McGuffey's Reader* and the Peter Parley and Rollo books with their catchy little homilies to thrift, perseverance, piety, and upward mobility.

The Success Ideology was virtually gospel. The nation's most influential clergymen preached self-help and industriousness as sure vehicles to wealth and respectability. Money was the divine reward come to the deserving. The celebrated evangelist Russell "Acres of Diamonds" Conwell barnstormed the country exhorting his audiences to achieve wealth in the name of God's commandments: "Money is power . . . and for a man to say, 'I do not want money,' is to say 'I do not wish to do any good for my fellow men.' "[13]

An unceasing cascade of "success literature"—pamphlets, books, and tracts—was gobbled up by an avid national audience. The wonderfully readable stories studded with stock characters, soap opera plots, and happy endings by Horatio Alger, the defrocked little minister turned novelist, enthused countless boys reading in haylofts or small-town porches.

According to the popular doctrine known as "New Thought," a certain "state of mind" must inevitably attract riches and property. "If you would attract success, keep your mind saturated with it," advised one New Thought tract. "When you think success, when you act it, when you live it, when you talk it, when it is in your bearing, then you are attracting it."[14]

Family-oriented magazines such as *Collier's*, *The Saturday Evening Post*, and the *American* ran innumerable articles stressing personal magnetism, decisiveness, and perseverance as the vital force behind the careers of such titans as Carnegie, Mellon, Swift, and Rockefeller. One article showcased the celebrated inventor/businessman Thomas Edison as exemplifying "tenacity of purpose." He is quoted as working on one project "from 18 to 20 hours a day for the last seven months." And his reward had duly arrived: "I held firm and I have succeeded."[15]

Stories of the Look-Where-They-Started-and-Where-They-Are-Now variety told about the rise of thirty-four-year-old Frank Vanderlip, assistant secretary of the United States Treasury, from the typesetting room of a Chicago newspaper; how Republican Party strategist and U.S. Assistant Postmaster Percy Heath had started out as a $1.25–a-week Indiana printers devil; and that one-time railroad clerk Charles M. Hays, now the Southern Pacific

Railroad president, was making more money than the nation's president.[16]

What the "respectable" media neglected, however, were the often unsavory details behind the careers of these "models of success." This partly reflected readers' fascination with the *fact* and not the *how* of wealth, but also the reluctance (as yet) of most publishers and editors to publish exposes of the rich and famous.

So when railroad magnate-shipbuilder Collis Huntington died in August 1900, newspapers and magazines had praise for his great acumen in building an industrial empire employing 100,000 men. His axiom for success—"Work with a will, do it better than anyone else has done it"—was quoted as a model for the young. What this neglected to mention was that the Huntington fortune of 60 or 70 million dollars had been constructed by a master intriguer and political manipulator, consummately skilled in securing the federal land grants and state favors that gave the Southern Pacific Railroad dominance in California. When the occasion demanded, it was not unknown for him to carry around suitcases of cash to buy the legislatures, congressmen, and judges he needed on his side.[17]

The success ethic also received uncritical sanction from prominent academics such as haughty, acerbic William Graham Sumner, professor at Yale University since 1872, and the nation's most prestigious social theorist. A leading disciple of the English Social Darwinist Herbert Spencer, Sumner sanctified the struggles for corporate supremacy as part of a divinely inspired evolutionary process leading to a great national destiny. "If we do not like the survival of the fittest," he wrote, "we have only one possible alternative, and that is the survival of the unfittest." Sumner praised the outcomes of individual selfishness in American life and was often heard exhorting his students at Yale to "get capital."[18]

Social Darwinism, if a hodgepodge of bastardized natural selection theory, religious fatalism, materialism, and individualism, meshed well enough with the interests and ethos of corporate business and was immensely influential in shaping popular thought. By 1900, it had penetrated the rising college football subculture. The gridiron at Yale and other colleges was viewed as a splendid training ground for the forceful, direct character (i.e., "the Anglo-Saxon spirit") that college men would have to develop to lead in the survivalist red-at-tooth-and-claw business world.[19]

So the official national mantra *circa* 1900: The opportunities for making it are wide open indeed, more open than ever before in any land in history. There was "room at the top" for white Americans.

A provocative question: Was the late nineteenth-century American dream merely a masterful media hype, a con perpetuated by a ruling business elite to justify its privileges? Assessing the evidence, one modern critic, John Tebbel, suggests that the nineteenth-century dream was an illusion whose power and magnetism allowed it to pass from generation to generation virtually unexamined:

> The American Dream was itself a chimera, without real substance, a delusion so strongly held that no one desired to question it, and so beloved for itself that no one wanted to doubt it.[20]

The dream *was* severely oversold and overpromoted and overbelieved ad nauseam. Obscuring the inequities in American society, it functioned as a potent instrument in the hands of the country's elite social classes for rationalizing their power and wealth. And the rags-to-riches journey was quite the exception: Irving Wyllie estimates less than 5 percent of the 1900–1910 corporate elite started poor. Steven Thernstrom notes that "there was little room at the top except for those who started very close to it."[21]

Yet, *some* substance was necessary for it to thrive. After all, there were boom years when the economy ran at full tide and the silver or brass ring of financial success was grabbable for any number of those reaching for it. Then, the American dream becomes transposed from myth to a sacred narrative of the American people. The years between 1899 and 1901 were like that.

Both good times and bad, people *did* rise in the world. If most workers remained roughly within the same occupational category, and mobility was mainly short range (e.g., from manual worker to foreman), it was still real and upward. By moving to the city, $20–a-month farm laborers could earn $30 or $40 and enjoy a diet more varied than corn bread and hog jowls. Native stock workers rose to supervisory and even white-collar positions as immigrants took their old jobs. Second-generation daughters of Irish domestics became secretaries or schoolteachers. College students might earn their way by typewriting or waiting tables. Home and land ownership became a reality for some skilled workers and rural people. The average man in 1900 was living a decade longer than his grandfather had.[22]

Americans did not easily foreclose their options: One's ship might yet come in. The outbreak of booms and boomlets illuminated the possibilities. Joseph Newton Pew, a prominent Pennsylvania natural gas dealer, was expanding his Sun Oil Company's leases into the farmlands of West Virginia in 1900, where some promising-looking wells had surfaced. "I may be able to buy some leases several miles from the well," reported his agent in the area, "but there is so much excitement here that it is impossible to buy on right terms."[23]

In June 1900, as soon as the ice broke in the Bering Sea, 6,000 gold miners at Dutch Harbor in Unalaska boarded ships headed to Cape Nome, the latest "Arctic Eldorado." The spur was a host of get-rich-quick stories coming out of the previous year's gold harvest. Reports told of one miner, formerly a $75–a-month engineer, sending his wife a gift of $45,000 in gold, while a New Jersey man had made $400,000 in a brief period of digging.

Cape Nome was the poor man's El Dorado. One wag called it "the only place in the world where a man can make a living with a frying pan." By July, the entire Nome sea-front area was covered with tents and itinerant miners digging the beachfront with picks and shovels, and people were still pouring in on $60 second-class passages from Seattle and Tacoma, many with no mining experience and lacking funds for the return passage.[24]

Public heroes exemplified the possibilities of future affluence. Take the well-known heavyweight boxing contender Jack Sharkey, who had landed only a few years before a penniless sailor from Ireland. Now, in 1900, he boasted a net worth of $85,000, and was bringing his parents over from the other side to live in his swank new Brooklyn home.

Really dramatic class leapfrogging acted as an economic aphrodisiac of sorts. Stories about someone who had "made it" rippled out into widening circles, affirming that hard work had real payoffs. "Well, if you don't work, you don't make it" was how a bookish, determined, Independence, Missouri, farm boy named Harry S. Truman put it in a letter. "You may do a lot of work and not make it too, but you have got to do it or you won't make it."[25]

If you could get some cash in 1900, it went far indeed. Coffee was a quarter a pound, steak a dime, turkey twelve cents, a frying chicken or a pound of cheese might cost fifteen cents. A respectable hotel room with meals might be had for $6 a week. Two or three thousand dollars represented a solid small-business credit line. Between $800 and $2,000 purchased a one- or two-story city cottage; 560 acres of Oregon wheat land went for $21,000.

American workers might remain deeply cynical about the duplicity of businessmen and politicians, and frustrated by conditions at their workplaces, while still embracing the society's dominant value structures. Taking the American dream as their own, they accepted its basic premise that one's achievements were due solely to one's efforts. When workers chafed, it was at their personal place in society rather than at the structure of power and money.

Life in the United States, furthermore, always had the advantage of comparison with "the other side," whence immigrants had come. Refugees from potato famine, Chinese civil wars, Prussian militarism, Hungarian landlords, and Cossack brutality often found these shores quite benign.

Indeed, the tough odds did not tend to alienate Americans from the game. Instead, they were quite willing to bend its rules and generally come to terms with its outcomes. After all, the struggle was viewed as being fought from the terrain of roughly equal opportunity and won by virtue. "Making it" became prima facie evidence of virtuousness. And around 1900, enough were advancing at some level or another to provide credibility.

This included women. If still strictly limited, there were more outlets for at least one segment of females to express their talents. Some higher educational institutions had recently been opened to women, as well as new professions; in a number of states they had more property rights. A small minority of working women had become established as professionals—lawyers, doctors, and teachers—and new jobs as "typewriters," salesclerks, and telephone operators were available to the native born. Commercial high schools featuring courses in typing and secretarial skills were attracting the young.

The gradual crumbling of Victorian rigidities meant young women might have more scope to seek out preferred suitors. The Sunday news supplements carried stories about working-class chorus girls and dancers from the wildly popular Floradora show at New York's Casino Theater who had been sumptuously wooed and won by millionaires. News about society women like Mrs. Astor and actress Lillian Russell received lavish coverage. So did the so-called "New Woman," athletic, confident, and attired in dark skirt and simple shirtwaist blouse on the model of the celebrated "Gibson Girl."

The transition was never easy, the female role remained strongly identified as being in the home, men resisted taking working women seriously. Certainly, working-class and farm women, and women of color, had far fewer options than upper middle-class urban white women did. Yet more than a sliver of progress toward equality with men was discernible.[26]

So most Americans in 1900 would not have devoted much time to deconstructing the dream ideology. The notion of weeding out the nation's fantastic post–Civil War wealth explosion from the force and drive provided by the dream was simply not on. And "the glitter of gold" that Jack London saw in the eyes of the miners who had flocked to the Alaskan Klondike— "They are borne along by uplifted ambition," he wrote[27]—was true of many of his contemporaries. The American man on the make would continue rearranging the world he encountered. The dream would be transformed to accommodate new realities and challenges, but remain curiously intact, inviolate.

By the early twentieth century, the dualism of the American dream, its role as both a force for stability *and* a mighty destabilizer, the vital impulse driving the nation onward *and* generator of acute tensions and conflicts, had become clear to some observers. Traveling through the United States, the brilliantly insightful and imaginative English writer H.G. Wells noted, "Each man is for himself, each enterprise; here is no order, no prevision, no common and universal plan."[28]

What Wells was describing was a war of all against all cheerfully sanctified by the scriptures of the dream. As an abstraction, the dream/success ideology was a powerful stimulus for harnessing individual talents and energies. But as an operational guide for organizing a society, it sabotoged the creation of anything resembling a decent, coherent, and harmonious nation.

One momentous issue was restricted availability. Access to the dream meant access to the package of economic, political, and human rights Benjamin Ringer has aptly called "the people's domain." This was definitely not on offer to all turn-of-the-century Americans. The logic of an "open frontier" was to annihilate and subdue the Native American tribes whose own economy and vision were obstacles to grabbing the continental resources the dream required. The "others," who dwelt outside "the people's domain"—blacks, Asians, Latinos, women, and first-generation eastern and southern European immigrants—limited their dreams of necessity. More often than not, they were simply instruments to carry out the dreams of others.[29]

Setting the dream in individual (male) terms created a second great *problematique*. No one expressed the extraordinary burden placed upon American men for achievement better than a Waterbury, Connecticut, businessman in a January 1900 letter:

> I firmly believe that any young man who is blessed with good health and fails, has but himself to blame for his failure. A man with a good education need never fail. The success or failure of any man, rests not upon the accident of birth, the lucky opportunity, or by the pulling of powerful or influential friends or relatives, but simply and absolutely upon himself.[30]

"Success" was thus cast in severely moralistic hues of light and darkness, the value of one's life work judged accordingly. The "failed" or "dependent" male became an object of contempt. Making the "unfettered" individual male the agent of the dream was a sure prescription for isolating and demoralizing him, making him chronically insecure. The loneliness was unspeakable. Too often, his self-respect could only be gained at the expense of those weaker.

Much of the era's preoccupation with "manliness" and virility, its morbid fears of "degeneration," flowed from the impossible tasks assigned to the American man. "Manliness" became constructed as transcending acts of surreal male bravado, such as the half-crazed Theodore Roosevelt hurling his Rough Riders up San Juan Hill in what amounted to a suicidal charge, or the oddly serene Georgia lynch mobs going about the business of protecting the virtue of "their" white women through ritualistic murder and mutilation of black victims.

Foreigners remarked on the humbleness of American men toward their wives and the deference women received in American society. Yet, of course, the cult of the male superman victimized fin de siècle American women, too, limiting (or making them deny) their own talents and aspirations to an independent, public role. Often, there was the lack of an authentic life apart from their husbands or fathers. So the widespread incidence of female nervous exhaustion and prostration, rising divorce rates, and the preoccupation of southern white females with the specter of black rapists is not terribly surprising.[31]

As a private, individual affair, equating freedom with "being left alone to do as one pleases," the dream could only superficially unify the American people. Since citizens, families, enterprises, all acted as *compartments*, little value was attached to mutual understanding, to acknowledging that others might have legitimate grievances. "Getting it" was an American issue back then, too.

Michael Lewis calls this "individual-as-central-sensibility" essential to understanding why poverty and disadvantage have been popularly dismissed as "abnormal" in the United States, and failure attributed to personal incompetence or immorality. What had evolved by 1900 was a "culture of inequality," which placed a moral stigma on being lower class. Not only did this attitude justify the shabby treatment of the poor (especially racial or ethnic "others"), it also encouraged working and lower middle-class folk to translate their insecurities into hostility and occasional violence against those lower in the economic pecking order.[32]

The glaring question was why, if "success" was so universally available, there were so many patently "unsuccessful" folk around. Much rhetoric and reams of newsprint were expended on explaining this. There was a *Saturday Evening Post* (at 200,000 copies an issue, one of the country's most popular magazines) series running through fall and winter 1899–1900 titled "Why Young Men Fail." Directed at students and young white collars aspiring to management, the articles featured corporate officials and businessmen analyzing the failure of their employees to get ahead. Invariably, the key factor was the character (or lack of such) of the young men themselves.

So a Maine streetcar company president pointed to his young employees' "lack of courage" and "lack of faith in the efficiency of work." The president of the United Press thought "incompetence" and "idleness" the main culprits. A telegraph company official blamed the "lack of concentration of purpose and energy." "I regret to state that there seems to be a lack of ambition on the part of a large percentage of the young men that come under my personal supervision," lamented one Detroit businessman."[33]

Solicited for his views, Indiana's brash young senator (and self-fancied man of destiny) Albert Beveridge advised "every young man to cultivate unselfishness, sincerity, truthfulness, write them on the tablets of your heart; get them into your blood." He concluded: "On the tablets of your courage is where we fail, not intellect."[34]

The essence of the *Post* series: "Success is normal, failure, abnormal; intelligent ernestness is essential and ultimately always wins." In the Horatio Alger tradition, the average young man with "persistence," industry," and "fidelity" would get his just reward.[35]

Perhaps, the ultimate test of the success mythology lay in its capacity to make believers of *those who could not afford to believe its truths.* Thus the young aspiring clerk should ignore sparse opportunities, office corruption, and the misuse of personal influence and remember that character must triumph over circumstances. So in the end, he alone was to blame for lack of career progress; he must transform himself and grab the always latent possibilities.

One response to the *Post* series coming from a Massachussetts man illustrates how deeply just such a message had been internalized as individual reality. He had "like a great many young men worked long hours for an unappreciative employer, so I know how it feels to work for ten dollars a week when I knew I was worth twenty dollars." While acknowledging he had "tasted despair," this young man advised others that "time will pay you back. Let us not be impatient for a quick success." His curiously truimphant conclusion: "Love your work and do it perfectly and the reward will come or natural law cease to exist."[36]

Since failure in the Great American Race was laid to either character defect or lack of personal capacity, the logic was to deny the disadvantaged any genuine public support. Aiding them would only further handicap their chances. William Graham Sumner again spoke the dominant libertarian wisdom here, asserting that "one man in a free state, cannot claim help from, and cannot be charged to give help to, another." What Americans owed each other was quite simply "good-will, mutual respect, and mutual grants of liberty."[37]

Turn-of-the-century businessmen and conservatives expected the federal government to protect business interests via tariffs, contracts, and land grants, and to promote American corporate interests abroad through an array of instruments that included military force. But social initiatives such as child labor laws, regulation of corporate trusts, or public ownership of Detroit streetcars were damned as interference with sancrosanct natural market laws and dangerous to the national character.[38]

It was in accord with this gospel that in 1893–1894, President Grover Cleveland, a not uncompassionate man, had refused to provide direct federal aid for the army of workless, hungry men and women and homeless tramps thrown up by the worst economic collapse in the country's history. Cleveland tinkered with tariffs and sold off bond issues, but took no initiatives to stimulate the economy and new jobs. Dominant figures in the U.S. Senate like Nelson Aldrich and Orville Platt assumed matters like poverty, labor conditions, and violence and discrimination against minorities to be outside the concerns of government. This caused sociologist Lester Ward to lament that "government today is powerless to perform the primary and original function of protecting society."[39]

Ward went on to argue that Sumner and the Social Darwinists really had it backward: Not only did competition choke freedom and progress, but "individual freedom can only come through social regulation." He thought "laissez-faire capitalism a dangerous anachronism" more relevant to the world of 1800 than 1900. The country was, in fact, "suffering from . . . undergovernment." In a complex industrial society, only government could play a stabilizing, balancing role. Economists Simon Patten and Richard Ely were voicing similar thoughts (and suffering inquisitions from the businessmen who dominated the universities where they worked).[40]

Thus the American dream ethos legitimated the imbalance between private and public spheres. Giving primacy to acquisitive individualism meant the privileging of individual ego and corporate goals over public policy and goods. Businessmen insisted on the sanctity of the marketplace and obtained almost complete freedom from restraints. As industrialist and presidential kingmaker Mark Hanna expressed it in his typically earthy style to a friend in March 1899: "I got sort of an idea that a man had a right to do what he pleased with his own."[41]

In the hands of pro-business conservative theorists, "natural law" was used to sanctify the social order and to insulate the rights of property. The task of building community should remain the prerogative of the marketplace. Corporations were really only *individuals* writ large, and bigness and economic power inherently positive. Self-interest guaranteed that resources would be properly channeled. Leave business to itself and it would usher in an era of great material progress. They championed the contributions the plutocrats were making to the nation's well-being against those who attacked them. Industrialists, William Graham Sumner reasoned, were "great generals" chosen by the natural selection of business competition to carry the "industrial war" to its successful conclusion. Such a metaphor found favor with an industrialist like John D. Rockefeller, who always regarded attacks on Standard Oil as incredible, equating the critics with gangsters practicing extortion.[42]

So despite rising challenges, the laissez-faire notion of businesses as freely developing, divinely inspired organisms still prevailed. The United States remained not merely a market economy, but a *market society*. Its political ruling class (incarnated by the U.S. Senate and Supreme Court) reflected business ideology, and was profoundly hostile to attempts to limit corporate powers.

Thus any semblance of social planning and development of resources continued to be regarded as un-American. Businessmen had a virtual carte blanche to define the patterns of local, regional, and national economic growth. Commercial pressures precluded learning from recent stupidities and environmental disasters.

By 1900, the consequences of such policy were visible in the chaotic, indiscriminate economic growth sprawling across the American industrial landscape. Nowhere was this more plain than in the country's second city and great hub, Chicago, described by the visiting H.G. Wells, as a "dark disorder of growth." Observing its vast industrial complex of stockyards, cattle trains, mountains of bituminous coal, grain elevators, flaming furnaces, and smoking chimneys, Wells thought Chicago represented "a scrambling, ill-mannered, undignified, unintelligent development of material resources." He noted the squalor of the working-class areas, the filth and pollution everywhere, the awful stench from the packing plants which carried two miles in every direction. "Growth forced itself upon me as the dominant American fact," he wrote wearily.[43]

The yellow brick American dreamroad has always been riddled with potholes; its promoters habitually promising more than they could deliver. The logical individual response has been to seize the moment, maximizing and fortifying one's returns and turf anyway one could. Greed and corruption were thus enshrined as central, *mainstream* elements of the culture.

The dream's very open-endedness, its "fuzziness," also served to legitimize avarice. The milestones of success were elusive, the race unceasing, and new "necessities" always seemed to be accumulating on the horizon. In a land where wealth and status comparison are endemic (others, of course, will always have "more"), the pressures to keep moving are mighty, indeed. A man who "has not piled up dollars to flaunt in the world's face," despairingly noted a New York literary lady in 1900, is not considered a "success."[44]

Public proclamations like John D. Rockefeller's—"I think it is a man's duty to make all the money he can"—gave the national treasure hunt sanction from on high. Indeed, the supreme winners in the wars of business *a l'outrance* were those like Rocky, Morgan, Carnegie, Huntington, and Hill who had gotten away with the most. The path of least resistance to money making was almost universal. Popular folk wisdom understood that behind the official facade of Christian piety and law, the boundaries between virtue and vice did not exist. "We are lawless," candidly remarked one social critic, "especially about everything that touches our business interests."[45]

Throughout the land, payoffs, kickbacks, and illegal rebates were the modus operandi. Mused *Harper's Weekly*, "We are all of us in need of a moral tuneup." Railroads gave prized customers large enough rebates to put rivals out of business. Wall Street promoters routinely overcapitalized stocks and rigged the market to take windfall profits. A state regulatory official described corporate management as "notoriously corrupt and dishonest and traitorous and traitors and villains." Factory foremen expected cigars, whiskey, and five-dollar bills in return for granting jobs to workers.[46]

The scale and openess of political corruption often made a mockery of any pretense of democratic process. There were the big-city, New York- and Chicago-type machines whose armies of precinct captains and wardheelers were financed by protection rackets collecting regular "donations" from saloons, brothels, and gambling dens. Red-light districts in San Francisco's Barbary Coast, Storyville in New Orleans, New York's Tenderloin, and Chicago's Levee operated in partnership with an array of predatory police, court, and other officials. Chicago was an "open city" where saloonkeeper-politicos controlled gangs of thieves and sold lucrative streetcar and utility franchises to those proferring the most grease money. "If the copper does me a favor I got to do him one, a'nit I?" one professional thief told a reporter. "The world is a graft anyway you take it."[47]

On New Year's Day 1900, the thick-set, green-eyed Richard Croker, street brawler and tunnel worker in his youth and Tammany Hall boss for the last fifteen years, fell from a horse on his lavish English estate and broke a leg. Control over "the most perfect voting machine on earth," 200,000 to 300,000 votes, made Croker overlord of the political life of New York City. Nobody did business in the world's second largest city without his imprimatur. Even the powerful Metropolitan Street Railway financial ring centered around William C. Whitney and Thomas Ryan paid blackmail to Tammany. An NYPD captaincy (really a license to blackmail pimps, whores, thieves, and assorted citizens) could be had for $12,000–15,000. In his suite at the Democratic party's midtown Manhattan headquarters, the dressed-in-high-fashion Croker, an unlighted cigar in his teeth, received supplicants for favors like a medieval lord bestowing boons on his subjects. His son, attending Cornell University Law School in 1900, resided in a country estate replete with servants.[48]

41

Republican state bosses Tom "The Easy Boss" Platt in New York and Matthew Quay in Pennsylvania protected favored companies and used the threat of legislative action to extort protection money from businesses. Using a $5 million loan from American Sugar, Senator Nelson Aldrich of Rhode Island (nicknamed "the political boss of the United States") built a ninety-four-room chateau on Narragansett Bay and outfitted a two-hundred-foot yacht. Railroads across the country ran state politics and routinely placed state legislators and congressmen on lucrative retainers. Corporate lobbyists spent lavishly in Washington.[49]

The "honest vote" was a major issue. Philadelphia (among other locales) was notorious for ballot stuffing. As 1900 began, the governor-elect of Kentucky was assassinated after a rigged state election, and Frankfort, the state capital, was occupied by armed camps backing different successors; the U.S. Senate investigated Senator William A. Clark, a mining magnate who had rather casually bought his Senate seat from the Montana state legislature for up to $50,000 per vote.[50]

The war with Spain had showcased this corruption at its most venal. Carnegie and other major war contractors had made outlandish profits on materiel furnished to the War Department. The inedible canned beef (popularly known as "embalmed beef") supplied by the beef trust to the U.S. Army launched a spate of fruitless investigations. And the culture of corruption traveled well. During the postwar U.S. occupation of Cuba, some of Mark Hanna's Ohio political patronage allies overseeing the Cuban post office system siphoned off large sums from the postal accounts.

The game that evoked the most passion among Americans, professional baseball, was, despite the open gambling going on throughout the ballparks, thought to be the sole sport not gambler controlled. But the National League team owners, the "magnates" whom the *Sporting News* labeled "a galaxy of bandits," were notorious for their under-the-table deals and encouragement of the John McGraw–style spike and knee 'em roughhouse play. An owner like Charles Ebbets in Brooklyn could be blackmailed by local politicians demanding free passes on the threat of running a road through the middle of his ballpark. The recurring scandals in college football centering on the use of paid semi-professional players by universities such as Georgia, Michigan, Wisconsin, and Chicago (and cover-ups by student managers) were causing faculties to demand control over the sport.[51]

By the century's turn, political corruption tied to the escalating money-making frenzy was evoking a sizable backlash. Reform movements had begun to mobilize, led by middle-class intellectuals and professionals resentful of the rise of the super rich, and indignant about sleazy alliances between business and politicians. Over the next decade or so, they would spearhead a Progressive movement dedicated to reforming the country's political institutions.

Among the era's most incisive critics was the brilliant but somewhat unstable John Jay Chapman, in 1900 a thirty-nine-year-old anti–Tammany Hall New York City political reformer. Chapman directly linked the extraordinary importance Americans gave to money with political corruption. "Dishonesty is a mere result of excessive devotion to money-making," he wrote. "The devotion of the individual to his bank account."

Observing the routine bribery of judges, councilmen, and other public officials, Chapman refused to make the usual convenient distinctions between virtuous businessman and "bad" politician. Rather, he insisted that "political corruption is a mere spur and offshoot of our business corruption" and that the corporate executives setting up phony subsidiaries to cheat stockholders, the blackmail practiced by railroad speculators, and so on, were part and parcel of the larger social and political corruption. "All our politics is business," was his assessment, "and our business is politics."[52]

Nonetheless, Jack Chapman, rapier wit and all, shared the impotence of other middle-class critics in the face of overwhelming realities of power, wealth, and dream values in American life. The dilemma that stumped Chapman, Ward, and other reformers: How to secure the wider social welfare when the country's citizens were still acting in accord with a worldview appropriate to an earlier age. Eventually, taking a path similar to Tom Watson's and that of other frustrated reformers, Chapman would begin looking for scapegoats to blame for the country's plight, and find them in Jews and other immigrants.

Corruption of personal and national morals was already the great theme of American literature. Novelists such as William Dean Howells, Theodore Dreiser, Stephen Crane, and Hamlin Garland struck hard at the brutality and crassness of social and economic life. One character in Howell's *A Hazard of New Fortunes* exclaims: "The dollar is the measure of every value, the stamp of every success." His novels increasingly highlighted individuals and families brutalized by the aggressive pursuit of success and wealth.

Dreiser's *Sister Carrie*, published in 1900, the raw, powerful story of a rural girl turned out of a $4.50–a-week Chicago shoe factory job to eventually become a successful actress, connected the plight of the working-class poor, the manipulation and sale of sex, and the centrality of money to the quality of one's life in America. The decline of a central character, George Hurstwood, from respected Chicago saloon manager to defeated panhandler represented the abyss so many Americans feared. Carrie herself, if economically well off at novel's end, is saddened and dispirited by her experiences. Bearing too many unwanted truths, the novel elicited little initial interest from reviewers and the reading public.

Meanwhile, social gospel ministers such as Yale Divinity School's Washington Gladden and Ohio clergyman Lyman Abbott, concerned about the decay of traditional ethical codes before the rising culture of consumption and hedonism, utilized their pulpits to assault the worship of "mammon" and the "almighty dollar" and to demand government regulation of private property. A spectrum of ministers, social workers, and academics even dared to suggest that lack of material success might be due not to individual failings, but to the workings of an impersonal, laissez-faire economic system—Lester Ward asserting that poverty itself was "a bar to opportunity." Reformers like Florence Kelley and Lillian Wald opened urban settlement houses and actively fostered new legislation protecting the unprotected.[53]

So the American mind remained profoundly split, distrusting, even demonizing Big Money, while pursuing the goal of success and, if possible, the Big Jackpot. Perhaps, nobody embodied this pattern better than Mark Twain. Always skeptical of the virtue and talents of the businessmen of his day, he would denounce the avarice, fraud, racketeering, and government corruption of the Gilded Age, using his scathing pen to argue for the primacy of human beings over property, then proceed to compulsively speculate his earnings away trying to capitalize on insiders' tips. The most gifted observer of his generation, Twain made a compelling case against the "truth" that economic mobility and the success ethic could create a decent society, but remained infatuated as anyone with their enchantments.

Americans took leave of the nineteenth century having constructed a national ethos that equated being free with being left alone to carve one's destiny. Personal achievement of wealth and status had become synonymous with the nation's progress. "Progress," in fact, came far closer than any word in American English to being a religious incantation.

A price was to be exacted for this: *A genuine moral center could never quite be located.* What "the sky's the limit" came to mean was freedom from virtually *any* limits. One insightful contemporary, John Graham Brooks, brooded that Americans had based their society on "an inadequate theory of freedom," and he feared the resulting chaos.

Since the logic was to exhalt the affluent and influential, while "losers" got blamed for character failings, the root causes of inequality and poverty could never be addressed head-on. The poignant gap between tough personal realities and cultural norms of abundance left a tinder-box of frustrations and anger nearly always at hand. The range of genuine "citizens' rights" was narrowed. Ultimately, what got sabotaged was a broader vision of the United States as a *national community*.

So Americans entered the new century bearing a mythomoteur that at once empowered and emboldened them, yet often left their intellectual, spiritual, and moral sensibilities flat and deadened. (Was this why one critic of the time credited his countrymen with "abundant wit, but very little humor"?) It was through this prism that Americans were to understand and act upon the critical issues confronting them.[54]

Part II

Fin de Siècle Dilemmas

Chapter 4

Kings of America

To make so much money, that you don't mind, don't mind anything—that is, absolutely, I think, the American formula.

—Henry James, circa 1900

The Millionaire is America's king
America is his to have and hold
His golden land! His Land of Gold!

—Eliakim Zunser
"For Whom Is the Gold Country" (widely sung in 1900)

All the wealth in the country will soon be
in the hands of a few men.

—*Munsey's,* 1900

A few years after the Civil War, the poet Walt Whitman, visionary spokesman for the America-that-might-yet-be, took pen in hand to imagine "a more universal ownership of property, general comfort, a vast intertwining rearticulation of wealth." Here was an expression of that uniquely American sense of the working out of equality as part of the national destiny.

By 1900, however, this Whitmanesque notion of a genuinely democratic and egalitarian society had, like so many other things, been swept away by the economic revolution that had overtaken the country. Rather than democracy and rough equality, the touchstones of American economic life were fast becoming hierarchy and gaping inequalities.

The United States, despite popular mythology, had, of course, never been classless. Yet since the days of Thomas Jefferson and Ben Franklin, the nation had prided itself on the independent, always fluid class character of its (white) population. Americans were, after all, supposed to be robustly on the make toward the better life. But now at the end of the nineteenth century, class lines were petrifying, being etched in granite. There was a splintering of society between rich and poor of unbridgeable proportions.[1]

The critical factor: the anarchic and compartmentalized manner in which the nation had been industrialized. Corporate and financial elites had used means fair and foul to pulverize opposition and dominate new raw-material sources, technologies, and markets, utilizing political allies, public resources, and high protective tariffs to erect business empires. In the process they had become wealthier than any group in human history.

The scene was what Americans a century later would have recognized as a "winner-takes-all economy." The victors, the newly minted oligarchy of railroad and tobacco barons, mining kings, dukes of coking coal and wire rods and copper, had emerged from the industrial/financial wars with a lockhold on a major share of the national wealth and income. The data are sketchy, but in 1890, the richest 1 percent of families controlled about one-half of the country's wealth, the richest 12 percent had 86 percent; the top 2 percent had about one-half of all income. A decade later, the top one-eighth of families in the economic hierarchy took 80 percent of national income.[2]

If dollars shaped life parameters, then incomes were dependent upon which economic compartment a person was situated in (a rich monopoly like Standard Oil offered better and more secure employment than a Pennsylvania mine), whether one was in the core or casual labor markets (a major railroad versus sharecoppping on a Mississippi plantation), and the bargaining power to be exerted from a specific job site (a plant chemist versus a bank teller).

The economy was simply generating strikingly different outcomes for people situated in its different compartments, a fact starkly highlighted wherever the American super-rich and destitute poor happened to be near neighbors.

An hour's walk from the ornate mansions of Boston's Beacon Hill were the damp, rundown hovels and starved faces of the Italian-immigrant North End. Nearby the chateaus lining Fifth Avenue lay the mean streets of Five Points and the West Side tenement districts. On frigid winter nights, fur-coated Broadway theatergoers sporting high silk toppers passed lines of raggedly clad men panhandling nickels for a night's flophouse lodging. In

Chicago and San Francisco, the opulence of Lakeshore Drive and Nob Hill quickly gave way to neighborhoods living at subsistence. Biltmore, the Vanderbilts' peerless North Carolina estate, its palatial main building containing forty master bedrooms and three huge fireplaces, was located athwart a community of impoverished Appalachian mountain people sheltering in rude cabins.[3]

The statistic that the "average family" commanded the sum of $3,000 to $4,000 in wealth seemed impressive on its face, but what if this meant one family possessing $50 million and 10,000 others virtually nothing? William Dean Howells was not alone in wondering about "that struggle for material prosperity" that had yielded "so many millionares and so many tramps." The record-breaking August 1900 heat wave that enveloped much of the United States witnessed tenement dwellers in New York and Chicago sleeping on rooftops to catch a breath of air while the native aristocracy gathered at Newport, Rhode Island, bathed at Bailey's beach, and attended the Astor Cup sailboat races.

The poor were legion. The incomes of a large majority of city and country unskilled/semiskilled workers were at or below the crucial $400–$500–per-annum line that signified poverty. Within this not-so-exclusive club were southern piney woods farmers, Pennsylvania coal miners, garment workers on New York's Lower East Side, and skilled or white-collar workers fallen on hard times. Georgia sharecroppers, Philadelphia laundresses, Chicago packinghouse and North Carolina mill workers were also members.[4]

The next economic layer was inhabited by folks earning about $550 to $800, sufficient to make if through if all went well and the family's luck held, but not enough to save anything, and thus sorely vulnerable in times of family crisis or economic downturn. Here were located skilled and semi-skilled workers, people like machinists, railroad brakemen and firemen, tailors, department store sales ladies, office clerks, plus modestly successful farmers.

The Industrial Age had also ushered in the Paper Age and one of the fastest growing occupational groups (708,000 by 1900) was clerical staff in offices. Although they dressed well, prized their status as salaried, "middle-class" employees, and had better working conditions than manual workers, these white-collars were mainly located in the $550–$800 category and struggling. Promotions, especially for women, were infrequent.[5]

Still higher in the class structure were the "middling" but generally comfortable group of households in the bracket between $800 and $5,000, a category expanding of late. Here, an older middle class of small businessmen and well-to-do farmers were being joined by factory managers, professionals, engineers, and insurance underwriters. Lifestyles at the high end (for example, President McKinley's worshipful secretary George Cortelyou and the $4,000–a-year department store division manager) resembled the upper middle class, servants and all. Meanwhile, the doctors, lawyers, factory engineers, salesmen, managers, the Chicago high school teacher (starting around $900) and the U.S. Treasury Department clerk ($1,500) occupying the lower end, led "respectable" but distinctly more modest economic lives.

Incomes in the $5,000–$50,000 range brought one into an upper middle class that had been a prime beneficiary of America's whirlwind economic revolution. Among this group were medium-sized entrepreneurs, middle to upper managers, some professionals, investors, prosperous farmers and landlords. The lady of the household would expect to have a full support system of servants available to service her large, commodious house and might often spend her afternoons shopping and "visiting." She might wear the latest Parisian fashions at club teas. There were mountain or lakeside resorts for the summer and private schools for the children.

At the apex of the economic pyramid were those households claiming $50,000 or more in income each year. Almost everyone here, whether Senator Clark from Montana, the mining magnate with a quarter million a year in income, or a John D. Rockefeller ($10 million per year), were owners of large financial or industrial holdings, but there were some top managers of large corporations, too, and corporate lawyer/lobbyists on sizable retainers, like the whiskey trust's Levi Mayer, rumored to be making nearly $1 million per annum. Class movement was dynamic, however, and quite affluent people might slide down and out of society, as well as up.[6]

No one symbolized the era better than its millionaires, some 4,000 by 1900. This was a heterogenous bunch, ranging from urban financiers and industrialists to shrewd, market-savy speculators and small-town entrepreneurs leapfrogging to sudden wealth. If they did not quite comprehend how the country had passed into their hands, much less what they would do with it, these upstarts were determined on maintaining their position in American life and protecting and expanding what they had.

They enjoyed being rich in a society where wealth was easily converted into status, power, and personal specialness. Few among them agreed with steelman Andrew Carnegie who (probably reiterating the views of his radical, long-dead Scots weaver father) declared that wealth was a public "trust" to be disposed of responsibly. They cared even less for Carnegie's dictum that to die rich was among the most heinous of sins.[7]

Indeed, by the century's turning, the new commercial elite had created a fantastically elaborate and ritualized lifestyle mimicking that of the European nobility, yet all the same quite distinctively American. Its emergence may be dated from the get-rich-quick seventies and eighties and the original set of American super rich, men like the demonically driven railroad magnate Jay Gould, Cornelius Vanderbilt's son, William, and J.P. Morgan, whose money allowed them to live as opulently as they wished while being insulated from criticism or attacks from what was, on the surface at least, still a Puritan-minded society. The material standards and lifestyle they and others established became obligatory benchmarks for others who followed.[8]

By the century's turning, every town of any size had its homegrown economic and social elites and the cultural institutions—residential suburbs, private day and prep schools, and business and country clubs—they had built. On late autumnal Saturdays, the squirearchy of rural counties like Maryland's Montgomery and Marlboro would don gray tweed coats and Bedford cord breeches, velvet hats and buckskin gloves, and ride to the foxes. Some local notables, like the Drexels of Philadelphia, or the Stanfords and Hearsts of San Francisco, were formidable on anybody's social chart. But the country's most wealthy and powerful men and women (or those with serious aspirations to be so) gravitated to New York, drawn by the twin towers of business and high society at their most scintillating.

The world of high society circa 1900 proved, in fact, every bit as brutally competitive as the Great American Business Wars these families had recently triumphed in. Wealth, while a basic prerequisite, did not in itself guarantee admission to the most rarefied circles of New York high society. Society was entered at one of its various rings of prestige and a strict regimen adhered to in order to demonstrate one's worthiness.

Along with the social reform and temperance movements, high society was one of the few quasi-public arenas of American life, given leadership by women. Venerable aristocrats like Mrs. Caroline Astor and Mrs. Stuyvesant Fish exercised dictatorial control over the byzantine process of screening people for invitations to events such as the Patriarchs Ball, cotillions, and tea parties. Violators of established rules could be quite brutally ejected from grace. Only by conforming to an already well established style of upper-class life could the newly monied "swells" hope for entree to highest society.

This entailed stocking their recently acquired Manhattan brownstones with art treasures of classic antiquity and English-style country manor houses with racehorses. One threw "strategic" parties at Delmonico's and the Waldorf-Astoria (strutting around that hotel's aptly named Peacock Alley in full-dress regalia); joined clubs such as the Metropolitan, with its classic Greek columns and iron grilles, and the Union (reputed to have the best wine cellar and French books in the United States); kept boxes at the Metropolitan Opera; attended the races at Saratoga; and summered at Bar Harbor, Maine, or the more desirable Newport, Rhode Island. Sons were packed off to Exeter and Groton and, later, Yale, Harvard, and Princeton, where they were admitted to elite clubs like Fly and Porcellian; daughters went off to finishing schools.[9]

Around 1900, the older and newer money were clearly amalgamating to form a broadened upper class. The recent infusion of wealth upped the ante. In the process of buying up virtually everyone and everything (including the work of artists they often despised) that would validate their status, the nouveau riche steeply ratcheted up the notion of what constituted elite consumption and display in the United States. William C. Whitney, the power-broker attorney turned Manhattan electric streetcar magnate, stocked a 10,000–acre Massachussetts estate with big-game buffalo, elk, and game birds. The stories were legion of fabled shoppers like a Mrs. O'Neill, wife of the man who dominated the country's barley sales, entering a shop in Chicago and in short order running up a tab of $25,000 in jewels and books.[10]

Meanwhile, the competition was on for who could throw the season's most lavish and sensational entertainments. Nothing seemed too outrageous as long as nobody had done it before, no expense excessive. The more outrageously wasteful an activity, the more it was prized. Society women, sniffed a dowager from one of society's oldest families, were "on the lookout for novelties in order to attract guests to their entertainments and to excite admiration of their own daring flights of fancy."[11]

Parties were minutely scripted and choreographed. One gala affair featured guests smoking cigars wrapped in hundred-dollar bills, another had a showgirl bursting out of a huge cake. Favorite themes included phantasmagorical recreations of the Arabian Nights and the eighteenth-century Versailles court of Marie Antoinette. At the block-long Vanderbilt mansion on 51st and Fifth Avenue, built along the lines of a palace on the Loire (two huge bronze doors by the Renaissance Italian artist Ghiberti framed the entrance), Mrs. Cornelius Vanderbilt threw phenomenally elaborate entertainments for six hundred to a thousand guests. Footmen clad in the maroon livery of the Vanderbilts and standing at rigid attention on each step of the mansion's great curving marble stairway gave these extravaganzas a true feel of the ancien regime.[12]

Inevitably, a newly monied class in search of legitimation would seek to identify with older aristocracies of blood lineage, which explains the resemblance of American palaces to those of French kings and English lords and the dressing of coachmen and servants in livery. The Elizabethan-style stables with finished oak changing rooms at great country estates like Albert Bostwick's on Long Island were virtual replicas of those in Yorkshire or Surrey. Mrs. Delia Caton, arbiter of fashion in Chicago's high society, threw Cleopatra parties while seated on a solitary throne. The upper classes went to comical lengths to establish genealogical linkages to European royalty, and spent summers in Paris and London and autumns in Sicily. A passel of Vanderbilt, Whitney, and Gould daughters married penniless but titled and castled English and continental men.

Watching this dance of the sugarplum fairies from afar, a youngish, bohemian-looking economics professor with some heretical notions, Thorstein Veblen, penned *The Theory of the Leisure Class*, a work that would eventually bring terms such as "conspicuous consumption" into the mainstream of American English.

Largely ignored or disparaged when published in 1899, *The Theory* was far more than a satire of the nouveau rich and famous. Veblen had an uncanny understanding of the critical function of conspicuous consumption and leisure in setting big money above and apart from other Americans. The obsession of this spanking American aristocracy, he reasoned, was with legitimacy, and wild, seemingly irrational, spending was clearly a principle instrument to acquire it. But Veblen's roots in a deeply traditional Norwegian-American farm community in Wisconsin also gave him a unique appreciation of the disastrous long-term consequences of upper-class hedonism on older traditions of pride in work and craftsmanship. He gauged, moreover, that the plutocrats would not manage the industrial system in the interests of the people as a whole.[13]

Meanwhile, social snobbery demanded locating "others" to exclude. Yale's idealistic new president Arthur Hadley might exhort his audiences about the virtues of "democratic equality" and demand that his institution not become a "rich man's college," but Yale and other Ivies had become class-ridden institutions where monied students monopolized the elite "eating clubs," and secret societies excluded students of modest means. In the larger society, since hefty fortunes by themselves were too plentiful to be used as a source of exclusion, the "differentness" of Jews was fastened upon to deny them access to elite clubs, hotels, and schools.[14]

Some contemporaries, noting high society's demand for perfection of clothes, companions, sports, etiquette, et al., thought its rituals a form of public self-imprisonment. Even on summer "holidays," the upper-class set moved in lockstep through carefully prescribed routines. In July 1900, a perceptive journalist observing them gathered from Boston, New York, Philadelphia, Chicago, and San Francisco to summer at Newport mused that the frenetic round of balls, dinners, and functions was "a form of slavery that is the most dangerous in the world because it is voluntary." Rich families "could not just rest and swim," because "the refinements of a curious civilization has made them slaves of the clock."

Rigid schedules were in force for gathering at Bailey's Beach (11 A.M.), and later at the Casino for formal lunch. At 4 P.M. daily, the gates along

Bellevue Avenue's "huddle of palaces" opened and coaches and broghams poured out to parade along the Cliffs. The competition for place and position was white hot and interminably strategized over. "There seems to be no escape from snobbishness in Newport," wrote the reporter. "People breathe it in with the air."[15]

Codes of public behavior were unbending and enforced by ostracism. Private, out-of-sight behaviors, however, were shrugged off and it was rumored that the reason so few men appeared at high-society functions was because they much preferred the intimate company of their showgirl mistresses. But the monied elite was not immune to the recent trend toward greater expression of self and sensuality originating among working-class folk. Witness the mildly iconclastic blueblood, Asa Astor, surrounded by a group of ten young men about town reverently nicknamed the "Knickerbocker dudes," who throughout 1900 gallivanted around late-night Manhattan clubs setting the tone of high style well beyond New York.[16]

These were the years when the plutocrats were developing elaborate vacation retreats. William Rockefeller, Cyrus McCormack, and J.P. Morgan, for example, patronized the Jekyll Island Club (nicknamed "The One Hundred Millionaires") off the Georgia coast. And yet a full-fledged leisure class along European lines had not yet emerged. American businessmen remained too riveted on locating new investments, cutting lucrative deals, and expanding enterprises to find new interests easily. It was the only life most of them knew and felt comfortable with. So they worked on, long after more money than they could ever spend had been secured.

As a young man, Andrew Carnegie had vowed to leave business at the age of thirty-five or so, or as soon as he had won enough money to lead a quiet, reflective life. Instead he had driven on for decades afterward to leadership of the nation's iron and steel industry, haunted by compulsions that he himself recognized only too well. "Whatever I engage in, I must push inordinately," he remarked once. Morgan, the forbidding "Jupiter" of the piercing eyes and bulbous nose, worked his partners to exhaustion in overseeing his increasingly complex and far-flung financial holdings.[17]

Businessmen continued to rise early and work late. Clubs like the Union and Metropolitan closed at 1 A.M. since members went to their offices early. "Our men of great wealth go into offices and seriously devote their talents and capacities to the accumulation of great wealth," noted the perceptive *Collier's* columnist Margaret Sangster. These were men, she thought, who found "the fierce aggression of business pressing on them."[18]

Meanwhile, Simon Patten, a highly innovative University of Pennsylvania economics professor, had by 1900 come to a rather momentous conclusion:

The revolution in American industrial production meant that for the first time in human history, abundance was possible for *all* in a rationally organized and managed economy. "The materials for humanity's rapid development are ample," he wrote. What must be done is to build a cooperative society where the social surplus could be used for the common welfare.[19]

This was also the view of a growing number of social thinkers. Lester Ward consistently argued that only a small minority of Americans were positioned to benefit from the economic revolution. "We want pianos, bicycles, jewelry, good clothes, and so forth," declared Herbert Casson, speaking for widening consumerism. "Only guarantee every citizen $20 a week in wages and there would be the greatest boom in business the world has ever known." Here was an exciting and quite revolutionary vision: a nation purged of poverty and based on plenty.[20]

Little of this, however, touched the industrialists and their managers, believing as they did that only the fears generated by an economy of scarcity could motivate men and women to labor. Any major alteration in the system was regarded as a threat to maintaining operational control over their businesses and employees, not to mention their own mystique of indispensability.

What *did* engage their attention, however, were the ideas of evolutionary social Darwinism, which they casually adopted, bantering around terms like "survival of the fittest." If competition was a natural law in which dysfunctional and diseased parts of the economic body were removed for the health of the whole organism, then their class must clearly embody the supremacy of the healthiest and fittest. It was they who had bestowed industries and jobs and prosperity on the American worker.[21]

The belief in the right to rule absolutely over any business enterprises in which they had a controlling interest became a fundamental article of faith. George Baer, president of the Philadelphia and Reading Railroad, a coal and railroad conglomerate, and known for his hard-nosed attitude toward labor, enunciated a "divine rights of management" theory under which "there cannot be two masters in the management of business." Workers, went the argument, contracted with employers of their own free will and had little, if any, right to complain about their conditions or lives.[22]

And for all Andrew Carnegie's hyperbole about the workingman's dignity and rights, he had not hesitated to use private armies and state militia in suppressing the Homestead steel strike in 1893. Eight years later, when he sold out to J.P. Morgan, nearly all signs of union organization had been rooted out of Carnegie Steel. He was hardly alone. Here, baseball again provided a metaphor for the larger society. Word surfaced before the 1900 season that some National League players, distressed by the "reserve clause" in their contracts—which severely restricted whom they might play for, thus under-cutting their bargaining position—were planning to unionize. Incensed club "magnates" immediately threatened to close down the league.[23]

Throughout industry, the drive to raise production and reduce costs was intense. This meant industrial managers seeking a greater degree of control over the worksite exercised their prerogatives ruthlessly. Carnegie and his right-hand man, the charismatic, piano-playing extrovert Charles Michael Schwab, relentlessly pushed their plant managers to raise production and cut costs, taunting and playing them against each other. Directives from the top were carried out at the shop floor by hard-driving foremen. "I must keep my men down," said one, ". . . keep down (their wages) or my report to the boss would be against me." Railroad general manager George H. Paine would describe his role as akin to a major general in wartime: The railroad, he told *Munsey's*, "must be much like that of an army of slaves to be successful." And as on any battlefield, there would be an acceptable rate of casualties.[24]

So America Inc.'s general response to the formidable wave of strikes and labor agitation across the country during 1899–1902 was to play hardball. Tactically, this entailed the widespread use of lockouts, blacklists, union-busting, court injunctions, state militias, and gun thugs. Management in in-dustries like mining and lumbering tended to use more antilabor violence than manufacturers, whose strategy was to introduce sophisticated new ma-chinery and "scientific" factory management techniques such as those being popularized by Midvale Steel engineer-manager Frederick Winslow Taylor to undermine the workers' knowledge base and bargaining position. As one employer said candidly, "I want machines so simple in their operation that any fool can run them."[25]

Not that industrialists were devoid of compassion as they understood it. Nor were they the puffed up dollar-engorging monsters caricatured by the anti–big-business press. The much reviled John D. Rockefeller, by 1900 chan-neling large sums into the University of Chicago and medical research, was also a generous employer, who valued his Standard Oil people and provided benefits for sickness and old age. Pittsburgh coking coal/steel baron Henry Clay Frick was known to make private donations to workers and widows in distress. Mark Hanna and others did the same. But they would at all costs protect their autocratic power.[26]

Which explains why even corporate "welfare" programs designed for employees had a definite social control agenda. About seventy companies led by John Patterson's National Cash Register Company in Dayton, Ohio, had initiated programs to provide (mostly female) workers with wholesome working conditions and access to gyms, libraries, musical concerts, and out-door recreation. "Social welfare secretaries" were hired to manage programs

and individual grievances. Some companies instituted bureaucratic personnel management practices in place of the "drive" system based on fear and
compulsion. Better work environments with electric lighting and lockers were
introduced. The Brooklyn Rapid Transit Company set up reading and smoking rooms for its men and offered lunches at cost: coffee for a penny, two-
cent sandwiches, pies for three cents.[27]

This corporate welfare idea and the "scientific management" schemes
embodied by Taylor and others reflected the rising turn-of-the-century mania for worker efficiency. Corporations concerned with a declining work
ethic and alienated workers designed programs to convince employees of
the "mutuality of interests" binding them to employers. What the sponsors
of corporate paternalism hoped to do was to recreate the ties and loyalties of
an earlier era and reinvigorate the "work ethic" *without having to alter the
mind- and soul-numbing nature of industrial work.* "It Pays!" became the
general slogan of corporate welfare managers. The expected payoff would
be reduced employee turnover, higher productivity, and less threat of union-
ization. John Patterson, a compulsively ruthless competitor who has been
compared to today's Microsoft magnate Bill Gates, and who utilized research
scientists, salesmen, and patent lawyers to build NCR's supremacy, started
his company's model welfare program as a response to shoddy workman-
ship and high employee turnover.[28]

So corporate responsibility was to be on the company's terms and defined
in the company's interest. Companies might bestow and might also take away.
In 1899, that bastion of enlightened capitalism, National Cash Register, fired
its unionized workers; two years later, it locked out 2,400 striking workers
and busted their unions. In those firms where welfarism carried the undisguised middle-class missionary spirit of a civilizing mission, contempt for
working-class values led its managers to reach down into intimate areas of
workers' lives. On occasion, this evoked fierce resistance.[29]

Workers continued to be viewed as both necessary cogs in the industrial
machine and, on occasion, as potential threats to elite power and privileges,
but rarely, if ever, as partners in a great ongoing experiment. In those mining
and manufacturing industries populated by foreign-born workers, Anglo-
Saxon managers tended to look upon them as predestined to be toilers. Indeed, it was the rare industrialist, like one Bridgeport, Connecticut, factory
owner, who would acknowledge that his employees "have had a large share
in enabling me to make my money and I feel I owe them some recognition of
that fact." Labor participation in decision-making was regarded as an abdi-
cation of management responsibility.[30]

What the upper class most definitely was *not*, however, was a governing
class in the mode of their turn-of-the-century counterparts in Europe and

elsewhere. Affluent and powerful, they were reshaping the country's economic life, and had to be listened to. Yet, they were curiously remote and silent. Their intellectual interests and conversation were so negligible as to cause a man of letters like Charles Francis Adams (who as a railroad president knew the business elite well) to lambast them privately as incredibly ignorant, one-dimensional boors. "Of course, I have no other interest in life but my business," proudly avowed Philip Armour, of the massive Chicago meat-packing house. Living in grand isolation from the massive dislocations caused by their industrial regime, plutocrats (and their top managers) simply disclaimed responsibility.[31]

Business was their passion, not politics. Yes, they begrudgingly paid for political protection and favors, demanded federal help in securing foreign markets and tariffs to shelter their manufactures from foreign competition, and grabbed off government contracts, but all the time holding politics and politicians beneath contempt. The "democratic" process amounted to a messy inconvenience better left to their skillful lobbyists and well-placed U.S. senators such as Nelson Aldrich, Matthew Quay, and Chauncey DePew to dispose of.

The exception was those occasions when they felt their interests to be genuinely threatened by some demon or other, as in 1896, when one appeared in the form of William Jennings Bryan and free silver. In that momentous political year, the big-business class had inserted itself directly into the political arena in the large, shambling, and wholly unique person of Marcus Alonzo Hanna.

Situated as the plutocrats were, in control of the economy's strategic resources and crucial products, the money flowed in rather effortlessly. No wonder contemporaries referred to them as "Midases." At the time of his death in 1899, Cornelius Vanderbilt had, with fairly minimal effort, succeeded in doubling the $90 million bequeathed to him fourteen years earlier by his father. John D. Rockefeller drew $3 million yearly in Standard Oil dividends.[32]

The existence of the super rich may have been an issue to some clergy, intellectuals, and socialists outraged by their follies and aristocratic posturing. But the explosion in personal wealth didn't seem to disturb most citizens. By 1900 the sheer opulence and wastefulness of rich and famous lifestyles had become indistinguishable from the nation's greatness, part of the legendary American brag. Redistribution of the American pie simply went too much against the grain of American dreaming. The decision by the U. S. Supreme Court a few years earlier declaring the federal income tax unconstitutional had caused no large-scale public outcry. The New York, Chicago, or Washington of 1900 were not the Paris of the *sans-culottes* of 1793.

As the nation's surrogate royalty, the plutocrats and the lives they led exerted a continuing fascination on the imagination of other Americans, who compulsively sought out the latest news and gossip about their comings and goings in newspapers and magazines. "All Americans," wrote Frank Lewis Ford in *Munsey's*, "are interested deeply and personally in the Vanderbilt family." This was reciprocated by the super rich and their public relations people, who generally encouraged such interest.[33]

On Sundays and holidays on upper Fifth Avenue, crowds gathered to spy out the "nobs" as they entered and alighted from their carriages. Mobs descended on churches where elite weddings were occurring. Debutantes had their diets reported in the newspapers. The road through a pinewood forest leading to the lavish Lakewood, New Jersey, Renaissance-style mansion of railroad heir and playboy George Gould was heavily trafficked by sightseers. The presence of the super rich at Newport was a draw for less affluent vacationers—the families of white- and blue-collar workers, who took to watching for the carriages of the rich and famous passing along the streets around Bellevue Avenue. They delighted in learning the names of the occupants, commenting on their satin-striped dresses and bonnets with veils, and speculating on the lives they led.[34]

So the bulk of citizens accorded the plutocracy the right to have as much as they had and to put it on full display, and would probably have agreed with Columbia University's John Bates Clark that "if a man can create a billion dollars, let him have it and welcome."[35]

But there was a caveat: In Clark's view, as for many Americans, the issue was whether or not the multimillionaire was "making a net addition to the wealth of the world." Only that gave validity to great wealth and power. Popular opinion did not condemn the pioneer industrialists who were judged to have reaped their rewards from "building" the country in open competition. No one rebuked Andrew Carnegie for claiming that the great fortunes were good for the progress of the "race." But turn-of-the-century upstart speculators, stock manipulators, and merger promoters making dazzling sums of money from corporate manipulations were widely viewed as a disreputable lot undermining the country's moral base. Widespread sentiment existed for curtailing their activities.[36]

Even those within the Republican political establishment, such as the U.S. Secretary of the Treasury Lyman Gage, a Chicago banker, became sensitive to public opinion on this matter. "The large fortunes accumulated within a comparatively short period by a few men . . . ," Gage wrote to a friend in Peekskill, New York, "affect the imagination and excite the belief that 'something is wrong,' that 'robbery is going on.'"[37]

This hostility toward "illegitimate" wealth was inseparable from the mounting resentment against the advent of business on a colossal scale, the "trusts." By 1900, big business had been around long enough to raise up a full hue and cry against it. Purchasing a pound of meat, a gallon of lighting oil, a railroad or streetcar ticket, tenpenny nails, breakfast cereal, meant tribute paid to one gigantic firm or another.

"We see in monopoly then," concluded the astute University of Wisconsin economist Richard Ely, "one of the chief reasons for the vast concentration of wealth in this country." Since the source of the new plutocracy's golden touch lay in its control over monopolies and oligopolies, any movement to restrict or dismantle them would generate shock waves throughout the American social structure.[38]

The fight over the trusts was to be critical terrain on which it would be decided who would control the nation's economy and politics and how American wealth was to be distributed.

Chapter 5

The Great Game

I am not willing to place the laboring men of this country at the
mercy of the heads of monopolies.

—William Jennings Bryan, 1899

Why there isn't a man who has money to invest in the country
who cannot build a tin mill if he wants to.

—Mark Hanna, 1900

These corporations they say have no souls, but the trust has a
soul—a devil's soul . . . seeking whom it may devour.

—Archbishop Spalding, 1900

"Competition," noted New York State civil service commissioner William
Miller Collier, writing a book about trusts in the spring of 1900, "is the mother
of trusts." The financial panics and depressions of the 1870s and 1880s had
first revealed that great plague of modern industry: overproduction. Manufacturers responding to disappearing markets by radically cutting prices and
invading each other's territories caused havoc and sent bankruptcy rates soaring. Surviving companies had strong incentives to "kill" competition and
formed pools, cartels, and trusts to maintain prices and profits.[1]

The original "trust" form of corporate organization had been initiated by

Standard Oil Company lawyers back in 1882. The taciturn, secretive John D. Rockefeller's obsession with dominating the oil business and maximizing profits had led him to cajole and coerce other oil refiners to exchange independent ownership for certificates in a new organization controlled by trustees. The whiskey, cottonseed oil, and sugar industries soon followed Standard's lead, until some years later, the trust form of organization was made illegal by the Sherman Antitrust Act.

Two chosen instruments then emerged for concentrating business power: holding companies maintaining a "community of interest" through stock ownership and common directors, and the merger, combining various firms into one massive corporation registered in states with highly favorable laws such as New Jersey and Delaware.[2]

But the word "trust" had stuck with the American public. It would serve as a generic term for those firms with enough market muscle to dominate entire industries, controlling the prices of raw materials, transportation costs, and the end product to the consumer. A Columbia University professor's cogent definition of "trust"—"any company that is big enough to be menacing"—would probably have sounded right to many citizens.[3]

The year 1898 marked the beginning of an unprecedented merger stampede. The immediate impetus was U.S. Supreme Court decisions outlawing cartels, but also rendering the Sherman Act a dead letter for prosecuting manufacturing companies. This was the signal that promoters needed that the federal government would not intervene to prevent horizontally merged corporations of huge size from being formed. Meanwhile, the recent depression had left many companies weakened and vulnerable to being mopped up.[4]

During wildly speculative 1899, the year of super-bulls run amok on Wall Street, there were 105 mergers (over 1,200 companies disappearing), the following year 34. New corporate monoliths such as the National Biscuit Company, American Steel and Wire, National Steel, American Ice, the International Paper Company, and United Fruit were ushered into existence. The largest four hundred companies, capitalized at between $9 and $10 billion, or one-quarter of the U.S. total in 1900, were now the commanding force in the national economy.[5]

The returns for those well situated to participate in the merger festivities were stunning. Opportunistic promoters, financiers, underwriters, and law firms specializing in corporate reorganization helped drive the boom. Lawyers like Sullivan and Cromwell, Adolphus Green, and W.H. Moore located the cash to entice various rival companies into making compacts, cemented the deals, and drew commissions in the form of shares of grossly overcapitalized (or "watered") stock in the new enterprises.

The formation of National Steel and Wire, for instance, netted the Gates Brothers a cool $15 million in common stock. W.H. Moore got $10 million for promoting the American Tin Plate Company. J.P. Morgan, kingpin of investment bankers, presided over consolidations of a slew of major railroads, and brought the National Tube company, American Bridge, and American Sheet Steel into existence. William C. Whitney, Thomas Fortune Ryan, and Charles Yerkes, businessmen boasting superb political connections, picked off the country's choice urban streetcar companies.[6]

If sheer avarice was a force driving merger mania, so was the American dream's "the sky's-the-limit" mentality. The Morgans, Dukes, Havemeyers, Gates, et al. were men of colossal egos and ambitions, and they were constructing enterprises to match. The fact that Morgan directors already serving on the boards of financial giants like First National Bank, National Bank of Chicago, and Chase Manhattan now took seats on boards of these newly created corporations gave Morgan and a small group of men unprecedented power over the national economy. John D. Rockefeller, with a background in evangelical Christianity, always believed oil was a "miracle," and he was doing the work of God in delivering it. Questioned by the United States Industrial Commission as to the origins of the wire trust, John "Bet a Million" Gates, chief of American Steel and Wire, answered crisply, "We wished to be the wire manufacturers of the world." This was no hyperbole: Gates had indeed been negotiating with German manufacturers to split up the global market. "It wasn't the money we were after, 'twas the power we were all playing for," mused John D. Stillman, a banker allied with Rockefeller. "It was a great game."[7]

This was in the best American dream tradition, egomania and profiteering sanctified by progress and human service. In concentrating industries such as railroads or steel, a J.P. Morgan was certain he was providing more efficient service to the nation, while exorcising wasteful competition among his banking customers. Ditto for Adolphus Green, the Chicago lawyer who organized the country's largest bakeries into the National Biscuit Company in 1898, and within two years had developed the new Uneeda brand cracker, conducted the first million-dollar advertising campaign to transform it into a household name, and sold over 10 million packages.[8]

But the most potent force underlying the push for corporate giganticism was the dynamically changing nature of American capitalism itself. Late nineteenth-century revolutions in communications, transportation, and production technology had created new ways of producing and distributing goods. State-of-the-art machinery and production processes introduced by the rising caste of professional corporate managers generated larger and larger outputs. The advent of advertising and new sales networks facilitated selling to

65

continental and global markets. "It is the widening of markets which is responsible for combinations among producers," argued an advisor to Washington policy-makers. In this new business world, sheer size and vertical integration with firms boasting complementary skills and markets offered major advantages in production and sales. Companies like American Tobacco, Quaker Oats, Diamond Match, Campbell's Soup, Colgate Palmolive, and Eastman Kodak actively developed mass markets.[9]

A second powerful business instinct was the one that had inspired the Rockefellers to suppress competition in the oil business several decades before: the need to bring order, stability, and predictibility to maturing industries with heavier fixed costs. Indeed, the specter of overproduction haunted businessmen more intensely around 1900 than ever before. Not without reason: Overcapacity was rife. The marvelously productive factories coming on-line in virtually every industry were capable of churning out far more than Americans could possibly absorb.

Still, consolidation may not have been inevitable had it not been for the bitter depression of the nineties, which had launched a series of major price wars among capital intensive industries. Major companies in fields like tinplate, newsprint, wire nails, and copper, which had only recently expanded and taken on heavy fixed costs, now cut prices sharply to keep their plants running. Bankruptcies rose, and businessmen became acutely aware of the dangers of all-out competition. A National Salt Company executive told the U.S. Industrial Commission that his combine had come together as a consequence of suicidal competition undermining both the price and quality of salt: "Economic conditions demanded the formation of the organization," he insisted.[10]

So corporate leaders in various industrial fields acted to escape or "kill" genuine competition. This did not usually require a total 100 percent monopoly à la Buck Duke's American Tobacco Company, which, having swallowed its rivals, commanded sales of cigarettes and plug tobacco in the United States, or Diamond Match's ownership of every match factory in the country.

Rather, it meant comfortable coexistence through oligopoly, the dominant firm exercising price leadership. In effect, prices listed by Standard Oil (80–90 percent of the oil market) or American Sugar (90 percent of sugar) became *the* prices. Price cutting ceased to be a problem. The norm was to use "gentlemen's agreements" and industry federations to allocate market shares and territories. What the last years of the nineteenth century amply demonstrate is how quickly "free markets" became unfree.[11]

The trusts had first become a politically explosive national issue during the eighties when the Populists had flayed the eastern "money power" and railroads in the name of southern and western farmers. By 1898, thirty-one states had passed antitrust laws, some, such as Texas, laying down sweeping prohibitions on restraint of competition and price fixing. But the division of powers between states and the federal government undermined effective regulation. Presidents Cleveland and McKinley had only infrequently and ineffectively used the Sherman Antitrust Act to attack monopolies. Supreme Court decisions, moreover, worked to narrow the judicial meaning of Sherman's "conspiracy to restrain trade."[12]

The earlier debate over trusts had revolved mainly around control over "natural monopolies" such as railroads and telegraphs. Now, in 1900, combinations in industries producing consumer necessities such as heating oil, wire, nails, and sugar were creating a sense of urgency about the "trust problem" that would last for the next dozen years and give wings to the Progressive political movement and politicians like Theodore Roosevelt and Woodrow Wilson. Democrats and Republicans alike competed to gain the distinction of being the party that would protect the public from the evils of monopoly.

The trusts found an array of articulate defenders both within their own ranks and outside. Those opposed to (or at least critical of) big capital were both numerous and spread across the continent, and included farmers, small businessmen, salesmen, traditional professionals, intellectuals, and some workers. A host of overstated arguments and counterarguments were offered to the public. A roiling nationwide debate spilled over from newspapers and magazines to public lecture halls, saloons, and family dinner tables, and around potbellied stoves in country stores. Raw-edged and highly politicized, it exposed some of the most painful inconsistencies at the heart of the American-dream world view.

A number of questions framed the Great Trust Debate. Were the corporate giants really "a menace to industrial progress and to human liberty"? Did their size put them beyond economic laws? Would they annihilate any and all competition? A basic issue was whether or not the trust was economically *efficient*. Efficiency was usually posed in terms of prices: Would the combines make products available to Americans at cheaper prices, or would their awesome market power be used to gouge them? A second issue was jobs. Did the trusts intend treating their employees fairly, and what would happen to workers from smaller firms who were being displaced?[13]

The antitrust discourse was multifaceted and persuasive in its assault on the dangers of big business and easily lent itself to fiery orations and editorials. In short, the birth of the corporate giants was a wholly artificial affair motivated not by the special skills and economies of scale, but rather by simple greed and selfishness. Sleazy deals based on watered stock, along with high tariff walls to keep out foreign goods, cutthroat competition, political favors, and, in the case of Standard Oil and others, railroad rebates had given these unnatural creatures life and pumped them up to bloated proportions. Meanwhile, ordinary people's lives got mangled.

"The trusts are fond of advancing prices," was how John Bates Clark, one of the country's most respected authorities on trusts, put it. The power to control prices, critics argued, was the power to fix prices in one's own interest. Artificially low prices were applied to areas where competition remained stiff, while in places where monopoly had been consolidated, prices shot up. That arch-villain trust Standard Oil was usually (and for good reason) cited as a practitioner of this art.[14]

Recently formed combines like Pittsburgh Glass, American Tin Plate, and American Wallpapering were shown to have used their leverage to initiate steep price rises and to squeeze consumers. American Steel and Wire had ratcheted up prices of barbed wire and wire nails high enough to enrage farmers and ranchers. Metals firms controlled by the same interlocking boards of directors forced suppliers' prices down. Reports from the Carolinas told of American Tobacco's dictating leaf prices to growers. The gist of the argument was, remove the monopolies, and prices of oil and other essential goods would come tumbling down.[15]

Corporate rationalization was widely feared for the havoc it would wreak among workers; after all, *somebody* was going to be rationalized:—for example, the commercial traveler or salesman, who in competitive times had been invaluable in making contacts with retailers, but now seemed merely a wasteful expense. Testifying before the U.S. Industrial Commission in June 1899, and then at a Chicago Antitrust conference soon afterward, P.C. Dowe, president of a salesmen's organization, charged that the recent merger wave had thrown 35,000 of his members out of work, and put 25,000 on reduced wages. He denounced the trusts as "animated only by selfishness. . . . Personally I consider that trusts are the worst, the greatest evil that has ever confronted the American people."[16]

Dowe's testimony reinforced suspicions that the vast resources and overcapacity of the new combines gave them a whip hand over their employees. Workers who struck would find themselves locked out for the duration, and work shifted to other plants. They could take the corporate wage or starve. Monopoly profits would not be passed on in wages and workers would still be better off in competitive industries.[17]

Throughout 1899 and 1900, merged firms were, in fact, selecting plants to be closed. At least in the case of American Tin Plate, which shuttered almost a third of of its mills, management did engage in blackmail, playing off mills against each other to reduce wages and disempower and punish workers with a history of militancy. Thus, over a thousand tinplate workers in two Pittsburgh plants who had refused wage cuts were left jobless to face the winter of 1899–1900.[18]

It was, critics charged, a vicious cycle: Manipulating prices and attacking competitors, great corporations like American Tobacco and Standard Oil would undermine the remaining competition and secure true monopoly corners. At that point, prices paid to suppliers could be reduced and prices extracted from consumers raised to "charge-what-the-traffic-will-bear" levels. The profits would roll in, the beneficiaries being top managers, promoters, big stockholders, and perhaps skilled employees.

The huge profits realized by companies like Standard Oil ($25 million on $150 million in sales in 1899 and dividends of 30 percent) and Carnegie Steel ($40 million in 1900) seemed to validate this scenario. As someone cogently put it: "A trust is a good thing for those inside of it, but bad for the people on the outside."[19]

Supporters of the trusts, or at least those who believed the corporate giants represented a natural and logical response to a new age, were apt to stress their inevitability. Wasn't this Darwin's "survival of the fittest" played out on the commercial stage? "The history of the trust is the history of the evolution of civilization," declared a writer in January 1900. "To abolish the trust is to step backward in civilization to a primitive condition."[20]

The massively robust Thomas Reed, now a corporate lawyer, and a few years before, as speaker of the U.S. House of Representatives, the most skillful parliamentarian in the country, ventured that big capitals were simply "the natural invention of the growing complication of human affairs: the result of growing civilization."[21]

Politics make strange bedfellows. Not only did business conservatives uphold trusts, but also socialists, who argued that they represented the ultimate stage in capitalism and were hastening the evolution to "cooperative ownership" of industry.[22]

The pro-trust discourse denied that market domination made abuses inevitable. Price gouging just didn't pay, not over the medium or long run. Ultimately, the "market mechanism" would function as a dependable safeguard: Any monopoly extracting exorbitant profits from the public would lose business and also set off a chain reaction generating lower-priced competition. Its market share would fade away.

Big business spokesmen vigorously denied exercising anything resembling monopoly power. Competition was still real, was their claim, had a momentum of its own, and would continue indefinitely. A Standard Oil vice president noted that his firm really had "a very restricted power," and that competition was "very active." Sneering at the attacks on big business as "a miserable clamor, this gabble about trusts," Henry Havemeyer, boss of the $70 million American Sugar Refining Corporation, informed the Industrial Commission that "anybody can go into that business that wants to."[23]

"Efficiency" became the mantra of business combination. Corporate leaders reiterated that the object of forming massive corporations was to raise profits by rationalizing production, closing inefficient plants, and achieving full production. Inefficiency and the inefficient had been wrung out of their industries. If they were successful (as John Gates remarked) it is because they were "running our business strictly on business principles." The size and resources of great business would enable it to consolidate existing plants and plan new ones better, conduct innovative research, utilize by-products, eliminate redundant bureaucracy—all of which translated into lower prices for consumers, and expansion throughout the economy.[24]

Proof was the steady decline of prices during the years of oil, salt, beef, coal, and sugar monopolies. Thomas Reed put the alternatives bluntly: "If such a monopoly is a crime, then you must give up your continual demand for lower and lower prices."[25]

A crucial item in the Big Business–Big Efficiency thesis was the role of trusts in the increasingly vital sphere of global trade. Since size and resources did matter in capturing foreign markets, the trusts were natural leaders of the current export bonanza. Standard Oil alone was accounting for a formidable $60 million worth of exports in 1899. If (as endlessly repeated) the United States with a population of 75 million people had a capacity to produce for 150 million, only the trusts were positioned to export the difference and keep factories running at full capacity. They were, thought a mild critic, "the greatest and most perfect organization to use in the contest for the world's industrial supremacy."[26]

The trusts could also claim with some justification to be providing good wages and secure employment for at least a portion of their employees. John D. Rockefeller declared that Standard Oil paid its employees "the best wages." The fact that firms like National Steel and Federal Steel, in a tight labor market for some skilled craftsmen, were paying union-scale wages and setting wages in agreement with workers committees created some enthusiasm for the big-business idea in labor union circles.

Trust advocates could also argue that the problem of skilled workers displaced or downsized out of jobs by mergers was buffered by the expansive economy of 1900. These folks were finding jobs in various sectors of commerce and industry. Some, in fact, wound up working for the bigs: former shopkeepers as buyers in department stores, young accountants in steel or mining company headquarters, machinists in industrial shops.

So Americans should draw the appropriate conclusions: Only vast corporations could provide both price and economic stability. Disturb their operations and you endanger the present American cornucopia. All in all, this amounted to a fairly devastating argument.

In retrospect, a century later, what is most revealing about the trust debate was the extraordinary vehemence of the antitrust camp. There is something visceral here, reminiscent of the cry of a wounded and cornered animal in the wild. At its deepest core, the trust controversy stemmed from the knowledge that the terms of the American dream were being irrevocably altered.

The rise of the corporate Molochs seemed to herald the final demise of that part of the dream epitomized by Franklin, Jefferson, and Lincoln, which spoke of autonomy and the right of every man to control his livelihood and build his own enterprise ground up. Perhaps the best expression of this was a simple statement to the U.S. Industrial Commission by an independent Ohio oil man who had battled for years against Standard Oil. "Every man should be allowed to place his goods upon the market with the opportunity to make an honest profit." Competition was nothing less than a national icon, as American as apple pie and the Fourth of July. Historically, it had been viewed as a moral force for good and essential to the working out of democracy and freedom. To see it vanish so suddenly was deeply disconcerting.[27]

Nothing less than the vaunted tradition of American individualism was at stake here. American Sugar's Havemeyer might be correct that "anybody" could contest the trusts on their own turf, but that "anybody" would be another trust in collusion with financiers to raise the $20 to $30 million necessary to finance a steel complex, or the $6 million for a tinplate mill.

Steeped in the truths of individualism, significant numbers of Americans felt *personally* violated by the "Money Power," their cherished hopes mocked. Much of the outrage against big business was fueled by this grief over what they saw as the annihilation of the myth of the diligent toiler rising from wage or salaried labor to independent enterpriser. The popular writer and socialist Jack London caught the sense of foreclosure here:

> Rockefeller has shut the door on oil, the American
> Tobacco Company on tobacco, and Carnegie on steel.
> After Carnegie came, Morgan triple locked the door.
> These doors will not open again and before them
> pause thousands of ambitious young men.[28]

Were these young men on-the-make to be merely anonymous employees of vast, impersonal corporations? "The clerk in the average big office," la-

71

mented one letter writer to the *Saturday Evening Post*, "learns that he is merely a paid automaton hired to grind out the greatest possible amount of routine work a day of which he is capable." Was their destiny to languish in a bureaucracy where perhaps one $10–a–week clerk in half a dozen could move into lower management? There was the candid remark by E.D. Ripley, president of the Atchison, Topeka, and Santa Fe Railroad: "Necessarily promotion comes slowly, and to many it doesn't come at all."[29]

The trusts *were* causing turmoil among various segments of the American people. And appearing as they did at a time of cataclysmic economic and social change, they became symbols of the loss of the known and perils of the unknown world to come. The real dilemma, however, lay in the maturing of industrial/financial capitalism U.S. style: The American dream had been rash enough to promise abundance *and* personal autonomy, but now, it seemed, the latter would have to be jettisoned for the possibility of the former. So basic psychic needs would go unmet. Unable or unwilling to restructure either their expectations or capitalism itself, more than a few Americans experienced feelings of helplessness and rage at the power of impersonal market forces. Thus, it was not so strange to find (in a nation where loss of individual opportunity was literally equated with the death of one's soul) the trusts being repeatedly damned as "soulless," and the men who had built them—Rockefeller, Morgan, Hanna, Frick—depicted as demons.

Here also was the basis for the widespread notion that business "despotism" was in the process of destroying the country's democratic institutions. The republic was being overthrown. Back during the 1896 election, William Jennings Bryan and the Democrats had seized upon such fears and made them into a major campaign issue, and would do so again in 1900.

Of course, this was no mere fantasy. The upper business class was profoundly antidemocratic and generally suspicious of any democratizing influences (including education) that might undermine their power. Big business did exercise immense leverage at crucial pressure points of state and national government, controlled a stable of obedient congressmen and judges, and retained the country's most proficient lobbyists and legal talent ("high-priced men," in the jargon of the day). It maintained a lockhold on the Republican party leadership in Washington, along with considerable influence among Democrats. The sugar trust, in the person of American Sugar, controlled key senators such as Matthew Quay and Nelson Aldrich, and gave promiscuously to both parties. Quay received under-the-table payments from Standard Oil, as did the immensely influential, statesman-looking U.S. senator from Ohio, Joseph Foraker, who was assigned to bury legislation the company disliked. "It needs to be looked after," wrote Standard Vice President John Archbold to Foraker about a piece of legislation in February 1900.

"I hope there will be no difficulty in killing it." California was a fiefdom of the Southern Pacific Railroad; the Pennsylvania Railroad ruled the state it was named after. "They rise above all law and defy all judicial control," charged Grant Miller Cleveland. "These soulless corporations select our members of the House, purchase for themselves our Senators, dictate the norms for the Presidency on both sides, own our courts."[30]

However, the charge that American democracy, such as it was, lay in dire peril of overthrow by grand alliances between machine politicians and plutocrats was fanciful. At local and state levels, there were a number of incorruptible, reform-minded politicians, such as Mayor Sam "Golden Rule" Jones, who had instituted civil service reforms in Toledo, Ohio, and fought streetcar franchise corruption; and innovative reform governors Hazen Pingree of Michigan and Robert LaFollette in Wisconsin, who opposed railroad domination of their states. Moreover, the machines prized their independence and greedily hoarded their own authority, while the plutocrats *already possessed what amounted to a veto over the political decisions that mattered to them*. Only an exceptional public outpouring, or a split in the ranks of the business class (as in the events leading to the war with Spain), could spell trouble.[31]

Remedies for the "trust problem" had become one of the country's prime staples of conversation. Not everybody, of course, believed action was needed. Trust spokesmen were content to do as little as possible and hope to ride out the storm. Senator Mark Hanna of Ohio, a close ally of John D. Rockefeller, and who, more than anyone, personified the corporate/political axis, continued to deny that monopolistic trusts even existed. His political comrade-in-arms, President William McKinley (whose personal heroes were Rockefeller and Morgan and who identified trusts with the natural law of progress), made speeches indicating his concern and launched all of three antitrust suits while in office.[32]

This had worked well enough in the past, but anxiety and outrage were mounting in the country. A tempest was brewing. University of Wisconsin economist Richard Ely, disturbed about the threat posed to national liberty by uncontrolled monopolies, and expressing a widespread sentiment, wrote that "the only question before us . . . is how to exercise the control."[33]

Two distinct political alignments would offer answers. The first, led by the Bryan faction of the Democratic party, Populist remnants, and advocates for small business and farmers, sought to hem in big business, dismantle the worst trusts, and restore the competition that existed before their rise. Speaking with characteristic moral fervor before a September 1899 meeting in Chicago held to exchange ideas about monopolies, William Jennings Bryan vowed to "put the man before the dollar, not the dollar before the man." To tumultuous applause, he declared: "Monopoly in private hands is indefensible from any standpoint, it is intolerable."[34]

In short, if not humbled, the great combines would oppress the people, extorting money from the farmers and workers and driving more into poverty. The economy must be democratized. This was the antitrust position at its most pristine and visceral. The Bryan instrument for crippling corporate power would be "an amendment to the constitution that will give to Congress the power to destroy every trust in the country." But as a good Democrat, he would also see that the states had wide powers to mount their own attack.[35]

Bryan would lead his party's charge into the 1900 election pledged to tightly regulate the trusts, placing natural monopolies like railroads under public ownership. The fate of such an agenda rested on his election to the presidency, in tandem with a Democrat-controlled Congress.

A second major camp championing governmental intervention surfaced, but from a position more complex than Bryan's, more nuanced and cautious. These were the reform-minded legions of the nascent Progressive movement, mainly middle-class and white-collar Protestant Republicans from the Northeast and Midwest. Increasingly vocal against monopolies and corrupt political bosses, they were determined to preserve the disappearing small republican and entrepreneurial values they prized.

A dead-serious bunch prone to belief in universal laws and the possibility of making the country absolutely virtuous, the Progressives never doubted they were involved in struggle for the "soul" of America. In 1900, they were still gaining confidence that they could lead the country away from the strife of the nineties and toward some vision of the good society.[36]

Progressives would draw selectively upon both pro- and antitrust discourses as it suited their basically conservative tastes. The measures they would take to check the trusts were constrained by the value they placed on order and individual opportunity. Well aware of the evils of unchecked competition, Progressives viewed large-scale corporations as the sole entities capable of delivering an astonishing array of goods at low costs.

The trusts also seemed indispensable in the key conflict shaping up over international markets—"the only effective agencies," thought William Miller Collier, "which can develop our much needed foreign markets . . . dispose of our surplus products, and thus give constant employment to our workers and toilers." So mighty corporations represented the promise of American abundance and were not going to be assaulted or dismantled on the Progressive watch.[37]

But they were not to be left alone either, because Progressives viewed the economic and political domination of organized money, not to mention the stifling conformity demanded by bureaucratic organization, as wholly un-American. Competition as the great catalyst for national progress and ingenuity must be protected.

Besides, Progressives were appalled by the corruption, hedonism, and sheer ill manners of the plutocrats, financiers, and promoters. When Theodore Roosevelt voiced anxiety over "our gold-ridden, capitalist bestridden, usurer-mastered future," he was speaking for multitudes. There was concern that these business upstarts, instead of contributing to general prosperity, might easily hoard the surpluses created by economies of scale, igniting a whole new wave of economic contraction and social upheaval reminiscent of the nineties.

Ultimately, the Progressive objective was to utilize the strengths of great corporate organization, while diminishing its dangerous and destructive features. The enactment of federal and state laws and vigorous implementation by governmental agencies would end practices that gave huge combines undue advantages, and force everybody to compete "on a level playing field." Fair competition (and the simpler, more harmonious America in which the Progressives really felt comfortable) might be restored.

In 1900 (and afterward), the realization of these objectives by Progressive forces would prove elusive. For one thing, while hugely energetic in reforming local and state government, they tended to divisiveness on solutions to major social problems. Rather than a coherent Progressive program for action, there was a grab bag of prescriptions: Abolish tariffs on trust products, end railroad rate discrimination, revoke public franchises, change the patent laws, limit profits and the size of corporations, and tax excessive earnings. Almost everybody's panacea was to use "publicity"—meaning the full disclosure of corporate financial affairs—to make officers and boards accountable.

One school of thought argued that the mission could be carried out by simply enforcing the existing Sherman Act; another believed in laws forbidding corporations to cut prices in select market areas or coerce local merchants. Theodore Roosevelt and the historian Charles Beard were fond of discoursing about "industrial democracy" and holding companies rigorously accountable for their actions.

Progressives simply could not bring themselves to come to grips with the elemental laws of modern capitalism, to wit the tendency of competition to beget monopoly and the enormous intrinsic advantages that biggness *in itself* gave firms in dominating markets. Since they were loath to examine the basic ethos of the American business culture or tackle the privileges of corporate sovereignty (or, as Stephen Diner says, "reflect on their own stake in the policies that they advocated"), the problem at its deepest level never was broached.[38]

What Progressives fastened upon instead was the rather simplistic duality between "good trusts" creating abundance, and "bad trusts" practicing monopoly. Government should leave the first alone, and act to restrain the second. That powerful corporations had been circumventing and manipulating antitrust laws for decades, confident of protection from pro-business federal judges, didn't seem to faze a Progressive reformer like Michigan governor Hazen Pingree, who blithely assured one audience that "the only way to kill the evil is to stamp it out. A federal law will do it."[39]

Richard Hofstadter has remarked that the "characteristic Progressive was often of two minds on many issues." Nowhere was this more true that on the trusts. But the Progressives simply shared the same maddening ambivalence that so many Americans had about the big capitals, admiring their power and grandeur, longing for the goods they could deliver, frustrated at the values they were eroding, and fearful of the power they now commanded. At the end of the day, however, they would not kill the corporate geese laying the golden eggs. Even as Progressivism feared the revolutionary dynamism of capitalism, it feared economic democracy still more. This lack of viable alternatives would paralyze them in real-world encounters with big business.[40]

Actually, beneath the blather of political rhetoric, neither Progressives nor Bryan Democrats really knew what to do about the trusts—*which is to say that no one knew how to utilize the dynamics of capitalism for the "public good."* The really difficult questions—such as how public institutions corrupted and manipulated by giant corporations could really control them for the public benefit—remained unanswered or simply unasked. And what could be achieved without restructuring the belief system at the heart of the culture—in brief, redefining the American dream?

Some of the most coherent responses were offered by former governor Altgeld of Illinois and the economist Richard Ely. Next to Bryan, Altgeld, a public man of rare courage and principle, was the Democrat whom Republicans most enjoyed demonizing. Regarding antitrust laws as an unworkable sham, he advocated direct state control and ownership of big capitals to serve the public good. This, of course, was absolute political dynamite.

Ely would argue that the problem had to be attacked at the base. Since concentrated wealth led to concentrated industry, income taxes must be aimed at breaking up the great fortunes. A federal bureau was needed as a watchdog over corporations, and child labor and sweatshops abolished. Ely's solution demanded nothing less than "a new way of looking at government. As our life is complex, our government must be elaborate." But even he faltered before the subservience of government to business in a business culture. "Property gives strength," he wrote, "Have we, or can we have, a class sufficiently strong to control those owners of immense property who are engaged in monopolistic undertakings?"[41]

Indeed, the difficulty of formulating a coherent program of action was evident at the fall 1899 Chicago antitrust conference, attended by delegations from thirty-five states, where lots of fire-and-brimstone rhetoric damning the trusts was accompanied by a remarkable lack of any agreement for controlling them.

And at least some corporate leaders were cleverly moving to appease public fears and head off any real regulation by channeling antitrust sentiments into harmless legislation and funneling increased funds into Republican party coffers. Political smokescreens—like the lighthearted introduction of a sweeping constitutional amendment by Republicans giving Congress the right to control trusts—were the order of the day. There was Senator Thurston of Nebraska, as senator and Standard Oil counsel a fierce opponent of antitrust legislation, framing a strongly worded antitrust plank at the Republican National Convention.[42]

Yet, the demand to rein in big capital appeared to be reaching critical mass. Almost every state political party platform strongly condemned the trusts. The Iowa Republican convention proclaimed that abusive corporations "must be restrained by natural laws, and if need be, abolished." In a message to the New York State legislature, Governor Theodore Roosevelt declared: "When a trust becomes a monopoly the state has an immediate right to interfere." He recommended inspections of those great corporations making "inordinate profits."[43]

Finger to the political wind, President McKinley, in his annual year-end message, hinted that since antitrust laws did not seem to be working, Congress might approach the issue with "studied deliberation." And with William Jennings Bryan preparing to contest McKinley for the White House, 1900 seemed to be the year America might finally confront the trust question one way or the other.[44]

Chapter 6

Other Americans

So far as the production of wealth is concerned, the present age is a phenomenal success. It is in the distribution of wealth produced where a failure is made.

—J.W. Keenan, *Saturday Evening Post*,
June 7, 1900

We can't even live decently on eighteen cents an hour working but three days a week, and then, here's the sickness and the deaths.

—Mother in packinghouse community,
The Commons, September 1900

It is a pity the men have to work like this, but there is no help for it. The machinery drives us at a gallop as well as the men. Our worst competition . . . drives harder than we do, and gets more out of his men.

—Iron industry manager, 1900

The late nineteenth/early twentieth-century experience in the United States bears out the axiom that not only do economic transformations and revolutions not occur pain-free, but the pain is never shared equally. Back in 1886,

President Rutherford Hayes had candidly acknowledged that "labor does not get its fair share of the wealth it creates." Thirteen years later, a U.S. Labor Department official was calling attention to how tragic it was that in an "age of invention, age of inventive genius," it was those who worked the hardest who had the least.[1]

Money largely defined peoples' lives circa 1900, and lack of it circumscribed them, often quite starkly. "It was not a matter of chance which threw me into the line which I follow today," went a letter to a leading magazine from someone signing himself, "Disagreeable Man." "Money had to be earned."[2]

There was Rose Cohen, a young Russian-Jewish immigrant seamstress worn down from the grind of working piece-rate in the sweatshops, reflecting upon the marriage match being proposed for her: "Father is poor and I am not strong. He is a nice young man and the main thing he is not a wage earner."[3]

The exact dollar figures of what constituted comfort and need were, of course, debatable. Living costs were considerably cheaper in the South than North or West, since the cost of food, land, and fuel was lower. Some workers had nonmonetary rights attached to their jobs; southern sharecroppers could utilize the land around their cabins for vegetable gardens and raising chickens, pigs, tobacco, and corn; miners' wives might take coal leavings. There was fishing and hunting in the country. To "make ends meet" it was the norm for working-class and farm wives to take in boarders and washing.

So there are varying estimates of the dollar amounts needed for certain lifestyles. *Forum* magazine opined that a family of four living at a "good living standard" in a northern city and putting away something for old age would require between $2,000 and $3,000 per annum; $1,200 was necessary for a degree of "economic independence," and $800 the minimum to maintain health, education, and good housing. As an adequate budget for a family of five, the state of Massachussetts arrived at the figure of $754, and a New York charity, $624.[4]

These figures were out of reach for the bulk of American households: At least nine of ten were earning under $1,200, and a fair majority below $800. The contemporary social thinker Simon Patten placed the poverty line at an even $500 a year; a recent analysis sets it at $553. *Ninety-five percent* of industrial and agricultural laborers earned $500 or less. The social writer and activist Robert Hunter concluded that over 10 million, or one in five people in the United States, lived in poverty. Other contemporary estimates were between 50 percent and 80 percent.[5]

What marked the typical working-class household was the inability of the primary family breadwinner to earn a *family wage*, or enough money on his/her own to decently provide for the entire household. So apart from a small group of highly skilled labor "aristocrats," such as glass blowers, the wage structure was simply inadequate to support more than basic needs. A third of all workers earned under $300. Skilled industrial workers averaged $360; the unskilled, $260. New York coat pressers took home $6 a week, and Chicago packinghouse workers $7.40. Cotton mill workers in the southern states (wages there being 25–40 percent lower than elsewhere) earned around $230, or seventy-five to ninety cents a day, but even this was attractive to farm tenants and sharecroppers twisting in a never-ending cycle of debt, squalor, and semipeonage.[6]

What exacerbated low piece and daily wages was the lack of steady, full-time work. A contemporary described the syndrome:

> At present, part of the laborers are overworked and have not time for enjoyment and culture, the other part have no work. The former are working . . . almost frenzied, lest they should be thrown out of employ, and the latter look longingly for employment.

During 1900, 6.5 million workers, or a *quarter* of all those over ten years of age, were unemployed at some time; more than 2 million of these from four to six months. Oil, meatpacking, furniture, glass, textile, men's clothing, and leather workers customarily had work for six to nine months per year. In the mills of Fall River, Massachussetts, regular work meant nine or ten months on the job. Stevedores, granary men, and sailors on the Great Lakes were unemployed during long winters, as were most agricultural laborers. Many carpenters, masons, and other skilled workers periodically crisscrossed states and regions looking for employment.[7]

The prosperous 1899–1901 period had its labor shortages; farmers harvesting crops in North Dakota and Maryland sought workers, so did new southern textile mills and steel mills producing at capacity. But the labor market was *generally* saturated and simply could not absorb all of those (including Ph.D.s seeking college and university positions) looking for work.

The competition for unskilled manual labor jobs was especially ferocious. Here large numbers of recently arrived immigrant workers were competing against each other and the native born. The words of a Boston trolley car motorman—"I am thankful to get this; if I dropped out, a hundred men would jump at my chance before supper"—are a reminder of the reserve labor army always present in the factory early-morning shadows or shape-ups on the docks.[8]

Businessmen might easily exploit such intense competition among a weak and divided workforce. In Pennsylvania and Illinois, Hungarians, Poles, and Slovaks were hired by mineowners at ninety cents a day as a check on native-born miners' wage demands; black strikebreakers were brought from the South to Chicago to coerce striking white building trades workers back to work; New England manufacturers gained leverage over textile workers by opening low-wage mills in the Carolinas.

If lay offs and downtime were frequent, when there was work it went at a fast tempo. Both European visitors and immigrant workers thought the speed and pace of work generally more intense in the United States. The "drive" system commonly used on factory shop floors relied upon foremen abusing and threatening workers to generate greater output. This accelerated during the 1900–era boom when employers sought to introduce newer and more specialized machinery as part of an all-out drive for production. Machine operators came under exhausting physical and emotional pressures. "We used to be able to take time to eat our meals like civilized beings," recalled one steelworker, "but now we can only snatch up a bite as we work." Following a twelve-hour shift, few Carnegie Steel workers were energetic enough to enjoy the public libraries Andrew Carnegie's philanthrophy had bestowed upon them.[9]

During 1900, San Francisco female telegraph operators incessantly monitored by supervisors ("One little slip no matter how trivial" resulted in being written up or fired), were having an unusual rate of breakdowns and hysteria. On early Carolina summer evenings, shirtsleeved mill workers re-cuperating in the aftermath of a ten-hour shift in 100–degree temperatures sat on the porches of their company shanties, immobile, staring vacantly off into space.[10]

In the North and West, immigrants from southern and eastern Europe and Mexico were assigned the dirtiest, toughest, and most dangerous jobs in mines, foundries, the oil, rubber, lumber, and chemical industries, and on the rail-roads. Poles and Bohemians worked for $1.50 a day in the sugar mills. In stockyards and mills, the "ethnic succession" moved from German and Irish laborers to Slavs and Italians. French Canadians were the workers of choice for New England's grimmest textile mill jobs. Popularly stereotyped as "lazy," "stupid," and "unstable," these immigrants were prone to begin and end their working lives at heavy manual, mind-numbing work.[11]

In the South, the seemingly endless supply of mountain and poor farm whites migrating into industrial centers depressed wages. So did the racial wage differential pitting blacks against whites (e.g., black bricklayers re-ceived fifty to seventy-five cents less a day). White agricultural workers seeking higher wages were told, "We cannot afford to pay you any more because I can get a negro for 60 cents a day."[12]

Prospering in the economy of 1900 increasingly seemed to demand either a solid specialization or a variety of skills. Remarked Dr. Edward Brook, the chief of Philadephia public schools, "In order to succeed nowadays the young man or young woman must have a special education in the direction of the particular line of business." Unskilled laborers, whether in iron and steel, meatpacking, soft coal, or the cotton mills, could expect low pay. "I think that wages everywhere, of common physical labor, are down at the point of actual subsistence," testified J.D. Redding to the U.S. Industrial Commission, "and no man rises above this level unless he becomes skilled, unless he displays extraordinary energy and ambition."[13]

Conditions at the blue-collar workplace were generally (with some notable exceptions) abominable: noxious fumes, poisonous chemicals, furnace-like temperatures, and unsafe machines operating in speed-up conditions. There were laws regulating factory conditions in the North, but only a few states such as Massachussets carried out rigorous inspections of worksites.

Considerably more railroad workers were killed (2,675) and injured (41,142) between June 1900 and June 1901 than fell in the war in the Philippines. One-armed and -legged men were common sights around railroad centers; perhaps one-half of all railroad accident victims received cash settlements from the companies. Fierce resistance by railroads to safety innovations like the block signal system and automatic couplets caused reforming journalist Robert Hunter to damn "this criminal policy of preferring murder to deferred dividends."[14]

The metal and textile industries were notorious for excruciatingly hard and long hours and producing a legion of maimed personnel. The two were indivisible. Ten- and twelve-hour shifts pouring molten iron, feeding furnaces, working lathes, or loading packinghouse railroad cars made workers prone to serious and lethal accidents, many occurring during the final hour. The frequency of explosions at minefaces across Appalachia, and the mass funerals at which pale men in their Sunday black frock coats marched behind the coffins of their workmates, illustrated the vulnerability of men digging three tons of coal and more per shift. [15]

Early burnout was common among men working sixty- and seventy-hour weeks since childhood. Even when sufficient food was available, diets were unbalanced. Salt pork, potatoes, and corn meal with tea and coffee were the miners' staple; southern mill workers ate fried chicken, pork, and cabbage. The air in workers' districts adjacent to factories was heavily polluted with industrial gases and chemicals, open sewers ran through muddy streets littered with tin cans, bottles, rocks, and garbage.

And there was the workingman's penchant for finding companionship, warmth, escape, not to mention a free (salty) lunch for the dime price of a whiskey in what Bishop Potter of New York referred to as "the poor man's club," the ubiquitous local barroom. "The saloon," sardonically noted Jacob Riis, "has had the monopoly up to date of all the cheer in the tenements."[16]

By age forty or forty-five, men in the steelworks, the building trades, saw and textile mills, mines, and railroads no longer had the strength and endurance to keep up with the work. It was axiomatic in the iron industry, for instance, that there were no rollers over forty. Older or former workers frequently had the "shakes" from performing too many repetitions of minute tasks. In the era's jargon, their "physical efficiency," or ability to perform at the pace American business demanded, was impaired. Replaced by a seventeen- or eighteen-year-old, the burned-out worker, with luck, got hired on at lesser pay as a sweeper or night watchman. Some lived off their children's wages, others became paupers, or died shortly after retiring. The life took its toll: One-third of all industrial workers were dead or incapacitated by age fifty.[17]

Musing on his employees who earned "just enough to exist," a Pennsylvania ironworks manager reflected, "If they have families I don't see how they do it." The gap between $400 and $600 might easily spell the difference between food and hunger, between an intact family and one thrown upon the dreaded charity system. Among working-class and poor households, the labor resources at a family's disposal made a crucial difference. The lack of a family wage and early burnout left mobilizing the entire family as a labor battalion as *the* rational strategy for economic survival.[18]

So the ability to utilize family labor power accounted for significant differences in living standards. One cigarmaker is documented as earning $440 a year and living with his sickly childen in a decrepit, unhealthy house, eating potato soup for dinner, while another in a family with three incomes (total: $1,870) had a six-room carpeted house and a varied diet that included fish, meat, and vegetables. Contrast the laborer at $270 per annum in a filthy tenement, eating a dinner of coffee and bread and whose children didn't attend school, with another from a three-income family pulling in $1,114 and owning a comfortable house and piano.[19]

Despite the official cult of marriage and family as female destiny, nearly one in five American women were working for wages in 1900. Some were self-supporting, others motivated by work as a vehicle of self-expression, but most simply supplementing the wages of fathers, husbands, and brothers. Sometimes, women were also, as *Harper's Bazaar* noted, replacements for technologically unemployed males:

> As frequently happens nowadays, when inventions fast multiply, the father who at the time of marriage was a skilled laborer commanding good pay finds himself displaced by a machine, and . . . his skill is made worthless.[20]

Women did work that they had traditionally done, as domestics and cooks, agricultural workers, seamstresses, prostitutes, and maids, and many worked at home fabricating piece goods. But the economic revolution had also installed them as production-line workers in consumer goods factories such as Heinz and Procter and Gamble, in textile mills, department stores such as Wanamaker's and Filene's, and as secretaries, stenographers, and clerks in business offices.

The inequalities among working women reflected the nation's: The place one entered the workforce was largely determined by class, ethnicity, and color. Thus, the prevalence of native English-speaking women with pinned-up hair and neat clothes in offices, department stores, and nursing jobs; the stereotypic maid as "dumb," brogue-talking Bridgit or Chloe from Cork or Galway; in the South the "Aunt Jemima" type; and throughout the South-west, women from Mexican *barrios*. There was the dominance of Jewish and Italian immigrants in the garment trade; the "white women only" policy in most mills and factories. Foreign-born and black women were more apt to be classed as mentally inferior and less "ladylike" than the native born.[21]

Working lives began early. Children from families with less than $500 or so in annual income customarily entered the workaday world by age ten or earlier—hence, the children picking cotton, shucking corn, laboring in textile mills and paint, print, and glass factories and coal mines, and as servants, waiters, and messenger boys. Every city had its ragged urchins selling newspapers. Legal limits on hours, where they existed, were ten hours a day, and it was not uncommon to find eleven-year-olds working night shifts in silk and lace factories.[22]

While conditions varied, it is clear that many of 1900's 6-million-plus working youngsters were being deprived of a genuine childhood. They marched off to work half-awake and might be too exhausted at night to eat dinner. A century later, they stare out at us from grainy old photographs, the sooty-faced eight- and nine-year-old Pennsylvania "breaker boys" sorting out impurities from chunks of coal and little southern girls tending the cotton mill spindles, resigned faces prematurely world-weary.[23]

By starting heavy work too early, these children would be marked body and spirit for life. The U.S. Navy was already turning down a startling percentage of young miners deformed from early toil. Eighteen-year-old women in the southern textile mills, veterans of seventy-hour workweeks, tended to have dull heavy eyes and yellow, blotched complexions; at thirty, they were frequently haggard. Boys working ten hours a day in lime tanks full of dye at the American Printing Company in Fall River, Massachussetts, had a curiously leached skin color. Nonetheless, working-class families, impelled by the need for their children's earnings, joined mill owners in opposing restrictions on child labor.[24]

William McKinley at his presidential inauguration in 1897. McKinley was a patient, highly skilled politician with the aura of a devout clergyman. He spoke in simplistic dualities in an age that thought in simplistic dualities. *(All photos courtesy of the Library of Congress.)*

Theodore Roosevelt giving a speech. He was the most exciting new personality in national politics. "I am as strong as a bull moose," he wrote Mark Hanna at the beginning of the 1900 campaign, "and you can use me to the limit."

William Jennings Bryan. "The Great Commoner," personifying popular resistance to the values of business monopoly and modern culture, he inspired greater devotion among rural and small town folk than any political figure since Andrew Jackson.

J.P. Morgan. The forbidding "Jupiter" of the piercing eyes and bulbous nose, he worked his partners to exhaustion in overseeing his increasingly complex and far-flung financial holdings.

Andrew Carnegie. He had vowed to leave business at the age of thirty-five or so to lead a quiet, reflective life. Instead he had driven on for decades after to leadership of the nation's iron and steel industry, haunted by compulsions he, himself, recognized only too well.

John D. Rockefeller. From a background of evangelical Christianity, he always believed oil was a "miracle," and he was doing the work of God in delivering it. He always regarded attacks on Standard Oil as incredible, equating critics with gangsters practicing extortion.

Booker T. Washington. He was a gifted opportunist, powerbroker, and manipulator, a tragic Faust-like figure who, in his obsession to locate a community of interest with the powerful, sanctioned the sacrifice of black rights and dignity.

Elihu Root. The brilliantly resourceful Wall Street lawyer tapped by McKinley as the architect of U.S. colonial policy; an unabashed white supremacist with little sympathy for people of color either at home or abroad.

American soldiers, dead Filipinos, and men digging graves, Philippines. "The American soldier," declared Elihu Root, "is different from all other soldiers of all other countries since the world began."

Boys working with molds in a factory. Legal limits on hours, where they existed, were ten hours a day, and it was not uncommon to find eleven-year-olds working night shifts in some factories.

Coal breaker boys, Kingston, Pennsylvania. It is clear that in 1900 many of the six-million-plus working youngsters were being deprived of a genuine childhood.

African-Americans picking cotton. The majority of southern blacks were share-croppers or tenants living at the edge of subsistence in flimsy shacks with broken furniture, no running water, and lean-to privies out back.

Man and woman at rural Virginia house, ca. 1900. In long swathes of the rural South, ramshackle tenants' and sharecroppers' cabins (many of them predating the Civil War) dotted dusty roads.

Chinese woman carrying child down street in Chinatown, San Francisco. By the end of the nineteenth century, the Chinese had become "perpetual foreigners," excluded from mainstream American life and opportunities, denied constitutional rights, and segregated in public schools.

Typewriting department, National Cash Register Company, Dayton, Ohio. The Industrial Age had ushered in the Paper Age; women were becoming an increasing presence in offices, and one of the fastest-growing occupational groups was clerical office workers.

The strategy of family labor mobilization successfully kept many household economies aloft. But women and children could not escape being labeled as "inferior labor." Both remained unorganized, and formed a virtually unlimited labor pool of individuals with similar skills competing against each other—thus, novelist Theodore Dreiser's depiction of the young, unskilled, and increasingly desperate Sister Carrie as "a lone figure in a thoughtless, tossing sea" that was the bowels of industrial Chicago.[25]

Certainly female high school or commercial school graduates with sought-after typing, bookeeping, and stenographical skills were eminently employable in offices, receiving steady work and paid vacations, and earning up to $15 a week in the North. Live-in nurses received double that, as did valuable department store staff. But they were an elite minority. Since females were assumed to be unsuited to exercising discretion or authority, upward mobility was strictly limited. The most technologically efficient jobs were reserved for men. And classifying women workers as "inferior" justified lower wages for equal work and restricted the vast majority to low-skilled positions: Domestic servants on duty sixteen hours a day received a few dollars a week, while dressmakers worked sixty-three-hour weeks at $4. Cheap female factory labor was the basis of the "New South's" heralded industrialization. One survey in a Minnesota box factory found males averaging $7.75 per week, and women $5.30. Jacob Riis mocked the notion of "liberty at sixty cents a day," the wage for many working women in urban areas.[26]

Meanwhile, children's tiny wages, while vital, added little to the family pot. Breakerboys in the mines earned fifty cents a day, a child in the North Carolina mills, thirty cents, and in southern agriculture, twenty cents for picking tea leaves.

So the family as labor battalion might valiantly soldier on, yet not win through. And family mobilization strategies had their own costs to the larger working-class struggle for betterment. The availability of cheaper female and child labor undercut wage rates for adult men, and factories increasingly tended to replace more expensive men with lesser paid females thought to be more docile.

Urban industrial life also tended to erode the older rituals and solidarities that had formerly sustained immigrant and rural families. Lives often seemed chained to an endless treadmill of work and endurance. Social workers and reformers began recognizing that "the unbroken round of monotonous work disintegrates the family." Working women did bone-weary double days of labor. Hundreds of thousands of mothers working in laundries, cigar factories, and so on were compelled to leave small children with caretakers for twelve or fourteen hours a day. One woman leaving off her two children told a journalist: "It's awful but I must work else we shall get nothing to eat and be turned into the street besides."[27]

This daily struggle for survival precluded a larger world view and often produced a ferociously defensive mentality; thus the mean-spirited hostility of the shanty Irish of Boston and New York to the arriving Jewish, Italian, and black immigrants. No wonder big-city slum families and poor widows were grateful to the only people in public life to offer a modicum of support, the ward heelers from the local political machine, who gave them small jobs and Christmas food baskets. On Election Day they returned these favors with their votes.

"We talk a good deal about prosperity and the blessings of American civilization," editorialized *Harper's Bazaar*, noting the arrest of a Manhattan janitoress for taking two loaves of bread from a baker's wagon to feed her children. "Can nothing be done to make prosperity the personal experience of the hungry mother and her child." The lack of ample, nutritious food was an important element in the vicious cycle undermining the poor family's "physical efficiency" and ability to work. There was hunger throughout parts of the South, in factory towns like Lawrence, Massachussetts, and on some Indian reservations. Sixty to seventy thousand children arrived hungry at New York City's public schools each morning. Evenings, scores of men queued up at the back door of a catering establishment at Broadway to receive free loaves of bread. The wives of fitfully employed immigrant Italian laborers in Chicago tied small salt bags on children's necks to drive away starvation. The twisted legs of malnourished working-class children signaled the ravages of rickets.[28]

Jacob Riis's famous book, *How The Other Half Lives* (1890) had made the dumbbell tenements of the most densely populated place on earth, the Lower East Side of Manhattan, notorious. Now, in 1900, three-quarters of New York City's residents were tenement dwellers, some living in damp, lightless attics and cellars, the air heavy with the stink and fumes of kerosene stoves.

If New York's housing crisis was the stuff of legend, then small, crowded, rundown houses along innumerable dirty, sewerless streets and alleys were to be found in scores of cities and towns. Among the most infamous were "Rat Row" along Cincinnati's riverfront, Boston's immigrant west end, the dumbbell tenement areas of Hartford, Connecticut, the Pittsburgh steel and Monongahela Valley mill towns, and the neighborhoods in Chicago near the stockyards. In long swaths of the rural South, ramshackle tenants' and share-croppers' cabins (many of them predating the Civil War) dotted dusty roads.[29]

The lives of the poor were lived in dense communion with each other and this was a source of strength, joy, and communal spirit. Yet, they also lived in claustrophobic intimacy: "There were five of us, the two boys in one cot and we three girls in the other, in the one room filled with the odor of cooling oil," recalled Rose Cohen, of her family's Lower East Side flat. "As I lay with my two sisters in the sagging cot with an unconscious limb of one or other thrown over me, I wept. Then I thought why need it be so?"[30]

Better sanitation, water systems, and garbage collection in urban areas were pushing life expectancy up, but individual and family immune systems continued to be eroded by working-class life. Sickness was a constant. Unventilated slum housing, where cooking, washing, and sleeping were done in the same room, and mill town houses built on clay and surrounded by tins and rubbish fostered epidemics of asthma, tuberculosis, cholera, and pneumonia.

Practically every trade seemed to have its own special affliction, whether rheumatism, muscle paralysis, hernia, or ulcers. Spinners in damp textile factories had astronomical levels of tuberculosis, often dying quite young. The onset of "blue gums" and teeth falling out was a sure sign of lead poisoning. Consumption (tuberculosis) was "the great modern plague," killing 150,000 in 1903, mainly the young and urban poor. The tenement dweller of delicate constitution, overworked and underfed, was a prime candidate. Measles, bronchitis, and pneumonia were also killers. "Slaughterhouses" was the popular appellation given to the lightless, airless tenements where men, women, and children died in startling numbers.[31]

Risen industrialists like Carnegie claimed that poverty ("a blessed heritage," he called it) stimulated discipline and furnished a sterling training ground for success. This did happen, but it was more likely to grind down even unusually capable and spirited men and women, diminish their lives, and end them prematurely. And poverty escalated the risk of falling into pauperism. Households with incomes below $800 or so a year simply could not build ample savings or property to resist unemployment, injuries, burnout, or widowhood. The period before young children could begin working was especially precarious.[32]

Not infrequently, the urban working-class family broke apart under these strains, the father retreating to the saloon or abandoning the family, the mother's health breaking down under the stresses of supporting the family. Robert Hunter suggested that such a family had "before them the choice of three evils—starvation, crime, or relief by charity."[33]

Crime was epidemic. Urban boys drawn out of their overcrowded stifling homes began by shooting craps in alleys and graduated to gangs (like lower Manhattan's Mulberry Bends and Mott Streets), where they were rewarded with shares of the "swag" (loot) a la Tammany Hall. Teenage boys and girls found their way into the maze of brothels, cheap hotels, "barrel houses" serving cheap whiskey, gambling, cocaine, and opium dens, and nickel lodging houses stinking of tobacco juice located in every town of any size.[34]

In 1900, "safety nets" were unheard of: Unless someone became utterly destitute and dependent on society, their problems and their family's were considered no one's but their own. Charity houses and alms, the last resort, were available only to the "deserving" (the crippled, deaf, blind, etc.). The able-bodied poor were given minimal charity by middle-class Puritan-minded charity managers often contemptuous of the values of those who came to them in need, especially immigrants, and were speedily hustled back into the workaday world. Charitable institutions were designed to efface every shred of human dignity, and working-class people went to extraordinary lengths (including breaking up their families) to avoid them. Significantly, a main character of 1901's bestselling novel, Alice Hegan Rice's *Mrs.Wiggs of the Cabbage Patch*, was Jimmy Wiggs, the teenage son of a poor widow who literally works himself to death rather than have his family be thrown upon charity.[35]

The world most American working men and women inhabited circa 1900 was an ongoing battleground where one's economic survival, not to mention gaining a degree of autonomy, depended on creatively utilizing various strategems.

Family labor mobilization, although crucial, was only one method. Workers developed the process of sabotoging the frenetic factory-drive/piece-rate system into an art form. Those who exceeded informal rates were ostracized or worse. Unionized machinists struggled to maintain their "one machine, one man" rule and prevent piecework. There were militant acts of resistance by working women and men. Immigrants found invaluable buffers against an alien environment in ethnic communities filled with benevolent societies, sporting clubs, fraternal orders, restaurants, and saloons, and used these networks and cultural institutions to locate jobs and credit. Workers fought to control what leisure time they had, and in order to cope with pulverizing jobs, might unilaterally extend Sunday into Monday.[36]

Mobility was the most common instrument of individual betterment. Mountain whites journeyed to southern mill towns; sharecropping blacks from plantations to Atlanta, Birmingham, and smaller southern cities, or out of the South altogether; Wisconsin small-town or farm folk decamped to Milwaukee or Racine. Stints in industry alternated with work on family farms. Workers, especially the unskilled, habitually changed jobs looking for something better; this led to a phenomenal turnover rate in many factories. While glitzy Heinz Company advertisements promoting the image of "the Girl in the White Cap" cheerfully assembling ketchup botttles drew some 20,000 curious visitors to its Pittsburgh factory in 1900, Heinz's drive system was causing massive turnover. Among immigrant Lithuanian, Slovenian, and Croatian immigrants in Pennsylvania steel plants, turnover approached *100 percent* annually.[37]

Sometimes, worker nomadism paid off: Thernstrom's study of Boston concludes that there were some laborers who did move into skilled work. But low-paying laboring jobs were, after all, low-paying laboring jobs *anywhere*, and improvement was probably the exception. Where one entered the labor market continued to be the key to one's subsequent career.[38]

None of these strategies, moreover, answered the dilemma of how workers could command the fairness and economic justice they felt was their due. Or as John Graham Brooks posed it, "Who shall have the new increment of gain which the machine brings?" Working people needed to find more collective and dynamic ways to bridge the radical disconnection between their meager living and working conditions and the fantastic new wealth they were producing.[39]

Workers were weak because they were disorganized, were hostile to ethnic and racial "others," and lacked the resources to confront a business class adept at using blacklists, strikebreaking, plant closures, and corporate welfarism to undermine worker solidarity. Political impotence was critical; despite their weight and numbers, workers had a startling lack of political clout.

Constructing powerful, effective trade unions that could become, as a labor newspaper said, "a wall of defense between the family and corporate greed" was key. Here, the history, since the disintegration of the Knights of Labor in the 1880s, had been dismal. The nineties had witnessed business/governmental repression destroy militant labor organizations like the American Railway Union.[40]

Unions were handicapped by the need to prove their legitimacy. In an American-dream culture priding itself on individualism, any organization carrying a message of brotherhood and collective rights had to be an anomaly. Salespeople and white collar clerks tended to identify with management and look down on manual workers. The American Federation of Labor (AFL), an umbrella organization for unions, had to remind its members not to "forget . . . that trade unionism is a perfectly legitimate and lawful mode of procedure. Labor is about the only capital a poor man has."[41]

Difficulties in organizing a working class driven by intense ethnic, religious, and cultural divisions were legion. Ethnic differences between native-stock workers and recent immigrants from southern and eastern Europe, as well as between whites and workers of color, mattered far more than common class position. Businessmen occasionally gloated about the advantages this brought: "It is one good result of race prejudice," Brooks quotes an executive of a large southern corporation, "that the negro will enable us in the long run to weaken the trade union so that it cannot harm us. We can keep wages down with the negro, and we can prevent too much organization."[42]

The incessant movement of workers around the country (or immigrants to and from their countries of origin), and the split between skilled and unskilled, were barriers to the kind of solidarity that stable unions needed. So was the surplus of the unskilled. Even the Portland *Oregonian*, a newspaper quite sympathetic to labor, thought strikes "foredoomed to failure" because "the labor market is thronged with a cheap supply of non-union labor."[43]

The big strikes had, in fact, assumed a ritualistic pattern: workers walking out, and employers responding by importing strikebreakers. The outburst of violence that usually followed alienated the public and tapped into its worst fears of labor hooliganism and radicalism. Hard-fisted state militias, sheriff's deputies, or federal troops then occupied the area, preparing the climate for federal judges to define the strike as "intimidation and violence" and issue blanket injunctions to crush it. Hungry and demoralized, those strikers who could, returned to work on whatever terms were available. Two major 1899 strikes highlighted just how acrimonious the conflict between capital and labor had become.

The Standard Oil Company–owned Bunker Hill mine in Idaho's ore-rich Silver Valley had been the scene of a fierce strike in 1892. Now, seven years later, in April 1899, when the company rejected a demand for a wage raise and recognition of the Western Federation of Miners, another violent strike ensued. Hundreds of masked, armed miners seized a train, packed it with dynamite, and blew up the Bunker Hill mill. Several men died. The governor of Idaho, Frank Steuenberg, a politician noted for his seven-foot height and closeness to Standard Oil, declared martial law and called in military force. Federal troops comanded by General Merriam arrived on the scene, arrested six hundred workers, and imprisoned them in bullpens in conditions that outraged labor union people around the country. Strike leaders received long prison terms. Miners returning to work had to apply for a work permit and renounce the union.[44]

A few months later in Cleveland, union members on the city's electric streetcar system were singled out for discharge by the Big Consolidated Street Railroad Company. This ignited an uprising of the city's working-class community in support of the trolley workers. Thousands blocked trolley cars along Euclid Avenue, a main downtown thoroughfare, and some cars were dynamited. Observers noted the presence in the crowds of militant, apron-clad neighborhood women. Workers from factories in the area joined the strikers in driving replacement motormen off the trolleys. When the militia arrived on the scene, there was a pitched battle, including exchanges of gunfire. Meanwhile, the strikers enforced a trolley boycott and violators were manhandled or ostracized. The strike stretched on through the fall and beyond, with occasional riot scenes and more trolley cars blown up.[45]

Workers circa 1900 were clearly receptive to change. Writer Charles Spahr, after visiting workplaces around the country, concluded that "the distinguishing spirit of America's working people is hopeful discontent." Prices rising faster than wages intensified resentments.[46]

Thus the impetus for exceptional union growth. New union locals were springing up across the country: teamsters in Portland, retail clerks in Tacoma, tailors in Davenport, Iowa, and bricklayers, plumbers, marble workers, and barbers. During 1900, 400,000 workers were recorded on strike at one time or another at 1,800 sites; the main issues were wages, hours, and union recognition. The following year, almost 3,000 strikes occurred. It was not uncommon for workers at one jobsite to walk off in a "sympathy" strike on behalf of workers striking at another, or for teamsters to refuse to deliver materials to a worksite on strike.[47]

At center stage was the AFL, presided over since the mid-eighties by rotund Samuel Gompers, gregarious former cigarmaker and an immensely shrewd and capable master of bureaucratic maneuver and survival. Its nucleus in traditional craft unions, typographers, miners, machinists, building trades, boilermakers, and cigarmakers, the federation's membership was now passing the 800,000 mark.

The official AFL line, appearing in its house newspaper and speeches by Gompers, promoted worker unity; the official slogan was the forthright, "Liberty for all, slavery for none." The definition, however, of precisely who constituted a genuine American worker was highly selective. Federation policies toward minorities and women reflected the world view of craft workers for whom the ethnic/racial and gender prejudices of American society were their prejudices too, and whose identities largely derived from job skills and being white and masculine. If threats to the work rules, seniority, and "ownership" of their jobs provoked ferocious resistance, so did the specter of minorities and women as union members, and little was done to organize them.[48]

So native-stock Chicago carpenters or Dayton machinists were classified as bonafide trade unionists, but not the recent immigrants who formed a growing proportion of the unskilled and semiskilled industrial workforce. Blacks were to be excluded from the union movement; Asians, widely regarded by labor as threatening American wage standards, from the country.

Some miners' and cigarmakers' locals in the South did remain racially integrated, and there were white trade unionists who regarded organizing blacks as essential. But the AFL contained few black members and its constitutional provision barring any of its member unions from discrimination had been eroded by the failure to take action against locals with exclusionary policies. Ignoring complaints from blacks, Gompers increasingly tended to blame the victim: Blacks were at fault for allowing themselves to be used as strikebreakers and lacking the skills to work in crafts. At the December 1900 convention in Louisville, segregation received official AFL sanction. Henceforth, racially separate locals would receive Federation charters. As President Gompers conceded, the AFL would not take on "social barriers existing between whites and blacks." This stance would harden with time. Five years later, Gompers was vowing in a speech that "the Caucasians are not going to let their standard of living be destroyed by negroes, Chinamen, Japs, or any others."[49]

Excluding the great bulk of American workers mocked the Federation's claim to represent the aspirations of *all* working men and women for economic security, respect, and full lives. It also undermined the AFL's ability to defend its existing membership. Gompers might grandiosely declare that rather than oppose the trusts, the labor unions would organize the trust workers. But keeping the AFL a bastion of white male craft unionism left it trying to preserve nineteenth-century craft privileges in the face of a dynamic industrial environment where the line between skilled and unskilled workers was blurring and new machines were transforming old craft skills like furniture making into factory labor.[50]

Likewise, official AFL rhetoric about "high wages, shorter hours, comfortable homes, and higher education and larger liberty" was unaccompanied by any willingness to fight for those goals politically. The leaders of various AFL craft unions, key players in Federation policy making, were a cautious, upward mobile bunch, often desperately anxious for personal respectability and dead set against political action. This mindset was reinforced by the activities of a Roman Catholic Church, solicitous of the welfare of its working-class parishoners, pro-union, and also an influential force against socialism and labor radicalism among both rank and file and leadership. AFL leaders continued to insist that only union economic power could improve conditions, and opposed minimum-wage legislation and government health and unemployment insurance. The stinging defeat suffered by President Gompers in his 1899 campaign to lobby Congress for an eight-hour-a-day work law showed the folly of this strategy, of trying to exert political pressure without being politically mobilized.[51]

At the 1900 AFL convention, where the official line was "better and more friendly relations between capital and labor," a self-satisfied Gompers told the delegates, "Ladies and gentlemen, your struggle during the past twenty years for shorter hours and better conditions for the toiling masses has been a successful one." The trend was clearly toward bread and butter unionism and away from an earlier focus on workers solidarity and control over the jobsite. Businesses providing union recognition to skilled employees were to be welcomed as partners, and the unskilled, immigrant, and racial minorities left to fend for themselves.[52]

This shift toward trading workers' autonomy off for security and higher wages was noted approvingly by major business figures like Mark Hanna, who realized the potential of labor leaders as allies of business against radicals and socialists inside and outside of the unions, and in helping to suppress the militant wave of sympathy strikes sweeping the country. On a more long-term level, the labor movement could be integrated into modern capitalism and utilized in raising productivity and profits.

The outlines of an organization to be called the National Civic Federation, composed of corporate and labor union leaders, began taking form in mid-1900 during a strike against the National Metal Trades Association by metal workers belonging to the International Association of Machinists. At the Murray Hill Hotel in Manhattan, an agreement was drawn up: In return for a national contract and improved wages and hours, union negotiators agreed to suppress sympathy strikes by workers and to remove limits on output. Within two years, the agreement would break down in mutual recriminations, and by 1903, a massive corporate offensive to smash unions would lead to a strike wave across the country.[53]

What the working classes in the United States circa 1900 desperately needed— a multiethnic, multiracial social movement based on trade unions of industrial and agricultural workers and capable of swinging elections and initiating broad policy changes—was simply not available. This condition guaranteed their continued marginalization.

Chapter 7

White Man's Country

I am strongly of the opinion that Negroes ought to be in Africa, yellow men in Asia, and white men in Europe and America.

—Harry Truman (future U.S. President, aged 17), 1901

In supreme crises the racial element will be found the most potent and will control action.

—Andrew Carnegie to President William McKinley, 1898

The Anglo-Saxon is pretty much the same wherever you find him, and he walks on the necks of every colored race he comes into contact with. Resistance to his will or institutions means destruction to the weaker race.

—U.S. Senator Ben Tillman, circa 1900

This is a white man's country and will always be controlled by whites.

—Virginia populist, 1900

Arriving in Honolulu toward the end of 1899, a correspondent for the *Nation* was startled by how different race and ethnic relations and norms were from the continental United States. He especially remarked upon the way "the brown people move about with a cheerful self-confidence whatever their race, accosting each other and the whites with an easy bearing indicative of reciprocal respect."

The writer did note, however, a source of anxiety among local people of color he met in the islands. The Americans, it was feared, would bring the "brutal race prejudices which have disgraced the United States" to their new Pacific possession.[1]

Looking back, how do we account for the sheer intensity and virulence (on occasion bordering insanity) of white racial feeling in this era? After all, European descendants were surely the continental masters of all they surveyed: The final defeat of Indian resistance had occurred years before, southern blacks had already been successfully stripped of any vestige of rights and powers they had acquired following the Civil War, and the Chinese "menace" had long since been excluded from entering the United States.

Every period, however, generates the racism it needs. The striking power of race in the life of this era stemmed less from threats to white hegemony and more from internal white struggles and fears due to acute dislocations and changes. In such an environment, racism provided both "a mechanism of convincing oneself . . . of one's self worth" and a familiar, comforting anchor.[2]

By 1900, certain racial traditions were deeply embedded in the national culture and psyche. Three centuries of racial hierarchy had made racial and cultural differences central to how Americans defined their identities and viewed the world about them. Boundaries were heavily sandbagged and not easily transcended.

Racism is, as Joel Kovel suggests, "an integral part of a stable and productive cultural order." It has provided a firm foundation for building white American dreams. Ideologies of biological and cultural supremacy formed the rationale for the special privileges claimed by whites in the new country, for the grabbing off of a continent and restricting the rights and opportunities of others. And white supremacy offered special psychological gratifications.[3]

So "whiteness" was the cultural norm in the United States of 1900, the measure of one's Americanness. The axiom "To be white is to be human and to be human is to be white" could have been inscribed on the walls of the U.S. Capitol and Supreme Court. In a society based on a dual, racially defined set of legal and everyday rights, privileges, and protections, the fact (or appearance) of being Caucasian was basic to full citizenship in the republic.[4]

In analyzing the "history of white supremacy," the race relations scholar George Fredrickson has assigned "a major causal role to tensions or divisions within the white social structure." Historically, periods of traumatic change in the United States have seen minorities used as stand-ins for what were essentially class and ethnic antagonisms among whites. Thus, the scapegoating of nonwhites has functioned as a ritual by which blame and frustrations were exorcised, white solidarities maintained, and deep-rooted problems evaded.[5]

The economic and cultural crises of the nineties had generated bitter political and cultural conflicts between different sets of whites, arraying small farmers and laborers against planters and merchants, industrial workers versus corporate employers. The unprecedented pace of change was creating anxieties and a sense of a world somewhat out of sync. For some Americans the rise of populism as a political force, then the 1896 Bryan campaign, had aroused great hopes for change, only to be dashed, leaving a sizable vacuum readily filled by the hunt for a variety of "others" to scapegoat.

The definition of "others" might include the one in seven Americans who in 1900 had been born abroad. What had changed during the nineties was the immigration mix. Now the people coming through the metal wicket gate at Ellis Island toting bundles and tin boxes were more likely to be arriving from Sicily, Kiev, and Bohemia than from Ireland or Germany. These new immigrants, many with swarthy complexions, bizarre-sounding native tongues, and outlandish customs, were widely viewed as less "desirable" than the old.

The real issue, of course, was assimilation: "How to absorb them all safely is the question," mused Jacob Riis, himself Danish by birth, watching the foreign born swelling to almost one-half the population of New York City. One out of three residents of Massachussetts and Rhode Island was foreign born. Towns like Passaic, New Jersey, and Manchester, New Hampshire, had majority foreign-born populations. Milwaukee, Chicago, Pittsburgh, and Cleveland were overwhelmingly populated by first- and second-generation Americans.[6]

Could these immigrants be successfully processed into Americans? Many native born had doubts, and stereotypes were thick on the ground. A prominent Buffalo man ridiculed the "crowd of illiterate peasants freshly raked in from Irish bogs, or Bohemian mines, or Italian robber nests." Was the country, old-stock folks wondered, being innundated by foreign anarchists, paupers, and criminals?[7]

During the turbulent, economically volatile decade before the Spanish-American War, nativism and anti-immigrant feeling reached an apex. Immigrants were pilloried for everything from being violent radical agitators intent on class warfare, to providing the mass voting base for corrupt Irish-run big city machines, and being agents and tools of some devlish Papist conspiracy.

Fraternal and nativist societies flourished. The elitist Immigration Restriction League headquartered in Boston led a legislative offensive to drastically tighten immigration laws. There was the meteoric rise and fall of the virulently anti-Roman Catholic American Protective Society (APA), a semisecret political organization, which at its peak boasted several million members nationwide and a political power base in the upper Midwest. Sensing the national mood, Congress passed a literacy bill for new immigrants in 1896, only to have President Cleveland veto it.[8]

The return of prosperity in 1898 blunted the force of the nativist drive. Public opinion seemed more confident in the capacity of American society to assimilate immigrants and vaguely in favor of a continuing inflow. Ethnic organizations lobbied for a continuing open door. So did manufacturers like Carnegie and mine owners and railroad barons who, finding they could not obtain enough workers during booming 1899–1901, advertised widely in Europe.

But the immigration issue was never far from the center of American life, particularly since renewed economic expansion was drawing a fresh wave of immigrants to the United States. Arrivals in 1899 were double the number coming two years earlier. An average of over 1,000 new immigrants were landing each day during 1900, while thousands more were in passage on ships stretched across the Atlantic sea lanes. This upsurge in arrivals helped revitalize the anti-immigration lobby.[9]

Convinced that new waves of cheap labor threatened American living standards, some trade unions took aggressive positions on immigration. "No self-respecting American citizen," complained one union leader, "could compete with the alien laborer brought in from Europe, to whom a fishgall would be a big luxury." In 1900, the AFL, its own leadership heavily immigrant and second generation, was publicly supporting literacy requirements for immigrants.[10]

But the mass base behind the exclusionist movement consisted of Protestant middle-class folk who had joined organizations like the APA during the nineties. Political leadership was supplied by powerful Boston bluebloods like U.S. Senator Henry Cabot Lodge and Brooks Adams of the Immigration Restriction League, whose objection to the new immigrants was, in the main, racial and cultural, and had everything to do with the fin de siècle obsession they shared with other native-stock Americans regarding the alleged glories of a recently invented category of people called the "Anglo-Saxons."[11]

The belief in the uniqueness and superiority of Anglo-Saxons was founded on the premise that over the last 1,500 or so years, the descendants of certain Germanic tribes had evolved a special genius for self-governance, state building, technology, and military conquest that marked them from other "races." "We are Teutons, God's kings of men," was the view of an ex–North Carolina Confederate officer, Colonel Robert Bingham, whose pamphlet, *An American Slaveholder's View of the Negro Question in the South*, was receiving some attention in high places. According to Bingham, manhood, suffrage, and responsibility had required centuries of preparation and violent struggle: "But every step towards the higher freedom was won in the best blood of our race." Theodore Roosevelt, in his popular series, *The Winning of the West*, declared the vanquishing of the Indian tribes to have been part of the "race destiny" of Europeans to dominate less civilized and virile peoples.[12]

"Anglo-Saxonism" was fully compatible with the new racial "sciences" weighted with Social Darwinist and racial evolutionary ideas and popularized by books like William Z. Ripley's *The Races of Empire*. American social and physical scientists, historians, and clergymen proclaimed "racial" (a word they invariably mixed up with "ethnic") categories to be natural and fixed. Freshly minted terms such as the "race problem," "race war," and "higher races" began filtering into the English language.

Territorial expansion by the "Anglo-Saxon powers"—Great Britain and the United States over the last decade had gained control over much of Africa, the Pacific, and the Caribbean—gave credence to the Anglo-Saxon superiority thesis. Rather than a consequence of a (temporary) Western monopoly over advanced technology and military organization, racial ideologues like Henry Cabot Lodge and Roosevelt regarded global supremacy as clinching the argument for the inherent superiority of Anglo-Saxon civilization. A textbook case was the recent thrashing of the dark-skinned Spanish "dons" by one of the "masterful fighting races." It was "the incarnate tradition of Anglo-Saxon seamanship" that was responsible for Dewey's victory at Manila Bay (the state of the decrepit, out-gunned Spanish fleet being ignored).[13]

What never seemed to be asked was whether or not the so-called "Anglo-Saxons" constituted an authentic human grouping—a writer in the *Nation* could courageously lash "the sanctimonious and condescending attitude of Anglo-Saxons towards the races they are pleased to call inferiors," while never questioning the authenticity of their existence.[14]

What, then, was to be the place of recent immigrants from Byelorussia, Slovakia, and Sicily in this republic of Anglo-Saxon mythmen and heroes?

The new immigrants could not avoid, of course, being faulted for lacking the proper bloodlines. Indeed, many native-stock Americans thought the recently arrived eastern and southern European immigrants to be debased human material, the "scum and offal of Europe, human garbage." This distinctly limited their empathy. The "Bohunk" laborer in a Pennsylvania coal mine or steel mill, or the "Eyetalian" working in a New England textile plant or cannery, was only doing work appropriate to his mental and moral capacity. That such people allowed themselves to be manipulated by political machines, ethnic labor contract bosses, and union agitators simply confirmed their deficiencies.[15]

Yet, the more crucial issue in a society obsessed with "whiteness" was whether or not the new immigrants were to gain inclusion to the all-important category of "white," and thus eligibility for genuine participation in the White Man's Country. The implications were momentous: Designating Italian immigrants as "white Negroes" in Louisiana during the nineties had made them vulnerable to occasional white mob violence and lynch law. Greek immigrants in the South and Slavs in the North were often referred to as "half-niggers." Designating Americans of Mexican extraction as nonwhites legitimated their victimization by official and vigilante violence and segregated schools in Texas towns like Corpus Christi. A famous "corrido" is still sung about the ill-starred Gregorio Cortez, who in 1901 shot down two Texas sheriffs to avenge his brother's murder.[16]

Plenty of Americans believed that the root of the immigrants' failings lay not in their Old World heritage, or newness to America, but in their tainted "blood." A chorus of intellectuals, clergymen, and politicians denounced mass immigration as posing dangers to the future of "the master race." "There is now being injected into the veins of the nation," declared the popular writer, the Reverend Josiah Strong, "a large amount of inferior blood every day of the year." Stanford University's distinguished Edward Ross cautioned that the twin evils of the closing of the frontier and mass immigration by inferior peoples must undermine the Nordic race and lead to "race suicide." Federal action was needed. Franklin Giddings, John Commons, and Richard Mayo-Smith, all numbered among the country's most eminent scholars, argued that the new immigrants could never fit into American culture. Lobbying for restrictions on immigration, the superintendent of the United States Census, Francis Walker, would claim there was no possibility of assimilating "alien breeds" who were "ignorant, unskilled, inert."[17]

But the experience of one non-Anglo-Saxon white group was already establishing the right of any and all Europeans to claim a degree of whiteness. The Irish, arriving en masse in midcentury after the Great Potato Famine, had originally been reviled as paupers and criminals fleeing a destitute, priest-ridden country. Allocated "white nigger" status and work and permanently consigned to the underclass of unskilled laborers and housemaids, they had been the object of abuse and violence from the anti-Catholic Know Nothings and other nativists. Yet over the course of the next two generations these Irish had used ferociously hard work, organizational skills, and their claim to whiteness to entrench themselves in the new country.[18]

There were still in 1900 an abundance of poor shanty and lower working-class Irish Americans residing in Chicago, Boston, New York, and elsewhere, and high rates of tuberculosis were registered among children of mothers born in Ireland. Big-city criminal gangs were often composed of second-generation Irishmen. Being Irish still carried a stigma in many places, and negative Irish stereotypes around strong drink and popery abounded. They continued to be excluded from established society. But Irish Americans controlled the politics and municipal bureaucracies of half a dozen major cities including Boston, Philadelphia, and New York (Charles Murphy would take over leadership of Tammany Hall from Richard Croker in 1901 and remain boss until 1924), boasted a business and professional class, skilled workmen and trade union leaders, powerful fraternal societies, and the country's most celebrated athletes, John L. Sullivan, John McGraw, Jim Corbett, Jim Jeffries, and Jack Sharkey.[19]

"In my work as Governor," Theodore Roosevelt confided to a friend, "some of the very best appointees whom I have to my credit are Irishmen." One of America's favorite and most widely syndicated newspaper columns featured the marvelous wit of Finley Peter Dunne's "Mr. Dooley," brogue and all, sagely discoursing on the issues of the day.[20]

The success of the Irish in situating themselves within the privileged circle of what Benjamin Ringer has called "We the People" had secured their claim to whiteness. Now, in a familiar American scenario, the recently oppressed were exchanging roles. By 1900, the Irish were dominating more recent Roman Catholic immigrants and arousing resentments. Irish-American bishops prohibited Polish and French from being spoken in immigrant churches and Irish foremen exercised dictatorial authority over French-Canadians and Italians in New England textile and paper mills.[21]

Nonetheless, the Irish had set a precedent for the country's acceptance of the non–English-speaking European immigrants of the late nineteenth and early twentieth centuries who might now follow the same broad pathway: Americanization through schools, settlement houses, hard work, and exercise of political muscle would in time raise their children to an acceptable level of Anglo-Saxon civilization. Kate Cleghorn, seeing the progress of the Irish as a benchmark, asked in the *Atlantic Monthly*, "Is there any reason to suppose that newer comers will not assimilate as readily?"[22]

Older-stock Americans would continue to be ambivalent, if not downright hostile, toward the new immigrants. But there was a measure of confidence that newcomers could be Americanized and make a contribution. Buttressing this were prominent theories of human evolution, like the early nineteenth-century French thinker Jean-Baptiste Lamarck's teachings that environment would ultimately prevail over heredity. For the Lamarckians, acquired traits could be passed down. Given time and the right associations, even physical features might be modified. So the stages of evolution from "savagery" to "barbarism" and ultimately to "social efficiency" would proceed in logical progression. The immigrants would yet become good Americans. In January 1900, Governor Theodore Roosevelt, a strong Lamarckian, wrote to a foreign friend: "Here our people of different race origins do get fused very soon."[23]

Roosevelt's voice here is also that of an astute politician in a nation where non–Anglo-Saxon white voters were now an increasingly potent force. In a similar vein, another ambitious politican, Indiana's Albert Beveridge, was declaring that "the great crucible of the American continent has produced a new race superior to all the rest." In the exuberance of U.S. imperial expansion, the trend was to fudge the definition of who exactly was "Anglo-Saxon," and focus on the virtues of generic "whiteness."[24]

Contrary to rumors back in Europe, eastern and southern Europeans would find most American streets paved with poverty and grinding work rather than gold. Ethnic segregation in the cities was intensifying, and signs such as "No Jews, No Italians" were going up at house and job sites. Nonetheless, they would not be turned into a caste of pariahs or denied access to resources for betterment. There would be a chance to rise. The Irish had provided a road map. And it was already noticed how attached some recent immigrant groups were to learning and how well they did in school.

By dint of their Europeanness, skin color, control of the vote, and commitment to labor, white ethnics might now claim a precarious right to full citizenship in the United States, one they would struggle to consolidate right through the post–World War II years. Assimilation would exact a stiff price—nothing less than the subordination of ethnic group life to American goals and values—but it would be an option.

There were, in 1900, in a country that had made whiteness the prerequisite for democratic rights and opportunities, almost 9.5 million people of color. They were Sioux, Oneida, Iroquois, and Hopi, along with black Americans and immigrants from China, Japan, and Mexico. Boundary lines between whites and nonwhites had been hardening of late and getting drawn fast and tight. If American dreaming easily crossed color lines, then the power to realize American dreams remained largely a white monopoly.

The nation was more complex now; thus, the mental images and mythologies of race so crucial to maintaining the system of white domination demanding more sophistication. Intellectual cover here was provided by the "race sciences" of heredity and biology. There was Henry Fairfield Osborn, paleontologist and director of New York's American Musuem of Natural

History, arguing that "primitive" races were retarded physically and mentally, and that different races represented fundamentally different species. Church leaders, especially from Protestant denominations, declared that "racial inequality is the work and the will of God," and cited Biblical authority to prove that races had been created with different qualities. At the grass roots, the folk imagery became more graphic: Rural wisdom had it that "the lord made a white man of dust, a nigger from mud, and then threw up what was left, and it came down a Chinaman."[25]

Certainly there were white men and women who worked to defend the rights of racial minorities and who challenged the prevailing ethnocentrism: "We are constantly haunted with a vain imagining that Europeans and Americans are possessed of a noble type, vastly superior to the dusky races," stated Charles De Kay in a June 1900 magazine article. "Why not confess that the world is smaller and the mixture of human races is more ancient and complete than our race vanities have permitted us to believe?" Reflections like this, however, amounted to howling into a great wind, the nation fixated as it was on constituting these "dusky races" as "problems."[26]

Of all the peoples of color, Native Americans seemed to be the likeliest to be allowed the opportunity to assimilate into the White Man's Country—and the ones most reluctant to do so.

Since the military defeat of the tribes, assimilation had been official federal policy. Indians were encouraged to abandon their heritage and tribal languages, splice their communal lands into individualized homesteads, and adopt white lifestyles. The design was to diminish both tribal resources and loyalties. Having lost their lands, Native Americans would now lose what remained of their collective identities. Proponents of Indian assimilation in Washington were easterners like senators Henry Dawes and Orville Platt and the ethnographer John Wesley Powell, true believers in Indians making a successful, beneficial transition to "civilization."[27]

The 1887 Dawes Act, mapping out a gradual but steady assimilation process under federal guidance, provided the legislative underpinning. It was envisioned that as tribes allocated land "allotments" of 160 acres to individual households and these yeoman Indians flourished (and became U.S. citizens), traditional tribal lifestyles and cultural influence would wither away. By educating Indian youth in English-speaking federal reservation and boarding schools, they would be removed from tribal influences and prepared for future lives as independent farmers.[28]

Whatever the program's good intentions, this was a victor's *diktat*: The subjects themselves were not consulted about their future and no alternatives were on the table. Based on absolute contempt for tribal traditions, heritage, and communal economy, the program ignored the desperate sacrifices Indians would be called upon to make.

By 1900, the assimilation program had gotten so badly twisted that even original sponsors like Dawes and Platt were dismayed. As the population of the West increased and good farming and ranching land became scarce, and new mineral discoveries were made, intense political pressures mounted for opening up Indian lands to settlement and mining. Vast acreages were carved out of reservations for white commercial use, and whites began economically dominating Indian communities.[29]

Meanwhile, there was generally increasing white pessimism about the possibility of backward, "primitive" races becoming "civilized." Indians were said to have failed in the contest with whites because of their basic inferiority. "The present generation of Indians," editorialized the *Rocky Mountain Daily News*, "never can be taught to work, and the average Indian as long as he can steal, will never work."[30]

Native Americans were allegedly unable to think abstractly or creatively, or to innovate. According to prominent "race" scientist Daniel Garrison Brinton, the establishment of Indian racial inferiority early in its "species" development made the condition irreversible. The use of cubical skull capacity tests, thought to be accurate indicators of intelligence, showed that Indians, although mentally above blacks, were markedly inferior to whites.[31]

Meanwhile, congressional hostility toward providing federally funded education to Native Americans was escalating. Convinced of Indians' limited intellectual capacity, the supervisors of the federal Indian schools deemphasized academics in favor of manual skills. This meant educating young people to perform cheap dependent labor for whites. Speaking to the 1900 National Education Association convention, Hollis Frissell, principal of the Negro school, Hampton Institute, expressed the prevailing wisdom:

> Indians are people of the child races. In looking forward to the future, I believe we should teach them to labor in order that they may be brought to manhood.[32]

Dawes and other supporters of assimilation had assumed that the protection of the federal government would be available until the assimilation process was completed. Federal authorities, however, lobbied relentlessly by western congressmen, soon abandoned trying to safeguard tribal property. By 1900, the 138 million acres owned by the tribes thirteen years before had dwindled to 78 million. William Jones, commissioner of Indian affairs, a McKinley patronage appointee, was acquiescing to continued grabs of reservation land and accelerating the distribution of allotments. Indian rights organizations ineffectually attempted to provide legal defenses against land theft, but hundreds of thousands of acres were passing out of Indian domain. Meanwhile, Congress was ratifying a fraudulent land cession from the Kiowas, and white squatters in Florida were evicting Seminoles. The Rosebud Sioux, the Flathead, and the Unitahs were coming under pressure to sell lands. Southern Ute reservation lands in the sagebrush country around Durango, Colorado, were being opened by the federal government to settlement. "Forty years hence," editorialized the *Nation*, "scarcely an Indian may have an acre of his allotment left."[33]

In cities far from the reservations, there was a measure of unease and guilt over the plight of the Indian. George Hoar, the U.S. Senate's foremost opponent of colonialism, cited Native Americans as a case in point to argue against acquiring the Philippines. "The Indian problem is not chiefly how to teach the Indian to be less savage in his treatment of the Saxon," commented Hoar, "but the Saxon to be less savage in his treatment of the Indian."[34]

But Hoar's was a lonely voice. "Hardly anyone in congress now takes the slightest interest in the dealing of our Government with the Indian tribes," went one report.

> The abuse had become so strongly entrenched as to be secure. Public opinion cannot be aroused . . . and there is much money to be made by administering their affairs.[35]

The Indian wars were distant enough in the past now to evoke nostalgia for Indians as primitives in an uncivilized state. Thus the popularity of curios sold at Niagara Falls and countless other places, and the innumerable sports teams named "Indians" or "Braves." Shows like William Cody's Wild West extravaganza toured the country. Tribal customs were caricatured: Before the 1899 football game with Carlisle, the Indian school, Harvard sophomores did Indian dances. A year earlier, at the Omaha Exposition, where Indians displayed in traditional settings were terrifically popular, tourists could get Geronimo's autograph for fifty cents and a picture taken with the legendary Apache warrior for a dollar.[36]

A few Native Americans made the transition well and used the rentals from land allotments to live in modest comfort. But for most, the past quarter century had been catastrophic. Neither assimilated into American culture nor allowed the resources to refashion their own cultural lives; they existed in a profound limbo that often led to cultural and personal despair. Dependence on whiskey, tobacco, and federal handouts became tribal hallmarks. Reservation poverty was epidemic. Given astronomic infant mortality and tuberculosis rates and abbreviated lifespans, the Indian population of 267,000 in 1900 was in decline. White scholars following the demographic curve predicted that the American Indian was destined for extinction.

This was to underestimate the resilience of Native Americans and their capacity for resistance. Only a few years before, Chippewas in Minnesota had fought and won a pitched battle with loggers and federal troops intruding into their lands. The isolation of tribal culture from mainstream America would help maintain a degree of integrity and a land base. It would not be the first time that a people would take advantage of its peripheral status to forge some autonomy. Yet, in 2000, Indians would still be attempting to recover from the ravages occurring in these years.

Over the last half of the nineteenth century, immigrants from Asia had not found the United States very hospitable. To the question of the place of the Chinese in the country, Americans brought their customary ignorance of other peoples and a tendency to generalize on the basis of rumors, half-truths, and emotional fears. Imagery of "gambling dens and slave pens . . . coolie labor and bloodthirsty tongs" had become identified with the Chinese early on and been etched hard into the white consciousness. China was a manifestly "queer" civilization; the men carried leprosy and the women venereal diseases.

Excursions by voyeuristic whites into Chinatown exotica amplified this notion that the "heathen Chinee" were captives to backward traditions, and could never be transformed into genuine citizens of a progressive democratic nation. A more menacing image was the specter of North America being innundated by 400 million Chinese. If favorable images of China as an ancient and wise civilization skilled at arts and scholarship were there, they were muted.[37]

After the great post–Civil War railroad-building spree ended and the Chinese had settled down, they had been subjected to public and private ridicule and abuse and the occasional violent pogrom. Anti-Chinese riots had forced expulsions from Seattle, Tacoma, Rock Springs, Wyoming, and other towns during the 1880s. Chinese living in San Francisco and Boston were harassed by police and refused protection from white thugs. In the West, white workers regarded them as a dire threat to wage standards and vigorously resisted their employment in mining and manufacturing. Many employers thought Chinese workers inferior and boycotted them.[38]

By the end of the century in California and elsewhere, the Chinese had become what Sucheng Chan has called "perpetual foreigners," excluded from mainstream American life and opportunities, denied constitutional rights, segregated in public schools, refused service in white restaurants and barbershops. Confined to the bottom of the labor hierarchy, they mainly worked in low-wage sweatshops, as seasonal agricultural laborers, and in hand laundries, restaurants, and groceries located in Chinatowns. Among affluent whites it had become fashionable to have Chinese cooks and servants ("a yellow blessing," in the words of *Harper's Bazaar*).[39]

The 1882 treaty excluding Chinese from immigrating into the United States and denying citizenship to those already here was the first official announcement that American nationality was to be racially based. Immigration restrictions played havoc, separating fathers from families in China and making those who could not prove they were in the United States before passage of restrictive legislation fearful of deportation. By 1900, the Chinese population, heavily male, and down to 119,000, had reached its lowest ebb in decades.

Both Chinese government officials in the United States and Chinese-American organizations such as Native Sons of the Golden State tried to fight exclusion but made scant headway against an almost solid wall of hostility driven by ignorance and fears of difference. Some missionaries and scholars familiar with China presented the view that the Chinese were intelligent and hard-working people from a culture priding itself on learning and arts, but this paled before politicians and newspapers actively frothing up public paranoia about the pending renewal of the Chinese Exclusion Treaty in 1902. Failure to renew, went the hysterical cry, meant inevitable Asian domination of the West Coast, the critical outer frontier of the white man's world. Anti-Chinese feeling was abetted by foreign-policy opinion leaders such as Mahan and Roosevelt voicing fears of "race war" and "race degeneracy."[40]

Geographic center of Sinophobia was San Francisco, which had 14,000 Chinese residents among a population of 342,000. In this, the country's most prolabor major city, where Irish trade union leaders and politicians had great power, an Italian-American entrepreneur named Giannini was carefully crafting what eventually became the Bank of America, and Jewish merchants were respected community members, anti-Asian traditions ran deep. The vanguard of the city's anti-Chinese agitation, as in earlier years, was skilled crafts workers and their union leaders, convinced that the presence of "Monglolian coolies" subsisting at starvation wages would quickly destroy the living standards they had struggled for.[41]

This, of course, was about considerably more than simply maintaining a white lockhold over blue-collar jobs. Coming at a time when Chinese were effectively barred from entrance to the United States and forced by law to register with the authorities, the sheer ferocity of the anti-Chinese movement reveals the presence of other agendas and fears. Positioning the Chinese as devils was, in fact, invaluable in maintaining the facade of unity, consensus, and common purpose among competitive, often fractious, white communities. In retrospect, what white San Franciscans "seeking protection against Asiatic hordes" were really seeking was protection against each other and the chaos of trying to live out the American dream.

This meant that any issue involving Chinese, such as the discovery in March 1900 of a few cases of bubonic plague, was immediately transformed into a racial cause célèbre, and used to inflame existing prejudices. Blaming the Chinese for the outbreak, San Francisco's reform mayor James Phelan had Chinatown roped off and policemen stationed at key intersections. Only Chinese were vaccinated against the plague. The local press largely treated the affair as a conspiracy against whites. "The almond eyed Mongolian is waiting for his opportunity," editorialized *Organized Labor*, "waiting to assassinate you and your children with one of his many maladies."[42]

Anti-Chinese antagonism was reinforced at the highest political levels. The summer 1900 Boxer revolt against the western powers in China seemed to affirm both the irrational savagery of the Chinese, who had massacred American and European missionaries, and their inferiority when a relatively small international force seized Peking and crushed the Boxers. President McKinley used the Boxer affair to disparage the "character of the Chinese races," and label the Chinese "a primitive people."[43]

The Japanese presence on the West Coast had been minimal until the nineties, when immigration moderately increased, raising Japanese visibility in cities like Seattle and San Francisco. In California's agricultural valleys, peasants arriving from southern Japan were working as laborers on sugar beet, bean, and hops farms, leasing and beginning to purchase cropland for truck farms. Japanese fishermen had also started to revolutionize the West Coast fishing industry. Then, annexation of Hawaii resulted in an influx of thousands more Japanese. Labor union leaders accused the Japanese of displacing whites from railroad employment.[44]

All of this provided the impetus for what had been a gathering white backlash to take off. An early (and lasting) theme became the deadly threat posed to white dominance by a calculating, greedy, and crafty group of people regarded as being more energetic and entrepreneurial than the Chinese. According to one labor newspaper, Chinese were a "menace to the country," but "the sniveling Japanese, who swarm along the streets is a far greater danger to the laboring portion of society than all the opium smoked pigtails." And the U.S. Industrial Commmission concluded that "the Japanese . . . have most of the vices of the Chinese and none of the virtues."[45]

Both Chinese and Japanese embodied the "yellow peril," a new term just coming into vogue to depict the threat from the Orient. Mayor Phelan, addressing a large anti-Asian rally on May 7, 1900, at Union Square Square, declared: "The Chinese and Japanese are not bonafide citizens. They are not the stuff of which American citizens can be made." Phelan demanded drastic action, or else the "Asiatic laborers will undermine our civilzation."

The main anti-Asian target increasingly became the Japanese. At the same

May 7 rally, there was the shrill charge of Stanford Professor Edward Alsworth Ross, the noted sociologist who had coined the term "race suicide": "Shall the worse come to worst, it would be better for us to turn our guns upon every vessel bringing Japanese to our shore rather than permit them to land." A resolution was passed by the audience to extend exclusion to the Japanese.[46]

California politicians picked up the beat; the legislature demanding that Congress "pass laws and resolutions for the protection of American labor against the immigration of oriental laborer," while the state's governor denounced "the unrestricted importation of Japanese laborers." In reply, the Japanese government dramatically curtailed immigration to the United States. Thus began what the noted California writer Carey McWilliams has referred to as "the state of undeclared war between California and Japan." In 1941, this would become a declared, shooting war between Washington and Tokyo, and 110,000 Japanese-Americans would experience deportation from their homes to concentration camps in the interior. The seeds of this calamity had been sown in the policies of the fin de siècle era.[47]

Chapter 8

Black in White Man's Country

Why is there a problem to solve as to the Negro race? From the Whiteman's standpoint, the Negro is good for nothing, but a servant or some menial position. Independent Negroes are considered dangerous.

—M.S. David, letter to *New York Times*,
January 1, 1899

Mr. Hennessey: "What's goin't to happen to th' naygur?"
Mr. Dooley: "Well, he'll ayther have to go to th' north an' be a subjick race, or stay in th' south 'an' be an objick lesson: 'Tis a harrd time he'll have annyhow. I'm not sure that I'd not as leave be gintly lynched in Mississippi as baten to death in New York. If I was a black man, I'd choose th' cotton belt in prifirince to th' belt on th' neck fr'm th' policeman's club . . . . "I freed the slave Hinnissy, but faith I think 't was like turrnin' him out iv a panthry into a cellar."

—Finley Peter Dunne, *Mr. Dooley*, September 1, 1900

One drop of negro blood makes a negro, it kinks the hair, flattens the nose, thickens the lip, puts out the light of intellect, and lights the fires of brutal passions.

—Thomas Dixon, Jr., *The Leopard's Spots*, 1902

> The rights of the Negroes are at a lower ebb than at any time
> during the thirty-five years of their freedom, and the race
> prejudice more intense and uncompromising.
>
> —Charles W. Chestnut (black writer), 1903

The nearly 9 million black Americans in 1900 constituted the vast majority of people of color. Heavily concentrated in the southern Black Belt cotton states, they formed majorities in South Carolina and Mississippi, and almost half the population of Louisiana and Georgia. Substantial black minorities were located in Alabama, Florida, North Carolina, Arkansas, Texas, and Tennessee.

If white Americans circa 1900 were in agreement on anything, it was on the basic inferiority of the African descendants on their continent. Firmly embedded were slave and post–Civil War stereotypes of blacks as "shiftless" and of limited intelligence. Antiblack race prejudice was widely viewed as a normal white instinct.

In the late nineties, scientific theory, in the form of Social Darwinism, had been used to buttress the movement toward extending and institutionalizing white supremacy. The ideas of Arthur de Gobineau, Gustave Le Bon, and August Weissman, European thinkers who assumed black inferiority and the innate right of whites to rule, circulated widely. Pronouncements by eminent American scientists such as professors Nathaniel Shaler of Harvard and Edward Cope of the University of Pennsylvania reinforced the notion that blacks were physically and mentally retarded.[1]

African-Americans were classified as lesser genetic material, the failed side of the natural-selection process. They were perpetual adolescents, lacking the mental competence to choose wisely. "God never tried to make the Negro the equal of the white man," said a Georgia governor, "and the southern Anglo Saxon has too much reverence to attempt such an improvement upon the Creator's handiwork."[2]

Crucial to the antiblack indictment was the charge that black morals, health, and character had significantly deteriorated during the generation since the Civil War ended. Ignoring a history of exploitation and deprivation, people attributed any and all black behaviors—high crime rates, out-of-wedlock births, et al.—to innate racial characteristics. "We delivered the African man over to the nation in 1865 orderly, fairly industrious, without vice, without disease, without crime," claimed one ex-slaveholder. "In the hands of the nation, he has become disorderly, idle, vicious, diseased."[3]

Lacking the restraining influence of their slave masters, blacks' innate jungle-like savagery had reappeared, said the commentators. They were simply incapable of controlling their lustful passions. Both males and females were depraved, their blackness a metaphor for the darkness lurking within. Said one contemporary: "There is common agreement in the public mind that the negro represents an accentuated type of human degradation." One slightly fringe school of southern racists liberally quoted the Bible to validate the claim that blacks were not really homo sapiens, but "bestial" ape men.[4]

In documenting an increase in the black population, the 1900 U.S. census put an end to (some wishful) white speculation that blacks, like American Indians, were fated to die out. But black life *was* cheap: the average lifespan, 34 years, or 14 less than the white. Poor and inadequate food, housing, and sanitation, and lack of medical care took a toll on barefoot ragged children living in sharecropper cabins. Twice as many black children as white were dying of typhoid fever and four times as many from diarrheal diseases. Pneumonia and tuberculosis afflicted all ages.[5]

A popular (if simplistic) northern notion had been that education by itself could solve the race problem. Ignoring the fact that only half of all black children in 1900 had access to schools, this now came under assault. John Roach Stratton, a Georgia professor, citing statistics showing that blacks committed over a third of the nation's homicides, told a national audience that nothing could overcome "the negro's tendency to immorality and crime." High rates of pulmonary and venereal disease demonstrated "the negro's moral decline." In any event, they could not hope to compete with Anglo-Saxons. Professor Paul Barringer of the University of Virginia declared to the 1900 Southern Education Association that "the Negro race is essentially a race of peasant farmers and laborers . . . everywhere else he is a foredained failure."[6]

This crusade to devalue African-Americans, while mainly engineered by southern true believers, resonated in the North where many whites were resistant to racial equality and enforcing civil rights in their own states, and by 1900 were prone to casually accept the southern white evaluation of blacks. A key block was those liberals who, having been defenders of southern black rights since the Civil War, thought of themselves as the nation's conscience in matters of race. Now, however, they had become steadily more passive, convinced that scientific evidence and the failures of emancipation had proven blacks to be emotionally unstable and incapable of functioning as citizens in a modern democratic nation. Allowances should be made for a few superior individuals, but the goals of equality and social justice given up for now.

Only a very slow, painful process of evolution might one day bring the races into rough equality. Meanwhile, since miscegenation was unnatural and could only debase the white bloodstream, intermarriage was simply not possible.[7]

This rush to demonize blacks reflected the fin de siècle pressures on whites themselves, and the pressing need to justify the roles they were forcing upon Americans of African descent. Whites, in short, intent on denying the equal rights of black citizens, were creating elaborate justifications for what they were doing. This meant erecting black stereotypes so powerfully negative that they defied first-hand personal evidence to the contrary. The sheer brilliance of Atlanta University sociologist W.E.B. DuBois made him something of a freak to the whites he occasionally lectured to, and they were clearly discombobulated upon meeting him. Having personally witnessed the courage and heroism under fire of the black Ninth and Tenth Cavalries during the Spanish-American War, Theodore Roosevelt still damned black cowardice and "the superstition and fear of the darkey."[8]

Nine of every ten black Americans lived in the southern states, and it had been the evolution of that region that defined their fate. The immediate aftermath of the Civil War had left the South a stricken region, defeated and economically impoverished. Blacks were propertyless, most lacking literacy, training, and skills. Attempts to re-enslave the freedmen under the draconian "black codes" were thwarted by Republican Congresses, which passed constitutional amendments and the Civil Rights Act of 1875 guaranteeing equal rights.

During Reconstruction, blacks throughout much of the South, defying intimidation and terror, achieved a measure of political power and elected a significant number of officeholders. Public facilities such as schools and hospitals were desegregated. But two developments essential to long-term black progress, the creation of a large, economically independent class of black farmers and the formation of an interracial lower-class political coalition, never happened.

The first—in essence, a revolution in southern social structure—required a federal policy of breaking up the plantations and providing land, equipment, and credit to ex-slaves. This was much further than northern Republicans were prepared to go. The second was frustrated by poor whites who viewed any assertion of black rights as threatening their own position and status. So African-Americans were terribly vulnerable when federal troops left the South after 1876, and political power was consolidated by the "Redeemers" or "Bourbons," affluent gentry who played on historic white loyalties and fears to restore Democratic party dominance.

White supremacy was enshrined as official Democratic party policy. In history books, novels, and folklore, the Reconstruction became an object lesson in the evils of "Negro domination." But while the Redeemers swept away black gains made during Reconstruction, they provided protection on their own terms. Black voting was generally permitted as long as it could be manipulated.[9]

From the 1880s on, economic recovery was well on its way. Sleepy country towns like Greensboro, North Carolina, became textile mill centers, new railroads crisscrossed the region, steel mills fired up in Birmingham, the lumber industry in Louisiana and Appalachian mining coming into its own. The tobacco industry's famous Bull Durham bull became recognizable the world round.

But the "New South" remained a virtual economic colony, dependent on the North for capital, technology, and markets. Redeemer governments offered northern companies huge land grants for railroads and free rein to exploit natural resources. Development was grossly uneven; the South remained the most rural and the poorest region of the United States, Alabama being the nation's poorest state. (In 1900, southern per-capita income of $509 was less than one-half that of the United States as a whole.) At least 5–6 million poor whites had no sure foothold in the economy.[10]

By the 1890s, the Redeemers, who ran (even for the times) unusually corrupt governments, were being challenged and sometimes overthrown by insurgent Populist farmers trying to gain protection from landlord and corporate control. Populist leaders in a number of states made enormously courageous efforts to transcend racial barriers and ally with black farmers. The most capable and progressive of these, Georgia's Tom Watson, was acutely aware of how the specter of "Negro rule" had suckered white farmers into voting against their own interests, and he spoke for political equality and against "lynch law." "You are made to hate each other," he told integrated audiences. The apex of racial solidarity may have been one night in October 1892, when 2,000 armed white farmers gathered before Watson's house to protect a Populist black preacher threatened with lynching.[11]

Such a revolutionary initiative naturally came under brutal assault from Democrats who damned Populists for breaking the united white front against blacks. Every attempt was made to use race hatred to detach poor farmers from populism. The repression was ferocious, Populist-won elections stolen, and Populist leaders murdered, and by 1897, populism was in retreat almost everywhere in the South.[12]

The Populist challenge to the Democratic party/white supremacy monolith alerted conservative Redeemers and radical white supremacists to the potential danger of anti-elite black-white lower class coalitions. On their part, defeated Populists were only too glad to scapegoat blacks for the loss of elections and the crumbling of the grand vision and drive them out of politics for good. Ultimately, the general pattern throughout the South was for white reconcilliation to take place on the basis of sacrificing what remained of black rights, and substituting white supremacy for economic justice.[13]

Starting in Missisippi in 1890, disenfranchisement rolled state by state through the region. Individual states moved to exclude blacks from the voter rolls and construct official, legal apartheid regimes. Poll taxes, literacy tests, and white primaries were used to strip black (and some white) voters of the vote. One story revealing the temper of the times told of a hopeful Missis- sippi black voter who innocently brought his tax receipts to the courthouse, only to be asked, "What are the provisions of the Magna Carta accepted in the fundamental law of Mississippi?" "I dunno, judge," he replied, "but is it that no colored person shall vote in this state?" "That's right," said the judge. "You are the first nigger that has answered right."[14]

In election year 1900, the most crucial test (with implications for the rest of the South) was to be in eastern North Carolina, where a Republican/Popu- list coalition had put the highly intelligent and vocal black congressman George A. White and local officials in office.

None of this meant that white supremacists had anything resembling a long-term vision of how Americans of different colors might coexist. Asked by another senator as to what *his* plan was to solve the "race problem," Pitch- fork Ben Tillman admitted despairingly: "I do not know what to tell you to do about it. I see no end of it," and plaintively asked his colleagues if they had a solution.[15]

A harshly separate and unequal racial dictatorship was crystallizing. What gave it the stamp of legitimacy was the landmark 1896 *Plessy* v. *Ferguson* Supreme Court decision upholding Louisiana's separate law for accommo- dations of black and white train passengers. Justice Brown, writing for the court majority, argued that the Fourteenth Amendment "could not have been intended to abolish distinctions based upon color, or to enforce social . . . equality . . . or a comingling of the two races upon terms unsatisfactory to either." "If one race be inferior to the other socially," said Brown, "the Con- stitution of the United States cannot put them on the same plane."

In his vigorous dissent, the Kentucky-born jurist John Harlan saw that the effect of Plessy would be "to place in a condition of legal inferiority a large body of American citizens." His prediction that "the present decision . . . will . . . stimulate aggression, more or less brutal and irrational, upon the admit- ted rights of colored citizens" was prophetic. Indeed, during the early 1900s, Jim Crow was imposed on public transportation across the South and all public places and institutions, with signs "White Only" and "Colored Only" going up everywhere.[16]

The patent illegality of eliminating blacks from public life caused ripples of concern in the North. Some northerners charged the South with nullifying the U.S. Constitution. "The color of the illiterate is the real test for admission to or exclusion from the right of suffrage," editorialized the *Seattle Post-Intelligencer*.[17]

But northerners were only too willing to cede control over the "Negro problem" to white southerners. "It is obviously demoralizing for southern whites to live with negroes as they do, but if the two races began to merge what would the end be?" asked the liberal *Harper's Weekly*, which concluded despairingly: "It is all a very big and intricate problem. It will have to be settled in the south, where it is best understood." Southerners fondly quoted sympathetic Yankees, such as rabidly antiblack Columbia University history professor William Dunning, who insisted that granting voting rights to blacks had been a profound mistake.[18]

The racial environment in the North had historically been hostile to black claims for dignity and equal rights. Intermarriage between blacks and whites remained illegal in twelve northern and western states. Now antiblack animus was heightening as blacks (in a pattern similar to the South) became the designated scapegoats for painful economic and social transformations. Mockery of black speech and culture was pervasive. "Coon" songs, like the popular "All Coons Look Alike To Me" and "I Wish My Color Would Fade," had great popularity. Vaudeville enactments of "The Darktown Firebrigade" showed hapless blacks turning hoses on each other. Demeaning jokes were told everywhere. Following the 1900 Boston election, the newly elected mayor quipped: "This campaign reminds me of the old southern darkey who was brought before the court for stealing chickens. Judge: 'Were you ever in court before for stealing chickens?' Black: 'No, sah, I'se been mighty lucky, sah.'"[19]

Newspaper and magazine articles highlighted black crime, while comic strips and advertisements consistently portrayed blacks as primitive and stupid. A Colburn Washing ad featured two small black children grinning idiotically; the caption: "One little nigger feeling rather blue whistled at another nigger that made two." Stock characters, such as white-bearded "Uncle Rastus" lisping, "yes, sah," "missy," "lordy lordy," "fit for de angels," and "this darkey" were common. A soap advertisement pictured a little white girl asking a black one: "Why don't your mama wash you with Fairy?"

White southerners were notoriously hypersensitive to how their region was perceived by outsiders. Sensing how widespread Negrophobia was, propagandists like South Carolina's one-eyed, fire-eating Senator Benjamin

Tillman carried the offensive northward aiming to convince the polite audiences they spoke to of the righteousness of the southern approach to the "Negro problem." Ultimately northern passivity amounted to complicity with the South's racial agenda. As a congressman in the early 1890s, William McKinley, a man with considerable compassion, had spoken out for "equality of opportunity" and backed legislation to penalize southern states disenfranchising blacks. As governor of Ohio, he had enforced antilynching laws and, as president, declared that "lynching must not be tolerated in a great and civilized country like the United States."[20]

Nevertheless, once in the White House, he remained content to believe that "the time is coming when the injustice will be corrected by the people of the south themselves," and to dole out federal patronage positions to black Republicans and urge individual self-help as the answer. The president might privately confide that he wished for "fair and impartial treatment of my colored fellow citizens," but he would not utilize the White House as a bully pulpit against racism. A black delegation seeking federal intervention against lynching received a fifteen-minute audience, and McKinley never remotely considered sending federal marshals or troops into counties where lynch law prevailed.[21]

In 1898, a conspiracy organized by leaders of the North Carolina Democratic party led to the armed overthrow of the black-white coalition government in Wilmington, the largest city in North Carolina, and one known for its progressive race relations. Neither the coup nor the accompanying massacre of blacks on Wilmington's streets moved the president to comment or act.[22]

In the face of a continuing rollback of black voting rights, the federal inaction infuriated black leaders like the editor of the *Cleveland Gazette*, who asked, "What in the wide world is the Attorney General of the United States for, if not for such cases?" The black-owned *Indianapolis World* flat-out accused the Republican party of "abandoning the Negroes of the south to their fate."[23]

Both McKinley and the man who succeeded him in 1901, Theodore Roosevelt, could be outraged by cruelty and injustice. They were not ignorant of the costs of splintering the nation by color. During the recent war, black soldiers in southern military base towns like Tampa and Macon, infuriated by the brutal racism they encountered, had deliberately violated Jim Crow laws, wrecked saloons and cafes that refused them service, and brawled with local citizens and white soldiers. "It mattered not if we were soldiers of the United States," recalled one former soldier later, "we were niggers as they called us and treated us with contempt." In late 1899, fighting broke out between black and white soldiers on transport ships carrying them to the Philippines.[24]

Yet, both presidents and the Republican congressional leadership refused to provide political and moral leadership to challenge black resubordination. Political expediency and limited imagination account for much of this paralysis. Prisoners of their own racial stereotypes and infatuation with American dream individualism, carrying a limited sense of proper government activism, they could not envision a federal role that would protect the rights of black citizens. Sectional reconciliation (i.e., southern acquiescence to northern leadership of national affairs) was a political priority, and trading black rights off amounted to a reasonable exchange. In the absence of black political clout or a white-black coalition, no political price would have to be paid.[25]

Ultimately, neither man could imagine the 9 million black Americans as genuine assets to the country, or anything other than an exasperating, long-term "problem." Confiding his helplessness in a letter to a correspondent, Roosevelt would write that he was "unable to think out any solution of the terrible problem offered by the presence of the negro on this continent."[26]

Other northern politicians were as apathetic. In February 1900, during the course of a tirade on the Senate floor boasting how South Carolinians had "disenfranchised all of the colored race," the jaw-snapping, index-finger-pointing Ben Tillman blared out, "We stuffed ballot boxes. We shot them. We are not ashamed of it." No senator rose to rebuke him. A bill to reduce southern representation in the U.S. Congress in accord with the decrease in (black) voters failed to get out of committee. The May 10 *New York Times* commented, "Northern men . . . no longer denounce the suppression of the negro vote in the south." Southerners were receiving clear signals that the rest of the country would not defend black rights and that they might act with impunity. "Who has heard any protest from McKinley or his advisors?" taunted Tillman in a *North American Review* article. "The south has applied drastic remedies to a deadly disease."[27]

Relationships between blacks and whites in the South were far more intimate than in the North. Well-to-do white families might provide charity to black people they knew. It was not uncommon for middle- and upper-class white men to be raised by black nannies, and as adults take young black women as mistresses. Indeed, it was common currency among white southerners that only they understood and knew what was best for black people. The proviso, of course, was that relationships remain white-controlled and hierarchical. "We are willing to treat the Negro well if he keeps his place," remarked one contemporary critic of these racial mores, "but we won't have him ride the same car as us."[28]

Black men and women in 1900 had to fit into the suffocating compartments designed for them. Racial etiquette was elaborate, covering virtually all social situations, and was directed toward emphasizing white status and power and black subservience. "Knowing one's place" meant being servile in encounters with whites. Apart from the economic advantages accruing to whites from racial hierarchy was its tremendous psychic value: In an unstable, rapidly changing world, blacks fulfilled the desperately needed role of what James Baldwin has called "a fixed star . . . an immovable pillar," providing a sense of white stability and self. Fearful of black resistance to such a role and the threat of competition, whites had cordoned off no-go zones and developed frightful means to deal with "bad niggers."[29]

Here, distinctive southern traditions of gun culture and knee-jerk violence were wedded to an American ethic of frontier retribution. Violence against blacks regarded as violating boundaries (to be moved according to individual white whim) could occur at any time. There was the Georgia state senator who caned a black woman senseless because she allegedly jostled his daughter on a sidewalk. During a brief killing season in fall 1898, when eleven southern blacks were murdered, one account read: "The whites in the neighborhood seem to be out gunning for blacks as if they were game." The sheer randomness of white violence was enormously effective in inculcating uncertainty and fear in black communities.[30]

Visible signs of black economic success were especially threatening to whites and meant black peril; thus the "whitecapping" phenomenon in Georgia, South Carolina, and Mississippi, in which red-shirted night riders drove prosperous black farmers off their land at gunpoint. In February 1899, the house of Frazier B. Baker, a black postmaster in Lake City, South Carolina, was torched and Baker was shot down when he tried to flee.[31]

Basking in social approval, perpetrators were usually immune from justice. "Death from hanging by persons unknown" was the customary coroner's verdict. Prominent local gentry often regarded violence against blacks as unproductive and excessive, bad for law and order and for the image of the "New South," but they seldom intervened to save victims or condemn vigilantes. Where southern Progressives and radical racists differed was not over white supremacy, but rather how it might best be enforced. Southern Baptist churches (which preached that racial inequality was "the work of God") studiously ignored local lynchings. Public officials who tried to protect blacks from mobs bent on murder did so at risk of their careers.[32]

As the ultimate method of social control, nothing rivaled lynching. Between 1893 and 1899, some nine hundred persons, the large majority black, were lynched in the South. Lynching had become a regional custom, a community and family affair in which carnival-like crowds (often run out to sites by special trains) cavorted about the charred corpse, mutilating it and carrying off body parts as trophies. Late in 1899 a young black man named

Richard Coleman, accused of murdering his employer's wife, was taken by a mob from the sheriff in Marysville, Kentucky, tortured, and burned at the stake. Several thousand people attended, and Coleman's body was repeatedly pushed back into the fire. A similar fate befell a Georgia agricultural laborer named Sam Hose, who had killed a white plantation owner in a dispute. His pickled knuckles were later displayed in a downtown Atlanta store. White southerners were clearly performing ritualistic exorcisms, using black victims as stand-ins for their own demons.[33]

The lynchers came from various social classes, and businessmen and professionals were certainly involved. But among the men who stormed jails and trains carrying off prisoners accused of rape or murder, and on isolated country roads strung up young black males accused of burglary or insulting a white man, many were small farmers, tenants, and working men.

These were folks marginal to the American dream and desperately fearful of being "niggerized" themselves, men who felt victimized by local landlords, merchants, and invisible northern railroad corporations and bankers, and powerless to protect their families from low cotton prices and usurious loans. The motto "We will do it ourselves" expressed their contempt for a corrupt justice system controlled by the upper classes. Given southern traditions and the absence of alternatives, their grievances and frustrations were channeled into lynching bees. Lynching was an act of power over their lives, an assertion of commitment to defend their womenfolk and way of life. Chaotic forces of economic and social change might be displaced into the form of the demonic black. In the process, the secret attractions whites felt for blacks and black culture (note the number of white revelers at New Orleans' Mardi Gras disguised as blacks) might also be obliterated.[34]

The process of hunting the victims down, then torturing and murdering them was often a deliberate business that might be spread out over days and weeks and was graphically reported in newspapers to a country passively following the unfolding drama. In July 1899, after three blacks had been lynched around Saffold, Georgia, an Oregon paper reported matter-of-factly: "A hundred men with bloodhounds are after the remaining five members of the gang, and if caught they will be lynched."[35]

The startling frequency of lynchings—in 1900, there were 116, in 1901, 130, or one every *three* days or so—did evoke protests outside the South and demands for federal laws and intervention. Northern black leaders like the fiery journalist Ida Wells-Barnett, who, run out of Memphis, continued the fight in Chicago and New York, but also white groups in places such as old abolitionist Boston protested. Clergy in the North managed to avoid public comment on lynching, but a few such as New York rabbi Joseph Silverman— who in a Thanksgiving 1899 sermon remarked: "For shame be it said that there is a man in this country that . . . cannot give justice to the colored man"—did speak out.[36]

Southerners recognized that lynching needed justifying to the rest of the nation. They defended it around 1900 in terms of the "good violence' rooted in American frontier mythology, and increasingly, the necessity to protect the virtue of southern white women from the uncontrollable libidos of "bestial" black males intent on "outrages." The choice of such a defense (despite only a minority of lynchings being linked to sexual assault) went to the heart of white denial about the nexus of race, sexual relations, and southern culture.

It was, of course, white men who had been determined to control female sexuality, white and black, since the earliest slave days. By 1900, one-third of the black population were mulattos, while large numbers of partially black men and women were knowingly or (unknowingly) seizing the opportunities that went with passing for white. In Montgomery, Alabama, a city of modest size, an estimated four hundred black women (and their children) were kept by white men. Black brothels across the South catered to whites.[37]

These realities had to be denied through compartmentalization. To admit that the wholesale blending of black and white had already occurred (and was ongoing) would be to undermine the power of "whiteness" and racial hierarchy. Thus the obsession with the cult of virtuous southern white womanhood, and on maintaining the fiction of the pure-blood Anglo-Saxon white South, the shrill hysteria against Negro aggressors. It was no coincidence that the Wilmington, North Carolina, pogrom of 1898 had been ignited by black newspaper editor Alex Manly's antilynching editorial daring to suggest that white women might be attracted to some black men.[38]

Lack of economic resources and independence crushingly impacted the eight in ten southern blacks living in rural areas. Some had successful cotton and tobacco farms, but three-quarters were sharecroppers or tenants living at the edge of subsistence in flimsy tenant shacks with broken furniture, no running water, and lean-to privies out back. Their ignorance, poverty, and lack of political power or access to alternative jobs (growth industries such as textiles, furniture, and oil and gas had white-only hiring policies) put them at the mercy of white planters and merchants.

The natural inclination of black tenants and sharecroppers was to move from farm to farm to obtain better conditions, and some did, but planters needing a steady and dependable cheap source of labor constructed a system to control mobility. The liens placed on crops in return for advances on what they needed to survive left tenants and croppers in perpetual debt akin to slavery. Indebted blacks who tried to flee and got caught wound up on convict labor gangs in plantations, sawmills, brickyards, and the dreaded turpentine camps, often owned by politicos or politically connected businessmen.[39]

The harshness and hopelessness of rural southern life circa 1900 was pushing a growing stream of blacks to towns and cities. In the larger towns, a small, but prosperous class of black retail store owners, clergy, undertakers, doctors and lawyers, insurance people, and grocers served their own communities, and gathered on Sundays in churches like the First Congregational of Atlanta. A stable working class of blacksmiths, wheelrights, and machinists, Pullman porters, and postal workers was also well established. Washington D.C., basically, a southern city, and one-third black, was known for its black lawyers and professors.[40]

But jobs in the larger working world were limited by the resistance of white workers and employers. When jobs did materialize, as in the Birmingham steel mills, where hundreds of blacks fed the furnaces, there were definite racial ceilings. Job opportunities for the pool of unskilled young black men fresh from the country were in the nature of waiting tables, janitoring, and bellhopping in hotels, and seldom paid more than $20–25 monthly. Skilled jobs as electricians, plumbers, steamfitters, railroad engineers, and firemen were categorized as "white jobs" and off limits. In Nashville, among other cities, scores of skilled black "mechanics" languished jobless.[41]

Far more work materialized for women as domestics and laundresses, and they became family breadwinners. Inevitably, a class of urban male tricksters and petty criminals emerged, involved in gambling, prostitution, and drugs, a subculture conveniently cited by whites as proof of low black morals and "degeneracy."

In these southern cities, blacks found themselves living in neighborhoods adjacent to white working-class folk carrying country prejudices and fearing black job competition. At points of direct contact, like the area of black and white saloons and dives around Atlanta's Decatur and Peters Streets, the tensions were palpable.[42]

Like other racial minorities, blacks sought protection from the perils of living in the White Man's Country and to fashion tools of resistance. The dominant strategy was plotted by Booker T. Washington, forty-four years old in 1900, a former West Virginia slave, the founder of Tuskegee Institute in Alabama, and the most powerful black man in the United States. Washington had staked out his claim to leadership in a widely publicized speech at the 1895 Cotton States Exposition, stressing that instead of seeking social equality, blacks must build their economic foundations and provide loyal and valuable service to the South. He urged them to be stoical and "suffer in silence."

"I fear that the Negro lays too much stress on his grievances and not enough on opportunities," he remarked.[43]

Conservative and pro–laissez-faire with extensive personal business interests, Booker T. Washington fervently promoted black entrepreneurship: Thrift, economy, and business success would open new doors. In September 1900, at a Boston meeting of three hundred businessmen, he founded the National Negro Business League. Washington's agenda also involved keeping blacks in the southern countryside, and the educational emphasis at Tuskegee was on artisanal skills such as blacksmithing, bricklaying, and carpentry.

Since none of this was in conflict with white supremacy, Washington was embraced by upper-class southern whites who viewed him as a safe and benign influence on the black masses. His program also endeared him to northern industrialists like Andrew Carnegie, Collis Huntington, and H.H. Rogers of Standard Oil, who had sizable investments in the South and looked for stability in race relations. They provided "the wizard of Tuskegee" with the funding that enabled him to spread his influence into black communities north and south.[44]

Washington's ties to elite political circles gave him further clout among black Americans. The White House consulted him on black political appointments, and in December 1898, President McKinley paid a visit to Tuskegee, where he assured his audience that "patience, moderation, self-control, knowledge, character, will surely win you victories and realize the best aspirations of your people."[45]

The emergence of a man as paramount black leader preaching retrenchment and acceptance of third-class lives speaks volumes about the straitjacket black people found themselves in in fin de siècle America. There was, of course, a logic to his program for "lifting up and regenerating a whole race." To shelter blacks from the racist firestorm, he would have them tread softly until a community of interest could be built with more enlightened whites. Washington did protest in articles and speeches against the worst antiblack demogoguery and disenfranchisement in some states. And Tuskegee was a fortress of respectability, its graduates in high demand.[46]

But this was an enormously flawed leadership. Given his reliance on those who owned the South and the nation, Booker T. Washington could never condemn the social structures perpetuating racism. The confidence he had in the good offices of the "thoughtful and cultured white men and women of the South" was simply misplaced. His assertions that blacks lacked the skills and intelligence to take care of themselves and "whites have the right to exercise the greatest control in government" seemed to validate white supremacy. Washington, curiously, was dispensing the same advice as a character in Tomas Dixon's super-racist bestselling novel of 1903, *The Leopard's Spots*, who told blacks, "be however patient, humble, and industrious and every whiteman in the south will be your friend."[47]

Washington regarded education as a panacea, but ignored the structural changes neccessary to make it vital. He understood that blacks had to survive in the industrial twentieth century, yet did not care to challenge the sharecropping system and black exclusion from the modern American economy. Tuskegee's vocational education program, in fact, looked back toward the agricultural nineteenth. The campus itself, surrounded by decrepit sharecropper shacks, amounted to a surreal facade.

Ultimately, Booker T. Washington was many things, gifted opportunist, power broker, and manipulator, and also a tragic Faust-like figure who, in his obsession to locate a "community of interest" with the powerful, sanctioned the sacrifice of black rights and dignity. Following a southern visit, the white writer Charles Spahr recognized that "the treatment of the negro as a man is the very cornerstone for the elevation of his manhood." This, of course, was precisely what "the wizard of Tuskegee" was not about to confront.[48]

By 1900, there were black notables such as W.E.B. Du Bois, the Atlanta sociologist, already beginning to chaff under Washington's compromises and manipulations and starting to advocate bolder, proactive measures toward securing black liberation and equal rights. In an era when opportunities for self-help and utilizing skills simply weren't available, Du Bois realized that continued submission to white supremacy must ultimately destroy black "manhood." The fiery Boston journalist William Moore Trotter publicly challenged him: "Are the rope and the torch all the race is to get under your leadership?"[49]

Some blacks were ready to resist white supremacy directly. In Savannah and other cities, they organized boycotts of newly segregated streetcar lines. On occasion, as around Darien, Georgia, in 1899–1900, small-scale race wars flared up as militant blacks using armed force organized to protect their communities.[50]

Leaving the South was yet another act of resistance. Some Louisiana blacks told Du Bois they were "willing to run any risk to get where they might breathe freer." This modest northward black migration, 185,000 during the 1890s, marked the beginning of a great historic migration as threads of community and kinfolk began to stretch across the Mason-Dixon line. New York and Philadelphia each hosted communities of blacks 60,000 strong, and Chicago had 30,000. The Mississippi migrant who disembarked in Chicago from an Illinois Central Railroad train noted with wonder and pleasure that he might casually sit next to a white on a streetcar. The constant fears southern blacks lived with abated in a generally more relaxed, less threatening atmosphere. Where blacks had opportunities to break into white-monopoly industries, at Philadelphia's Midvale Steel plant, for example, they did well. And there were occasional epiphanies: one March day in 1900, for instance, when a black man joined with two white men to save six children from a fire in Harlem. A newspaper account: "The Negro made a derrick of his body, his legs held by the white men and swings the children to safety."[51]

But the emigrant who came "to better my condition" was arriving at a time when skilled black artisans were declining and blacks were being evicted from laboring and traditional service jobs in favor of fresh-off-the-boat immigrants. What remained were low-wage personal domestic service jobs. In New York City and Boston, the large majority of black workers were servants, janitors, and porters.[52]

Boycotted by both employers and unions, even blacks with skills and southern union cards were frozen out. "From all or nearly all trades, the colored man is shut out," was the story from Baltimore. "No Negro apprentices will be found at bricklaying, painting, tinning, smithing etc." White union members bought into popular antiblack folk myths and viewed black workers as unskilled "cheap labor" who would degrade wages. The railroad brotherhoods barred black members, and the railroads no longer hired black firemen. A vicious cycle was in place: Black men seeking to break into work on the Buffalo docks or Chicago building trades could do so only as strikebreakers, thus reinforcing white hostilities.[53]

The 1900 era marked the beginnings of the phenomenon of white flight. "Whenever a negro moves into a street the whites flutter away," said a Baltimore source. "They simply vanish . . . the whites verge more and more towards the suburbs." Inner-city neighborhoods might remain integrated, but boundary lines between white immigrants and blacks were hardening. Black ghettos began solidifying along a narrow strip of Chicago around State Street south of the Loop, in the tenement area of Manhattan's West 60s, and in the rows of cheap, one-story frame tenements known as "Bucktown" in Indianapolis.[54]

Greater black visibility generated backlash from northern whites anxious to maintain skin privileges and fearful of labor competition. Gangs in Indianapolis and Philadelphia, shouting "kill the nigger," staged assaults in parks and on streetcars. A Trenton, New Jersey, mob's attempt to lynch a black man accused of murder in December 1899 led to a hundred police barricading a building to save his life. Blacks living in the North soon learned the rules: After defeating a blond Californian, Joe Choyinski, in a heavyweight boxing match, Joe Walcott, originally from Barbados, told the *Sporting News* that he had a "punch dat I nebber use for fear dat I'll kill dem . . . and if a blackboy kill a white man, he get de rope husks t'rown into him."[55]

If anyone doubted blacks' status as America's chosen scapegoat, there was the long hot summer of 1900. Exceptionally warm weather lingered over much of the country, and in sweltering cities like New York and Chicago numerous heat-related deaths occurred among the poor. It was also a summer *horribilis* for black Americans, who were at the center of a series of racial flashpoints.

Throughout the late spring, omens of danger were plentiful. At the American Social Science Association Meeting in Washington, one panelist argued that higher education for blacks had failed and they should be trained in the "decencies" of life. The once problack *Harper's Weekly* confessed its sympathy with this, further arguing that the black man should be "relieved" of his vote: "Very gradually a great many northern readers have come to suspect that the average Negro is considerably cruder and less competent than the average Anglo-Saxon."[56]

In Mississippi, two black men suspected in the murder of a white girl were tortured and lynched by a mob that knew that at least one of them was innocent. Forty white men burst into a Douglas, Georgia jail, took Marshall Jones out, and lynched and riddled him with bullets. Hysteria ruled in Ripley, Tennessee, the scene of a double lynching, where incoming trains brought in armed men who engaged in a general hunt for blacks. Meanwhile, Ben Tillman was regaling audiences in Michigan with tales of black savagery.[57]

During the first week of May, a highly publicized conference in Montgomery, Alabama met to consider the future of black southerners. "The Negro's condition is improving," opined ex-Governor McCorkle of West Virginia, by far the most optimistic of all the speakers. "He is becoming better and as a rule more industrious." The black right to vote, he argued, "is as sacred as ours and should be as sacredly guarded."

McCorkle's, however, was a lonely voice at Montgomery, where the predominant attitide of "kill the vote of the colored" and protect white supremacy was expressed by Mayor Alfred Wadell of Wilmington, North Carolina, the same fellow who had led the overthrow of that city's government two years before and a violent assault against blacks. Another speaker, Georgian John Temple Graves, called the enfranchisement of the Negro "the American mistake of the century." Since the black "is the weakest and ours the strongest race on earth," he asked, ". . . where is the hope for the Negro?" For Clifton Breckenridge, a former minister to Russia, the black was a "monstrous beast crazed with lust." U.S. Senator Bourke Cochran came down from New York to demand repeal of the Fifteenth Amendment so whites would have "the supremacy to which they are entitled." Other speakers argued for deportation of blacks, and at least one believed they were destined for biological extinction.[58]

Throughout the spring and into the summer, attention was focused on North Carolina, where Democratic party strategists were using fears of "negro rule" as an instrument to destroy the Republican-Populist political opposition and eliminate 120,000 black voters from the rolls. A state constitutional amendment containing educational and property qualifications (but containing a clause designed to grandfather in 75,000 illiterate whites and keep them on the rolls) was up for vote. It is "our plan for ending all possible danger of future Negro domination, for establishing on a permanent basis White Supremacy," explained the state Democratic Party boss. The state's leading newspaper, the *Raleigh News and Observer*, urged "every really white man" to vote for the amendment. Armed "red shirts" held white-supremacy parades and assaulted opposition speakers. To nobody's surprise, the August election secured a 50,000 pro-amendment majority; white supremacist railroad lawyer Charles Aycock became the new governor. Intimidated or resigned, blacks stayed away from polls. The following year found Alabama and Tennessee excluding blacks from the voting rolls. Black voting rights in the South would be effectively ended for the next two generations.[59]

The summer's first major race riot occurred in New Orleans, the largest city in the South, dirty, unhealthy, and disorderly, chock full of brothels and drugs, and run by gangster-like politicians, but also with more tolerant racial traditions than in most of the South: 85,000 blacks were numbered among a population of 300,000. There was still a fair degree of residential integration in the working-class districts and black and whites rode to and from work on mule-drawn streetcars, and trolleys. But whites singled out inmigrating rural black workers as depressing wages and taking their jobs (white employers preferring cheaper black labor) and racial tensions were escalating. There was also a plan afoot to segregate streetcars, and whites were threatening retribution against blacks alleged to be harassing white women in the city's parks.

One of the recent black immigrants was Robert Charles, a tall, sturdily built, thirty-three-year-old manual laborer with a droopy mustache, who like so many Mississippians had come to New Orleans to breathe freer air. A tough, proud, intelligent man with a history of not backing down in the face of white threats, Charles was attached to a Back to Africa movement and sold its newspaper, *Voice of Missions*. Recent reports of lynchings enraged him. On July 24, sitting on a doorstoop near his girlfriend's house with a friend, Charles was assaulted by a policeman and gunshots exchanged. He fled and later that night killed two of the policemen sent to take him. Robert

Charles immediately became the target of a massive police manhunt, with the local press unleashing a bloodthirsty call for retribution and tribalistic violence. The *New Orleans Times* called him "one of the most formidable monsters that has ever been loosed on the community," while the *New Orleans Democrat* challenged whites to assert their manhood against "the regime of the free Negro."[60]

By the evening of the 24th, several thousand whites were roaming the city streets, pulling blacks off streetcars and shooting and beating pedestrians. Three blacks were killed and fifty beaten that night. Some white laborers and clergy defended black workers. When a sailor from New York named McCarthy voiced the thought that Charles deserved a fair trial, this "white nigger" was nearly lynched. Even after the mayor deputized special police and called in 1,500 state militia, mobs controlled parts of the French Quarter. Eventually, another 43 blacks were killed and many injured.[61]

Throughout the rioting, a wounded Robert Charles had been hiding in the secret compartment of a house. His whereabouts discovered, a huge mob gathered outside the building shouting "burn him." Positioning himself at a window, Charles coolly continued to fire his Winchester, killing five more whites and wounding twenty before being shot to death.[62]

Black and white reactions to the Charles affair were at stark counterpoint. A fearless, powerful black man skillfully picking off white targets under heavy gunfire was the ultimate southern white nightmare come to life, a refutation of the passive black sterotype they had worked so hard to fashion. This was a demon to be exorcised and Charles' body was severely mutilated after his death, one policeman firing a double barreled shotgun into his corpse. But the sheer courage and sangfroid of the man thrilled blacks, many of whom only regretted that he hadn't taken more whites with him. Among northern blacks, Robert Charles became a folk hero with a song sung about his exploits. The *Cleveland Gazette* offered this eulogy:

> Would every Negro of the south had the manhood and courage of Charles. Knowing that no justice would be meted out to him, knowing of the external hatred against his race he resolved to die fighting for his liberty. Charles has stood up for manhood wherever insulted.[63]

Race relations in New York City, never good in the best of times, had been polarized by a recent influx of southern blacks who clustered together on the west side of Manhattan. Ethnic whites were hostile and the New York Police Department, a center of corruption immune to the reform efforts of even Theodore Roosevelt, was notoriously abusive to blacks.

In August, the hottest weather in two decades gripped the city. Tensions escalated after a black man stabbed a police officer in a fracas in a park. On

August 15, an incident outside the house where the body of the slain police-man was lying led to police violence against blacks in the local neighbor-hood and provided sanction for white toughs who began assaulting blacks along Eighth Avenue and pulling them off streetcars. Over a thousand whites milled around the area. Two blacks at Thirty-fourth Street and Eighth Avenue were grabbed off trolleys and nearly lynched. Not only did the police refuse to restrain the rioters, but they gladly clubbed and arrested the black victims. One black woman who asked the police for help was told, "Go to hell, damn you." Those arrested were severely beaten at the police station: "We would like to get even with these black devils," a policeman told a reporter.[64]

Blacks in tenements on West Thirty-seventh Street responded by throw-ing missiles at police from windows, while others bought guns or took ref-uge elsewhere. The popular song-and-dance team Bert Williams and George Walker, playing in the musical comedy *Sons of Ham*, were among those hiding out from the mob. Questioned by newsmen, the city's police chief blamed the riot on recent arrivals from the South: "The colored people who live in this precinct are a bad class." He denied any police brutality: "There is no discrimination on the part of the force." A judge confronting the lack of white prisoners in the docket saw it differently. "I don't see why you have no white men here," he told police officials. "Apparently they acted like beasts jumping on cars and attacking colored passengers indiscriminately." It was "the wildest disorder that this city has witnessed in years," summed up the *New York Times*, which denounced the "brutality of the police."[65]

Ten days later, the shooting of John Brennan, a twenty-nine-year-old mes-senger boy, on West Sixty-second Street sparked another riot by Irish mobs who assaulted blacks and stoned businesses around Amsterdam Avenue. One policeman arresting a black man named William Hopson for being "sassy" found himself surrounded by an angry crowd of blacks and drew his re-volver in warning.[66]

Sandwiched between the two Manhattan riots was an eruption in Akron, a city in the industrial heartland of Ohio, which had grown rapidly during the nineties. Among the 40,000 residents were about 450 blacks. Louis Peck, a young black man from Cleveland, was accused of having raped a six-year-old white girl and was jailed in city hall. A crowd of hundreds gathered outside, besieging the building and demanding that Peck (who had already been hustled out of a back exit and sent to Cleveland under armed guard) be delivered to their justice. Peck's disappearance only further agitated the mob (shouting "Lynch any nigger"), which tried to use a battering ram to break down the city hall door. When police attempted to clear the street by firing gunshots, they mistakenly shot two children. The now thoroughly enraged besiegers used arms seized from a hardware store and began shooting from roofs of adjacent buildings at firemen and police. The mayor and police escaped after midnight. City hall was dynamited and an adjacent building set on fire. Declaring martial law, the governor of Ohio sent a dozen militia companies in to patrol the streets. Later, Peck, heavily guarded, was brought back for an instant trial in which he pleaded guilty, and was sentenced to life in prison.[67]

"The most alarming feature of the Akron outbreak," editorialized the *Cleveland Plain Dealer*, "was the swift transformation of race hatred into rebellion against authority and destruction simply for destruction's sake." What the Akron uprising had exposed was how thin the veneer of white solidarity was and the depth of animosity toward political authority. Remove the designated black scapegoat-target from the scene and, given the right circumstances, a lynch mob could become semi-insurrectionary. At his trial, Vernendo Kempf, a man identified as one of the mob's leaders, said:

> I admit that after those cowards the police shot into the crowd and killed children, I plugged lead into the city building as fast as I could and am willing to go to the penitentiary for it.[68]

Southerners like Ben Tillman greeted the news of northern racial violence gleefully. Newspaper editors sanctimoniously assured their readers that this proved that not only were blacks better off in the South, but that northern whites shared southern racial antipathies. " . . . a white man is a white man and a nigger is a nigger equally in New Orleans, New York, and Akron," crowed the *Louisville Courier Journal*'s Henry Waterson, one of the nation's most well-known editors.[69]

In parts of Georgia that August, sheer hysteria reigned over pretended or actual black assaults on white females. Murder by lynching was so common that Governor Candler appealed to white citizens to stop and urged officeholders to bring lynchers to justice. But southern blacks were not passive. On August 14, following the shooting of a black worker at a Greenville, South Carolina, cotton mill, his fellow black workers, wielding axes and shotguns, faced off armed whites in the area. In Liberty, Georgia, local blacks, reacting to a spate of lynchings, conducted a guerrilla war from forests and swamps, ambushing policemen, and firing local towns, forcing the calling in of state militia. Two thousand students at a normal school in Texas struck after white examiners were substituted for black ones.[70]

The imposition of apartheid in the American South completed a circle: White southerners had reclaimed the total control they had had before the Civil War. They composed by virtue of skin pigmentation a *herrenvolk* elite, racial dictators, supreme and unchallenged. White manhood was triumphant and might now proceed to construct a true southern way of life based on Anglo-Saxon solidarity.

This proved yet another illusion. The quality of many white southern lives remained abysmal. "This whole policy of the black man's repression . . ." mused the writer George W. Cable, "it . . . is constantly escaping from its intended boundaries and running into a fierce and general oppression of the laboring classes, black and white."[71]

Behind the shiny facade of the "New South," symbolized by Atlanta's downtown office buildings and North Carolina's mills, were much the same relations of power and inequality, characteristic of the Old South. In the early twentieth century, merchant-banker-planter elites held sway while appalling conditions prevailed in the factories and slums inhabited by the white working class. In mill towns, "dirty children with torn clothes but often with hair in curl-papers, play about the streets, until a shrill voice calls them to fetch water from the well at the corner or mind the ever present baby." One in three mill workers were children. Almost one-fifth of the white population was illiterate. The numbers of white farm tenants pulling poor crops from exhausted soil and trapped in debt constantly grew. White public schools were underfinanced and substandard: Alabama schools, during the 1900–1901 school year, allocated $3.10 (or three cents a day) per child, against $21.19 for the nation as a whole.[72]

Populist leaders and farmers had imagined that disenfranchising blacks would unify the white lower classes and help them to topple the reigning Bourbon elites, and during the early years of the century under leaders like John Vardaman and Jeff Davis in Mississippi and Arkansas this had happened. But whites' voting dropped dramatically as they withdrew in apathy from politics, leaving it in control of corrupt courthouse gangs and business-run state machines. Elections became a circus-like spectacle featuring flamboyant characters and little substance. The South was destined to have a one-party system for the next six decades (in a celebrated work, W.J. Cash called it "a so-called democratic country without an opposition party") and to be largely isolated from the progressive currents of political change in the country.[73]

Making race the southern way of "knowing and organizing the social world" proved profoundly destructive. The cry of "negro domination" halted every new initiative for change, every attempt at bettering work conditions or schools. The wall of white unity meant enforced allegiance of all whites to a corrupt and mean-spirited system. Ultimately, the price of white specialness was white conformity and retreat from reality into fantasies such as "the lost cause" of 1861–1865. Meanwhile, southern whites would remain the poorest white people in the United States.[74]

"Radicals," concludes Joel Williamson in his illuminating study, *The Crucible of Race*, "had worked effectively to unplug the south from the real world at large by generating an unreal racial world." The possibility of black and white southerners living together in mutual respect and learning from each other was foreclosed. Whites were unable to acknowledge the African roots of so much of southern culture, or black contributions to the general American culture. Those who treated blacks as equals risked forfeiting their whiteness. Triumphing over community or common sense, racism had foreclosed the possibility of whites coming to terms with themselves.[75]

Black Americans circa 1900 understood themselves to be in a state of siege, virtually friendless and powerless. Some despairingly internalized the message of black inferiority and turned it inward upon themselves. Others defended themselves any way they could: Black grassroots organizations based on churches, lodges, women's clubs organized to build schools and help indigent blacks. Where they could, they fought for rights. In Ohio, for example, antilynching laws were used to press civil suits against whites. A Hampton College graduate named Robert S. Abbott was founding what would become the nation's most widely read black newspaper, the *Chicago Defender*. In defiance of oppression, a vibrant black literary and artistic American culture appeared north and south.[76]

But mistrustful of whites, cynical about their future possibilities, black Americans were hunkering down, carving out institutions parallel to the dominant white ones. Some blacks were giving up on the idea of an integrated society and advocated separation. The Rev. Henry Turner in Atlanta ran a modest Back to Africa movement, and there were initiatives to set up black-only communities in Oklahoma and elsewhere. Following his study of the situation of black Philadelphians, W.E.B. Du Bois, himself the epitome of the European-trained western intellectual, was questioning the goal of integration within American national culture and calling on blacks to return to the creative powers of their own heritage. The problem of the coming century, he prophesized in 1903, would be the problem of "the color line."

But even as the United States circa 1900 was demonstrating its severe antipathy for black Americans and other people of color, it was in the process of absorbing still millions more from overseas. This, too, curiously enough, had its own logic.

Chapter 9

"A New Power of the First Order"

Damn, damn the Filipino
Pockmarked kodiac ladrone (thief)
Underneath the starry flag
Civilize him with a krag (rifle)
And return us to our own beloved home.

—Popular U.S. Army song, circa 1900

Expansion is the law of Saxon life. God sent him about the job
of subduing and saving the world, and he is out and at it.

—Senator Albert Beveridge, 1900

We shall be glad to see the last of your soliders; their presence
is neither for our own good, nor for your own. You came to our
country, you ask acceptance, profit by our aid in the defeat of
your enemy . . . when your enemy is defeated, you turn upon
us, shoot us down by the thousands.

—Sixto Lopez to Theodore Roosevelt, 1900

We've made a pretty mess at home. Let's make a mess abroad.

—Ernest Crosby (reform lawyer), 1902

"In future, America will play a part in the general affairs of the world such as she has never played before." So *The London Times* editorialized exactly one week after that May morning in 1898 when Admiral George Dewey's Pacific squadron had rather leisurely annihilated a Spanish fleet at Manila Bay. "What passes before our eyes . . . ," reflected the French newspaper *Le Temps*, "is the appearance on the scene of a new power of the first order."[1]

Overnight, United States stock on the world power exchange boomed. In imperial capitals such as Berlin, Vienna, Paris, Rome, Moscow, and Tokyo, the Americans were now reckoned as a serious factor in the intricate war of military and colonial competition, bluster, and shifting alliances known as the Great Power Game.

Great Britain, recognizing an altered power balance with the old colonies, and beset by nasty threats from France, Russia, and Germany, was making definite overtures to the Yankees. To defuse some of the fairly widespread anti-British feeling in the United States, the English statesman Joseph Chamberlain lauded cultural ties between the two nations and offered what amounted to an informal Anglo-American friendship pact. Both the German kaiser and Russian tsar, uneasy at the awesome combination of resources and the industrial and financial strength possessed by the rising American republic, weighed the option of either allying with Uncle Sam or seeking defensive alliances against him.[2]

While many Americans found the role of a major player on the global stage slightly intoxicating, ominous signs were already appearing of a future price to be paid. Immediately following Dewey's victory, a macho war of nerves between the American fleet blockading Manila Bay and German warships (hoping perhaps to pick up some pieces of a crumbled Spanish empire) came close to escalating to all-out fighting. There was the spate of tension with Japan shortly before Hawaii's annexation. Russian expansion into northern China seemed threatening to American interests. In a shrunken globe rife with great power rivalries, controlling overseas territory meant the likelihood of future military conflicts.

The lions of the imperial party, most prominently Teddy Roosevelt, Captain Alfred Mahan, Senator Henry Cabot Lodge, General Leonard Wood, Whitelaw Reid, publisher of the *New York Herald Tribune*, and diplomat John Hay, were delighted to pay such a price; indeed, they embraced greater international risks as both inevitable and welcome. In their view, a wholly new stage of American history had begun in which the nation's security and prosperity would come not from protected isolation, but from victory in economic and military competition with great powers across the globe.

The imperial agenda had been developing for years. Its concrete objectives were the annexation of Hawaii, establishment of bases across the Pacific and at key Caribbean points, construction of a U.S.-controlled isthmian canal, and a world-class navy that could guard vital trade lanes and "be superior to any which can be brought against it." The lands bordering the Pacific (which they called "an ocean of destiny") held particular fascination. "The enemies we may have to face will come from Asia," Roosevelt told the War College. "Our interests are as great in the Pacific as in the Atlantic."[3]

If, prior to 1898, achievement of such a program seemed possible only in the misty future, the war with Spain had suddenly telescoped it into the present. Americans troops occupied Cuba, the Philippines, Puerto Rico, and Guam, the lynchpins of a strategy of Pacific and Caribbean domination. The war had amply demonstrated the military necessity of a U.S. canal to connect the Atlantic and Pacific (the only question remaining was whether its location was to be in Nicaragua or Panama). A Pacific cable was being laid from Guam to Midway. National pride in the triumphs of the Navy, reinforced by the political influence of shipyards and military contractors, were driving an ongoing $200 million naval building program in which battleships, cruisers, and torpedo boats were being constructed.

In prewar days, the weakness of the imperials had been their elite status and narrow base among the American people. Victory and overseas conquest, however, had greatly magnified the appeal of their program to businessmen, some clergy, and a wide range of ordinary citizens, creating a powerful (if temporary) coalition around an expansionist foreign policy.

The depression of the mid-1890s had built a nationwide consensus among the business and political classes that domestic consumption of wire nails, locomotives, cotton, and so on, would simply not suffice and U.S. overproduction could only be remedied by locating dynamic new export markets. There was also concern about the lack of outlets for what U.S. State Department advisor Charles Conant called "the great mass of capital seeking employment, and unable to find it at home." In the wake of the war, American businessmen had begun looking beyond Canada and western Europe toward what might in a later day be called "emerging markets." Northwest lumbermen and wheat farmers, along with California fruitgrowers, Georgia cotton mill owners, and Oregon wheat farmers, had become vociferous supporters of an interocean canal that would cut the distance to domestic and foreign markets by thousands of miles.[4]

Certainly one target area for export of capital and goods was Latin America, whose promising markets had received special attention from recent U.S. secretaries of state and where American firms like W.R. Grace, Guggenheim, and United Fruit were increasingly active. Cotton and woolen exports were mounting fast, and ports such as Savannah and Tampa handled more Caribbean-bound cargoes. A major point of interest would be Cuba, where

U.S. firms had already invested tens of millions of dollars in sugar and coffee plantations, and American occupation authorities were encouraging still more.[5]

Shimmering across the Pacific was the fabled China market, popularly fantasized as a vast commercial vacuum of around 400 million consumers ready to suck up American exports of every shape and kind. Although China only accounted for 3 percent of U.S. trade, southern cotton mills and northwestern flour merchants had already found substantial outlets there. Promoters flaunting lofty Republican party connections were planning railroads deep in the interior. Cities like San Francisco and Seattle (while ferociously resisting Chinese immigrants) viewed their future prosperity as tied to China's modernization. In the midst of such euphoria, the few sober voices questioning how much trade could be carried on with an underdeveloped country of dismally low incomes and productivity tended to be ignored.[6]

Access to the China market meant keeping it open for American goods and investment. But the haplessness of the Manchu regime had turned the empire into an arena of great power rivalries: Germany, Japan, and Russia had begun shearing off territorial spheres of influence, and the prospect of the country's being partitioned was increasingly real. Demands were raised on the U.S. Senate floor and in business journals that Chinese markets not be closed off. John Hay, the sickly, high-strung secretary of state, sent a series of notes to each of the Great Powers asking that they agree to an open door for foreign commerce in China. Meanwhile, the imperial party insisted that protection of U.S. interests and trading rights in China demanded both continued control of the Philippines as a nearby entrepôt and battleships with an attack capacity.[7]

"We imagine that God has called us to rulership of the world," declared the president of Ohio Wesleyan University. "He sends us to serve the world and thus rule the world." If economics was one engine driving expansionism, yet another was the compelling urge in a nation whose self-image was bound up with its godliness to spread the gospel to "benighted" lands. The capture of the Philippines excited Protestant churchmen who (much to the alarm of the American Roman Catholic clergy) saw the "hand of God in history" and viewed the islands as fertile missionizing turf.[8]

China, in particular, had become the major theater of operations for American missionaries, "the heathen Chinee" singled out for proseletyzing by an array of Catholic, Baptist, Presbyterian, Methodist, and Episcopalian missions wielding considerable political influence back home. The burgeoning YMCA Student Volunteer Movement maintained a small army of missionaries there, and one of its officials, John R. Mott, spoke of "the evangelization of the whole world in this generation." The religious press carried frequent stories about the progress in saving Chinese souls.[9]

The boundary lines separating the commercial and spiritual aspects of the U.S. world-saving mission often got blurred. Influential religious figures such as the Reverend Josiah Strong, best-selling author of *Our Country*, had the knack of almost seamlessly combining Christian evangelism and corporate profits. Christianity and the American dream became indivisible instruments for both global spirituality and prosperity. D.Z. Sheffield, president of North China College, could start a message to Americans with "We are a Christian nation . . . great in the moral purposes . . . of our people," and end up lauding the great potential market of "four hundred millions of people in China (who) clothe themselves in cotton goods."[10]

Ultimately, both impulses, to export products and religion overseas, were enfolded within something larger: the romantic nationalism that cast such a potent spell over fin de siècle Americans. Romantic nationalists of various kinds might have doubts about both the present and immediate future, but remained deeply convinced of America's unique mission of spreading "the blessings of freedom to other lands." U.S. power would be projected over-seas to regenerate (i.e., Americanize) older nations in decline, and civilize inferior peoples in the islands of the tropical seas. American dreams and institutions were destined to revitalize the world.[11]

Here was a messianic spirit rooted in the seventeenth-century Puritan no-tion of "the City on the Hill"—the preordained national destiny to make the world whole again. The United States was thus the *indispensable* nation, its history and global history running together on parallel tracks, representative of the divinely ordered Progress of mankind. No one expressed this more fervently than a soldier engaged in putting down Filipino resistance to U.S. rule in 1900. "There is not a man of us who in his heart does not feel, and deeply know," he avowed, "that our nation is God's chosen nation for the doing of His inscrutable work."[12]

An imperialism offering Americans foreign markets, divine inspiration, and messianic mission had as its most fervent spokesman Albert Beveridge, the boyishly photogenic, relentlessly self-promoting senator from Indiana, and, in an era of supremely powerful orators, a real mesmerizer. If Beveridge's star was soaring in these years (he desperately sought to be taken seriously as presidential timber), it was due to both his personal charisma and his abil-ity to project the vision of romantic nationalism.

Beveridge used every means—speeches on the Senate floor, magazine articles, and highly publicized visits to the 'boys" in the Philippines—to identify himself (and his career) with unlimited expansionism. The Beveridge stock-in-trade was the use of mystical, rapturous, evangelical language, weighted with phrases such as "the divine destiny of the American people," and "the highest, strongest noblest tide of all is rising today in the reign of the American."[13]

His point of departure was conventional Social Darwinism: The United States was engaged in a protracted war of survival against other peoples and ways of life. But as "a race in its youth," the fittest of all, Americans were destined to be "the sovereign people of the world." U.S. global mastery would inevitably lead to the spread of American-style institutions, commerce, and "liberty" worldwide. For romantic nationalists like Beveridge, there was literally no alternative. To deny or betray the nation's global destiny was to fundamentally undermine American civilization.[14]

This was "White Man's Burden" American style, a potpourri of narrow self-righteousness, idealistic uplift, and crass dollar signs, and it resonated with many of the military men, missionaries, colonial officials, and businessmen at the vanguard of the "civilizing mission" in the new U.S. possessions.

Take Richard Leary, a U.S. Navy captain, whose ship, the *Charleston*, had, during the war with Spain, seized the Pacific island of Guam with nary a shot fired. Leary, a wiry fellow sporting a waxed mustache, apparently took his role as a civilizing agent quite seriously. Soon perceiving that the easy-going Guamanians were not up to the mark, he decreed that all couples living in sin were to be formally married, and "shiftless" people would immediately begin doing productive labor. Classes were formed in English and music, and alcohol banned. It was, remarked one observer, "paternal government with a vengeance."[15]

Leary's social engineering was a variation on the policies Leonard Wood as governor of Cuba, Charles Allen in Puerto Rico, and William Howard Taft in the Philippines would carry out over the next few years. Campaigns to clean up streets, raise sanitation levels, eradicate epidemic diseases, and build hospitals, schools, and roads justified U.S. claims to being a "civilizing force." American administrators always insisted that they were acting out of the loftiest humanitarian motives ("We have gone down to that island for the purpose of giving those people liberty," intoned Leonard Wood) and had the best interests of the natives at heart. Many, in their own way, did.

What remained undisguised, however, was the colonizers' contempt for the abilities and character of the peoples they ruled. That tropical peoples lacked the capacity or moral fiber to govern themselves and desperately needed the long-term tutelage of "civilized nations" was an axiom accepted not only by Belgians in the Congo, the French in Indo-China, and Englishmen in India, but by the U.S. colonial establishment and most Americans at home, too. Inevitably, the cultural beliefs and practices of Filipinos, Cubans,

137

Hawaiians, Guamanians, Puerto Ricans, and Samoans were to be found wanting and in dire need of reformation. "The more I see of them the better I like them," the military-governor of the Philippines island of Negros commented of the people under his control. He casually predicted that in ten years, "they will be the most American Americans in the world."[16]

"The people are naturally kind hearted," wrote Governor Allen to President McKinley of the Puerto Ricans. "They need to be treated with kindness, tact, and greatest patience." Members of the Hawaii's *haole* oligarchy lobbied hard in Washington to exclude the native Hawaiians, frivolous and patently "unfit for suffrage," from the right to vote. Native Hawaiian children returning from summer vacation in 1900 were forbidden to speak Hawaiian in the public schools and severely punished for doing it. An "expert" on the Cuban situation informed the readers of the *Atlantic Monthly* that:

> We must base our dealings with the Cubans on the understanding that they are but children. . . . They yield without opposition or question to a strong hand . . . utterly unfit to be masters of themselves or of anybody else. They are by inheritance unfit for responsibility.[17]

This was, of course, precisely the language of "social efficiency" and "undercivilization" that white Americans in Georgia and South Dakota were using to justify the subordination of local blacks and Indians. U.S. racial traditions were being exported. Those who believed in a natural racial hierarchy and white supremacy at home carried their ideological baggage overseas, fortified by the exaltation of being conquerors in alien, exotic lands. "Many of our officers, especially the younger ones have an arrogance, a sort of swagger," observed an American visitor to Cuba, "that they did not have at home, and there is a distinct tone of condescension toward 'these people down here . . .' as if they were all inferiors." Filipinos and Cubans soon enough learned the meaning of the epithet "nigger" that American soldiers so often flung at them.[18]

So U.S. colonial administrators in 1900 were undertaking the task of "uplifting" peoples to whom their basic attitude was curiously one of contempt. Overlords of the colonial project such as Governor Leonard Wood of Cuba and Secretary of War Elihu Root remained unabashed white supremacists with little sympathy for people of color either at home or abroad. Root, the brilliantly resourceful New York corporate lawyer well known for his exceptional grasp of detail and formidable memory, had been tapped by McKinley as the architect of U.S. colonial policy. In 1899, he had to be explicitly ordered by the president to raise black regiments for the Philippines. Depending on the circumstances, Root might deride the Filipinos as "but little advanced from pure savagery, and of the same characteristics of children," or hold them up as "little brown brothers" learning "the principle of American liberty." In any event, their identities and cultures were slated for reconstruction.[19]

From the moment the fighting with Spain ended, the critical issue became the disposition of the Spanish colonies captured during the 113–day war. The fate of Puerto Rico and Guam was never in question; the U.S. would keep them. But what was to be the future status of Cuba and the Philippines? Here were millions of people of color carrying traditions vastly different from middle Americans.

It was remarkable how quickly the florid rhetoric about liberating Cubans and Filipinos from Spanish oppression gave way to a sober assessment of how the long-term U.S. policy objective of controlling both island peoples might be achieved. The war had given Lodge, Beveridge, Roosevelt, Mahan, et al., advocates of direct colonial rule, the momentum needed to frame the debate. Control over the new colonies, they loudly claimed, would usher in permanent prosperity. Business and the churches could be offered incentives in the form of markets and potential Christian converts.

Overseas expansion was also quite compatible with the most cherished American mythologies. Advocates of empire presented the taking of ocean islands as representing continuity with the nation's mythic movement outward toward new frontiers. By universalizing American institutions, Frederick Jackson Turner's gloomy "end of the frontier" thesis might yet be trumped.

The Harvard philosopher William James, one of the country's most insightful thinkers and an outspoken anti-imperialist, fully appreciated the ability of pro-expansion forces to manipulate these always potent national myths. He would wonder aloud at the "peculiar . . . belief" Americans had "in a national destiny which must be 'big' at any cost"; and which "for some inscrutable reason" they could not "disbelieve in or refuse."[20]

The initial revelation of just how much momentum expansionism had was provided by the annexation of Hawaii. Five years earlier, the United States had sponsored the armed overthrow of Queen Liliuokalani by a mostly American group of businessmen. The expected aftermath to the coup, quick annexation to the United States, had been frustrated first by President Cleveland's refusal to take "stolen property," and then, in 1897, by congressional opposition and stonewalling.

But the euphoric May 1898 victory of arms at Manila Bay, followed by the dispatch of troops to the Philippines in June, had created an irresistible impetus for the taking of Hawaii. The islands' strategic value as the "key of the Pacific" was showcased when the *haole* elite running the Republic of Hawaii made it a base for U.S. naval operations against Spain. Declaring annexation to be "Manifest Destiny," McKinley adroitly used manufactured scares about Japanese imperialist designs to win over doubtful senators. The hostility of native Hawaiians to annexation was ignored. Congressional opposition worn down, or coopted by promises of political offices, a joint resolution passed in early July 1898 making Hawaii part of the United States.[20a]

This amounted to a fantastic and precedent-setting triumph for the imperial party. A territory lying 2,400 watery miles from North America had been annexed. Manifest Destiny had gone overseas.

Yet the stiff congressional opposition to the taking of Hawaii demonstrated that imperialism had nothing like a clear field. Opponents of overseas expansion would fight a tenacious, rearguard battle right up to 1902 when they were finally vanquished. The Anti-Imperialist League founded in June 1898 recruited tens of thousands of members and played a major role in disseminating propaganda and speakers throughout the country. While its centers were located among upper middle-class reform circles in Boston and New York, the anti-imperialist movement itself was nationwide and drew on a wide variety of Americans with varying motivations.

There were proper Bostonians, people such as Morefield Storey and George Hoar, representatives of the old anti-slavery–liberationist New England tradition, profoundly disturbed by the threat of empire to the integrity of republican institutions and ready to assert that all people were capable of self-government. In challenging white supremacy doctrines, they frequently argued that a nation incapable of protecting the rights of its own people of color could not possibly govern others well. Some of the country's leading writers and intellectuals, among whom were numbered Mark Twain, Finley Peter Dunne, and William Dean Howells, had been badly disillusioned by the outcome of what they had originally believed to be a war for human freedom, and voiced similar views. The daring socialist Morrison I. Swift, balancing on the edge of treason, denounced "the expansion of billionaires" and urged soldiers to refuse to fight.[21]

Businessmen like New England manufacturer Edward Atkinson, editor of the bitingly acerbic newsletter *The Anti-imperialist*, argued that it was the economic productivity and clout of the United States, rather than burdensome colonies, that would bring future prosperity. In speeches around the country, William Jennings Bryan emphasized that empires were profitable for army contractors, shipowners, and colonial officials, not workers or farmers.[22]

Anti-imperialism, a broad tent indeed, also contained white supremacists disturbed by the danger that colonization posed to America's remaining the White Man's Country. During the Hawaii debate, for instance, opponents made it clear that they regarded "a country an overwhelming majority of whose population consists of kanakas, Chinese, Japanese, and Portuguese" to be poorly suited for inclusion in the United States.[23]

Not surprisingly, South Carolina boss Ben Tillman (mischievously arguing that federal suppression of the democratic rights of colored peoples abroad was no more than what Mississippians and South Carolinians were doing at home) was in the vanguard here. "You deal with the Filipinos just as we deal with the Negroes," Tillman told the Senate, "only you treat them a heap worse." Tillman's argument that the country did not need "another race problem," nor "any more colored men in the body politic," was seconded by ex-U.S. House Speaker Thomas Reed, a New York City corporate lawyer. "I s'posed we had niggers enough in this country without bringin' any more of 'em."[24]

There was also the rambunctious former secretary of the interior, Carl Schurz, himself an immigrant, denying the capacity of "degenerate" tropical peoples such as "Spanish creoles and the negroes of the West Indies islands to participate in the conduct of our government." Holding these peoples as subjects would require "peculiar institutions" and subvert the Constitution. Andrew Carnegie, a prime financier of the anti-imperialist movement, viewed the colonization of alien peoples as a tragic diversion from developing the United States itself.[25]

Racial fears likewise propelled the anti-imperialism of trade union leaders like Samuel Gompers, who damned the Filipinos as "savages and barbarians" and maintained that The Philippines' incorporation must bring an "innundation" of low-wage nonwhite workers.[26]

The debate would pivot around the Administration's plans for the conquered territories. Before the Spanish war, President McKinley, convinced that U.S. economic recovery made peace essential, had been lukewarm to jingoism and expansionism. One of his biographers argues that "the war appeared to change McKinley, he seemed to become an imperialist." If this amounted to a conversion, it was surely a calculated one: William McKinley was the consummate political tactician, a "straddler" by instinct, legendary for his caution. The most enigmatic of presidents, he never (except for allusions to "divine" guidance) revealed his motivations for taking up the imperialist banner. We can surmise that what drove him were the imperatives of being national leader at a time of industrial-scientific-technological revolution. McKinley as a politician of *realpolitik* understood (and was prisoner of) the compelling demands of U.S. economic expansion. American dreams had to be fed, business profits kept high, industrial stagnation averted at all costs, and, to this end, he was prepared to enlarge the federal government's role as (in Emily Rosenberg's fine phrase) "a promotional state." So if protecting the American dream in this new era meant bold overseas initiatives, grabbing colonies, negotiating reciprocity treaties, and prying open new markets and areas for investment of capital, McKinley would do it. "What we want is new markets," he said, adding smugly, "and as trade follows the flag, it looks very much as if we are going to have new markets."[27]

So given the great power scramble for colonies and the trade and investment potential in the Pacific Rim and Caribbean/Latin America, William McKinley came down in favor of "holding on to what we get." Here, he was acting in the tradition of presidents stretching back to Jefferson, who had acted under the assumption that commercial and political expansion were imperative.[28]

McKinley was also being acutely sensitive here to the postwar public upswell in favor of geographic expansion, which presented advantages and risks to his presidency and party. West of the Rockies, commercial interests favored cementing a trade axis with Asia/Pacific, while in the Middle West and Atlantic seaboard, sentiments of national mission and uplift were strong. If there were alternatives to expansion that would protect his political flank, he didn't see them. Moreover, pressures to take the Philippines were coming from powerful senators like Henry Cabot Lodge, who insisted, "We must on no account let the Islands go. We hold the other side of the Pacific and the value to this country is almost beyond imagination." And renouncing the spoils of war simply wasn't done (especially since other nations seemed likely to snap them up).[29]

With McKinley, as most other public figures, it is nearly impossible to determine where, on the issues of the day, the public facade ended and a degree of sincere personal commitment began. *By the standards of his time* the president was certainly no racist demagogue, but rather a conventional, reasonably generous, white Protestant middle American who took the "duty" explicit in the White Man's Burden seriously. He never doubted that to be governed by tribunes of the noble, dynamic American civilization was clearly in the interest of the Filipinos and Cubans. Both would benefit from "our blessed mission of liberty and humanity." The alternative was anarchy.[30]

McKinley, like most Americans, assumed that the U.S. model of economic development could be universalized and American corporate investment and technologies were inherently positive. An identity of interest stretched between Americans and Cubans or Filipinos. So when the president referred to the Filipinos as "the ward of the nation," and declared that "we accepted the Philippines from high duty in the interests of the inhabitants and for humanity and civilization," his words can be taken at face value.[31]

Right up to his assasination in fall 1901, McKinley's confidence in his

colonial policy did not waver, and to attain its goals he would not flinch from
what he had to do to achieve them.

Cuba and the Philippines had some striking similarities. Both had been ruled
by Spain and misdeveloped for the sake of the mother country for four centuries. They had mixed-race populations. Likewise, both were, in 1898, in
the final stages of popular revolutions against Spanish control that would
have led to independence within a brief time. Where they differed was in
their historic relationship to the United States.

The Philippines, located 8,000 miles from New York and Washington,
had limited historical, commercial, and cultural ties with the United States.
(McKinley admitted that he "could not have told where those darn islands
were within 2,000 miles.") Cuba, in comparison, lay ninety miles from Florida
and strategically athwart sea lanes to the Caribbean and Gulf of Mexico. The
Cuban/American nexus, through trade, investment, immigration, and cultural ties, had grown tighter over the nineteenth century, and the island was
integrated into the U.S. economic system as a supplier of sugar and tobacco
and an importer of industrial and consumer goods.

Over the years Cuba had come to be regarded in elite U.S. circles as a
natural extension of the North American mainland. So even while it was
understood that the United States would protect Spanish dominion there as
long as Spain could hold it, presidents such as Jefferson, Polk, Pierce, and
Grant had either talked about acquiring Cuba or made overtures to the Spanish. In 1898, it was only at the point when Spain was bankrupt, its army
demoralized, and control over Cuba doomed, that the United States entered
the war against it. The eminent scholar Louis Perez argues persuasively that
this was not (as McKinley claimed) to facilitate *Cuba Libre*, but rather "to
stop Cuba from winning its independence" and incorporate the island into
the United States.[32]

Annexation had powerful backers in Washington. To American imperialists, an independent sovereign Cuba could not hope to provide the "stability" Cubans needed to develop along U.S. lines, or the security American
investors demanded. Neither would it effectively bar foreign powers like
Germany from using the island as a potential base against the United States.
The imperial party argued that Cuba could be "Americanized" and turned
into a state. Southerners envisioned it as an attractive area for immigration
and investment. Cuba was viewed as vital to formation of a U.S.-dominated
Pan-American economic system. In telling Congress "the new Cuba . . .
must be bound to us by ties of singular intimacy and strength," McKinley
was advocating something beyond the normal relations between two sovereign nations.[33]

Two major obstacles blocked immediate annexation. One was a U.S. Senate amendment sponsored by Colorado's Senator Henry M. Teller disclaiming any intent to interfere with Cuban independence. Thus there could be no unilateral American seizure of the island; the initiative for annexation must come from the Cubans. Here lay the second barrier. The popular *Cuba Libre* revolution against Spain had generated terrific grass-roots idealism and aspirations for national sovereignty and social justice. A clear majority of Cubans (including an armed revolutionary army of 40,000 veterans) were *independistas* set on establishing national sovereignty. Like Jose Marti, the late revolutionary hero who, even while fighting the Spanish, had feared U.S. economic penetration and political designs ("Once the U.S. is in Cuba, who will get it out?"), they questioned American intentions. Meanwhile, the pro-U.S., pro-annexationist upper classes remained disorganized and numerically weak.[34]

These facts would condition U.S. strategies during the occupation of Cuba, which began on January 1, 1899, with the hauling down of the Spanish flag flying over the Morro Castle in Havana harbor. Throughout the first year of military occupation, despite vague instructions from Washington and bureaucratic infighting among various U.S. generals commanding Cuban provinces, the policy thrust was clearly toward demonstrating the superiority of American-style government, thus gaining popular support for annexation. Engineers, public health officials, doctors, and teachers went to work at reconstruction and disease control. The sheer devastation of the island economy forced Cubans into a desperate struggle for survival and gave the U.S. military government the opportunity to co-opt many independistas. Destitute revolutionary soldiers were paid to bring their arms in for collection; middle-class Cubans returning from exile were awarded jobs in the military government.[35]

But the U.S. campaign to win Cuban hearts and minds was undermined from the start by its inherent contradictions. Historically, the notion of taking Cuba had been largely predicated on the assumption that it was far too critical to the United States to be left to the (unfit) Cubans to govern. So the U.S. military treated the raggedly clothed revolutionary army with open contempt, neither granting them status as official allies nor allowing them to participate in taking the Spanish surrender of key cities. *Yanqui* cultural arrogance was monumental: An American educational system was imposed on the island; half-drunken soldiers waved dollar bills at Cuban women on the city streets. The Cubans were proclaimed to be "a dying race" by one U.S. general. "The Cubans are stupid, given to saying and doing all things in the wrong way," lamented George M. Barbour, commissioner of sanitation in Santiago, adding optimistically, "Under our supervision . . . the people of Cuba may become a useful race and a credit to the world."[36]

Cultural contempt was laced with racial animus. Describing the Cuban revolutionaries as "a lot of degenerates," General Samuel B. M. Young added, "They are no more capable of self-government than the savages of Africa." The allusion was not accidental: One-third of the Cuban population (and a substantial part of the rebel army) were descendants of African slaves. The view from the White Man's Country was that centuries of mixing "dagos and niggers" had yielded a depraved population. Leave them in control of Cuba, and it would surely turn into a zone of chaos like nearby Haiti. "The scheme," shrewly observed the *Nation*, "is to set up a crippled dependency on the United States and call it an independent and sovereign state."[37]

The naming of Teddy Roosevelt's old friend and fellow Roughrider, the forceful, autocratic Leonard Wood, as military governor of Cuba in December 1899 signaled a new urgency in U.S. policy. Tensions between occupiers and independistas had been escalating, and the White House, already suppressing one revolt in the Philippines, feared the outbreak of yet another in Cuba. Under instructions from McKinley to "get out of the islands as soon as we safely can," Wood's mission was to utilize his office to lay down secure foundations for annexation.[38]

Over the next two and one-half years he relentlessly labored to create a viable coalition among "the leading citizens of Cuba," pro-American planters, merchants, bankers, and businessmen, that could command political power and consummate annexation. Wood urged them in speeches and meetings to unite, spoke for their candidates in elections, and intervened with the Congress to secure favorable tariffs for their products. Americanization was accelerated with the importation of school textbooks and curricula from Ohio and summer seminars in the United States for schoolteachers. U.S. corporations and speculators were encouraged to make substantial investments.[39]

To the end, Governor-General Wood continued to indulge the illusion that Yanqui institutions and attitudes could be smoothly transplanted and that the Cubans, so ill-suited to rule themselves, would choose annexation. Only a tiny minority, the "unruly rabble" and "troublemakers," were opposed, he assured Elihu Root. When progress dragged, Wood blamed the Cuban character, writing William McKinley:

> We are going ahead as fast as we can but we are dealing with a race that has steadily been going downhill for a hundred years and into which we have to infuse new life."[40]

In June came municipal elections, the first under American rule. Wood had spared no effort (including restricting access to the vote) to ensure victory by his Cuban protégés' running the pro-U.S. party. The voters, however, gave them minimal support, while independista parties made an impressive showing. The following November saw elections for the all-important convention to frame a new constitution for the future Cuban republic. Again, Wood campaigned relentlessly for convention candidates' supporting strong links to the United States, and once more, the Cuban people plumped decisively for candidates advocating absolute independence.[41]

By late 1900, United States policy in Cuba was in shambles. It was now apparent that popular sentiments for *Cuba Libre* were simply too powerful to be tamed by using Cuban elites to effect annexation. Governor Wood lamented the absence of the "land owning industrial and commercial classes" among convention delegates and voiced anxiety that the "worst political element in the island" had taken control. Secretary of War Elihu Root fretted over Cuban independence coming before the guarantees for U.S. interests that his administration demanded were in place. So the era of conciliation and persuasion was rapidly closed down and the convention informed that, in the absence of a constitution satisfactory to the United States, military occupation might continue indefinitely.[42]

Elihu Root was in his element here. As a phenomenally energetic, workaholic Wall Street lawyer, he had proved enormously resourceful in helping clients like the sugar trust and Whitney traction syndicate secure injunctions and franchises and reduce taxes. Throughout his career, the larger moral issues, the long-term consequences of his acts, seemed to escape him. Now he would secure order and stability in Cuba. In consultation with imperial friends, he authored a document (based on British indirect rule over Egypt) giving the United States the right to unrestricted action vis-à-vis Cuba: Future U.S. governments would have a blank check to intervene whenever they perceived its internal stability to be at risk, and the right to veto Cuban international treaties and to maintain a naval base on the island. As the Platt Amendment, it sailed through Congress. The Cuban convention was then given the ultimatum of either incorporating Platt into its final document or having its work rejected.[43]

In Cuba, Platt was correctly perceived to be outright blackmail, an American diktat grossly mutilating Cuban sovereignty. There was great resistance. Demonstrations and protests flared up. Prominent revolutionary leaders protested that this was not the republic they had fought for, and there was some talk of taking up arms once more. However, the convention's resolve steadily eroded under intense pressure from Root and the wining and dining of its leaders in Washington. After Root refused to consider modifying the amendment, the delegates, following intense debate, reluctantly agreed in June 1901 to accept Platt as the law of the Cuban republic. "If it is either annexation or a Republic with an amendment, I prefer the latter," explained one delegate. Outgoing Governor-General Wood, still in denial about the strength of independista feeling, informed McKinley, "There is of course little or no independence left in Cuba under the Platt Amendment," and smugly predicted annexation to be imminent.[44]

It did not come. The Cubans remained adamantly opposed. By 1902, expansionist fever was receding in the United States itself. Actually, the United States had the Cuba it wanted. The Cuban republic would remain sovereign only in theory, a protectorate of the northern colossus. Cuba had, as Elihu Root remarked, "become part of our political and military system." The Reciprocity Treaty of 1903 confirmed the island's status as an economic satellite: The lion's share of Cuba's sugar, coffee, and tobacco production would be controlled by American companies and directed to the United States, while U.S. imports dominated Cuban consumer markets.[45]

Rather than stability, however, U.S. policy ensured chronic political instabilty. A dependent agro-export economy meant economic underdevelopment, widespread underemployment, and the uneasy coexistence of wealth and poverty. In the absence of economic diversification, there was fierce competition among various political factions for control of government and the spoils of office. Inevitably, in times of crisis, they sought the support of the U.S. paterfamilias. The United States ambassador in Cuba became a supremely powerful figure, making and unmaking governments.

During the constitutional convention, the nationalist Juan Gualberto Gomez had remarked prophetically, "We are asked to give the U.S. the key to our house, with the right to come in whenever they choose." In 1906, Cuban political instability led President Theodore Roosevelt to order the landing of U.S. troops, and a three-year military occupation followed. When nationalist president Ramon Grau San Martin had the temerity in 1933 to declare the Platt Amendment null and void and threaten American interests, the United States conspired with Sergeant Fulgencio Batista to overthrow him.[46]

The consequences of turn-of-the-century U.S. policy toward Cuba began to unfold on January 1, 1959. Fidel Castro and his guerrilla columns moved out of the Sierra Maestra mountains to reclaim Cuba from the fleeing Batista, and entered Santiago. In his speech that night, Castro, the radical nationalist determined to liberate Cuba once and for all, talked about how General Calixto Garcia had been prevented from being present at the surrender of Santiago in 1898, "when the North Americans came and made themselves masters of our country." But "this time the revolution will not be thwarted," promised Castro, and "the republic would be really free."[47]

The Philippines: In the months following the end of the war with Spain, the president and his deeply divided cabinet made a reappraisal of what they would demand from Spain at the Paris peace talks. Given the McKinley "conversion" and the pressures of the imperial party, what initially began as the demand for a base in Manila Bay soon escalated to cession of the island of Luzon, and then the entire archipelago.[48]

The first major test of public opinion on the Philippines occurred during a fall 1898 presidential speaking tour of the Midwest. McKinley, a highly effective orator, spoke glowingly of expansion to large and enthusiastic crowds and promised it would bring "blessings that are now beyond calculation." When he rhetorically queried a huge audience at the Omaha Exposition, "Shall we deny ourselves what the rest of the world so freely and so justly accords us?" the crowd responded with a thunderous "No!" McKinley intoned dramatically. "Now then we will do our duty."[49]

Besides fortifying the president's confidence that a broad band of support existed for holding the Philippines, the western tour allowed him to fashion the administration's line on expansion. McKinley's speeches reveal a masterful understanding of his public, their myths and conceits. "We have expanded," he told an Iowa City audience and, conscious of the deep American aversion to limits and shrinkage of any kind, asked, "If there is any question at all, it is a question of contraction; and who is going to contract?"[50]

Administration strategy was to emphasize the nation's "duty" and "destiny" overseas. By insisting on a sacred obligation to raise up the Filipino people and create "good government" on the U.S model, McKinley was tapping into a racialized American paternalism that viewed dark-skinned tropicals as children needing support and tutelage in learning the arts of "civilization." Such a policy of "benevolent assimilation" gave the administration the moral high ground, differentiating it from white supremacists à la Tillman.[51]

McKinley had the good fortune to be a man who spoke in simplistic dualities in an age that thought in simplistic dualities. By casting a complex question as a simple moralism ("We must choose between manly doing and base desertion"), he was simultaneously stoking Americans' pride and playing on their insecurities. "It is not possible," he remarked, that "seventy-five millions of American freemen are unable to establish liberty and justice and good government in our new possesions." Nor was the president above claiming "the hand of almighty God" in the coming of U.S. rule to the Philippines. Thus did William McKinley make certain that real alternatives to annexation (for example, independence under international guarantees) were excluded from serious dialogue.[52]

In early February 1899 after several months of highly charged, often scathing debate on the floor of the Senate, the Treaty of Paris with Spain giving the Philippines to the United States came up for a vote. McKinley, aware that he lacked the two-thirds of the Senate needed for passage, wheeled and dealed from the White House, and had Republican leaders Hanna, Aldrich, and Orville Pratt in the Senate promise patronage plums and judgeships for votes. A critical intervention was that of the president's past and future Democratic challenger, William Jennings Bryan, who opposed annexation, but, reasoning that once the war with Spain was ended and the Philippines were in U.S. possession, independence could be granted, urged Democratic senators to vote yes.[53]

Ratification was aided two days before the Senate vote by the outbreak of fighting between Filipino and American soldiers who had for months been tensely confronting each other in trenches outside of Manila. Some historians have argued that the incident was deliberately provoked by the United States to ensure treaty passage. McKinley, always prone to self-righteous melodrama, claimed that "the first blow was struck by the insurgents . . . our kindness was . . . repaid by cruelty, our mercy with a Mauser."[54]

The decision in Washington to keep the islands had made an American-Filipino war inevitable. Earlier in the decade, a Filipino national movement had launched a protracted war for independence against Spain, and, despite numerous internal intrigues and struggles, had fought the Spanish to a stalemate, isolating them in Manila and other towns. Clearly, by the outset of the Spanish-American War, Spain's days in the Philippines, as in Cuba, were numbered. After Dewey's triumph at Manila Bay, he had initiated collaboration with the guerillas, and Emiliano Aguinaldo, a prominent young nationalist leader, had been brought back from exile.

However, the initial gratitude of Aguinaldo and the Filipino revolutionaries to "the Almighty and Human North American Nation" quickly turned to hostility when they saw that the Americans were intent on replacing the Spanish as colonizers. What particularly incensed the Filipinos was being utterly ignored during the Paris peace negotiations. Not only was no offer of eventual self-government made, but on December 21 McKinley proclamed military government over "the whole ceded territory"—a virtual declaration of war. A few weeks later, an independent Philippines republic based at Malolos in Luzon was defiantly proclaimed.[55]

An army led by generals who had made their careers in the American West fighting Indian tribes certainly didn't expect much resistance from a group of small, bronze-complexioned men wearing shabby checkered blue calico uniforms and Manila hats. Even the Mauser rifles they carried seemed too big for them. The Filipino army was hopelessly outgunned, lacked artillery, and would be forced to live off the land. To U.S. military brass and politicians, this was merely to be a repetition of routine police actions against the Apache and Sioux. There might be a few pockets of resistance to mop up before the enemy submitted to the Stars and Stripes.[56]

149

So at the onset, the Filipinos and their commitment and willingness to sacrifice and fight heroically against huge odds were vastly underestimated. "The bravest men I have ever seen" was how the veteran commander of the eighth Corps, General Thomas Lawton (killed in action late in 1899 at San Mateo in Luzon), assessed them, adding subversively that "such men have the right to be heard."[57]

Throughout the spring and summer of 1899, American troops won a series of small pitched battles, pushing their zone of control out from Manila, but they could not bring the decentralized Filipino battalions to decisive battle. General E.S. Otis, the stubbornly inflexible U.S. military governor, sent numerous messages to the White House promising victory, while asking for more soldiers to deliver it. The end of the rainy season in November saw a three-pronged drive across Luzon aimed at destroying the Filipino army and capturing the nationalist leadership. McKinley received reports of the disintegration of the "rebels," but Aguinaldo escaped encirclement and fled northward, Filipino units fighting suicidal rearguard actions, the survivors eventually regrouping in the mountains and native barrios.[58]

What U.S. field commanders now faced was the first modern "people's war" waged by guerrillas who were indistinguishable from the general populace and occasionally sallied forth to engage in ambushes and firefights.

Elihu Root at the War Department kept close watch on the Philippines situation, and by January 1900 had raised U.S. troop strength there to 65,000. U.S. forces seized more territory garrisoning strongpoints around Luzon and other islands. By March, General Joe Wheeler (ironically, as a onetime Civil War Confederate officer, a former rebel himself), opined: "I believe the back of the rebellion in the Philippines is broken." During early spring, fighting continued in central Luzon and the Visayas—the official count for one week in mid-April was 378 Filipinos killed and 256 captured. But by August, Luzon was virtually under U. S. control.[59]

Still, there were few signs of Filipino surrender. Offers of amnesty were generally ignored. "Though Aguinaldo is a fugitive, his influence is appreciable," admitted General Arthur MacArthur, the new army commander. "Throughout the entire archipelago, the people are surprisingly loyal to him." U.S. patrols were often ambushed by guerrillas who easily melted back into the general population. "There is no way to tell hostile citizens," complained the *Oregonian*, "when all dress alike and claim to be 'amigo' and all wear that Oriental smile."[60]

American frustrations at the resilience and elusiveness of the Filipinos and the tactics of the people's war engendered increasingly ruthless behavior. The September 1900 *Harper's Bazaar* reported "a spirit of bloodthirstiness is said to have taken possession of the U.S. army in the Philippines."

MacArthur viewed the Philippines as a zone under military occupation and treated the Filipinos as a hostile people. Acts of terror by U.S. soldiers became both widespread—villages burnt and bombarded as reprisals for nearby American casualties, water torture and bayoneting used to extract information from prisoners and villagers suspected of pro-guerrilla sympathies—and condoned and protected by staff and line officers.[61]

Widespread use of terror was scarcely surprising, however, in a situation where an entire population was targeted for dehumanization. The U.S. military, a white supremacist outfit deeply conscious of its role as the the vanguard of Anglo-Saxon superiority (black American officers in the Philippines were routinely snubbed by white officers and refused obedience by white enlisted men), was wholly contemptuous of Filipino "goo-goos" and "niggers." Noted the *Boston Herald:* "Our troops in the field look upon the Filipinos as niggers and entitled to all the contempt and harsh treatment administered by white overlords to the most inferior races."[62]

Such racial antipathies received sanction from political leaders at home such as Governor Teddy Roosevelt, who readily compared the Filipino "rebellion" to the uprising of the Apaches and likened Aguinaldo's fate to Geronimo's. Secretary of War Root tersely dismissed Aguinaldo's credibility with the statement that he was only "a Chinese half breed."[63]

And U.S. media reports reinforced the widely prevailing notion of the Filipinos as being something other than fully human. Typically, *Lesley Illustrated Weekly's* correspondent Sydney Adamson wrote of the Filipinos as "cruel and savage, of poor mental endowment . . . incapable of appreciating customs and sentiments of civilized warfare."[64]

There was a revealing tendency to compare Filipinos to animals in the wild. Cartoonists portrayed them as monkey men and naked cannibals. Adamson, observing a massacre of Filipino insurgents by the U.S. infantry, wrote, "The work had the excitement . . . of shooting birds as they broke from cover." In *Harper's Weekly*, George Hillyer would describe the deaths of young Filipino soldiers near the Santa Cruz River: "They die the way a wild animal dies—in such a position as one finds a deer or an antelope which one has shot in the woods." Accounts of battles referred to American soldiers being killed by "treacherous natives." Such reportage provided a rationale for the U.S. military's systematic violation of "civilized warfare."[65]

In retrospect, the American-Filipino war amounted to a massive exercise in denial by its U.S. advocates from McKinley on down. Of essence was the denial that the Filipinos constituted an authentic nation in the process of achieving self-determination. To acknowledge this, was, of course, to admit that the war was really between the armies of two national states. The United States would then stand indicted as an aggressor and empire builder. So right up to 1902, the administration would seek to portray the fighting as a regrettable, but necessary, police action conducted against rebels who had misunderstood the purity of U.S. objectives and were resisting Washington's legitimate sovereignty. McKinley (using an Indian analogy) cavalierly dismissed the conflict as the work of "a single tribe out of eighty or more."[66]

There was also denial that in the name of uplift and civilization (or what one reporter called the "stupendous task of instilling into the brown races the vital importance of justice and soap"), Americans had turned the Philippines into a bloody abattoir. McKinley and Root used warfront censorship to keep battlefield information from the public and their policies unaccountable to anyone. To counter those reports of American atrocities trickling home in letters or personal stories of returned infantrymen, official spokesmen steadfastly denied that Americans could be committing such atrocious acts in a war being fought on behalf of the Filipino people. "The American soldier," Root commented, "is different from all other soldiers of all other countries since the world began." The United States was merely pushing the frontiers of Anglo-Saxon civilization forward in opposition to the anarchy and terror spread by Filipino tribesmen.[67]

Occasionally, however, in revealing offhand statements, this veneer is pierced, and one catches glimpses into the arrogance and violent racism at the core of the civilizing mission. A comment by General Keith Funston, the most celebrated U.S. hero of the war: "[Let's] rawhide these bullet headed Asians until they yell for mercy, I'll warrant that the new generation of natives will know better than to get in the way of the bandwagon of Anglo/Saxon progress and decency."[68]

In a letter to Governor Theodore Roosevelt, John H. Parker, an officer serving in the Philippines, claimed the Filipinos did not surrender because "their reasoning faculties have become warped by centuries of bad training. . . . They must be so thoroughly licked that each and every individual is ready to say 'enough.'"[69]

Protracted fighting in the Philippines reignited the voices of dissent to the whole colonial project. Opponents charged that a misguided policy of overseas adventurism had caused the war and the entire mess could have been avoided by dealing honestly with Aguinaldo back in 1898. Democratic ideals were being tainted and dangerous patterns of U.S. intervention overseas established.

Senator Hoar, ex-President Benjamin Harrison, and Carl Schurz all agreed the Constitution must follow the flag: A free country did not have subjects. To govern without consent was "un-American," and contrary to the founding principles of the country. The hugely respected and dignified Hoar told a

Massachussetts audience: "When now they say to me that the Philippine islands are ours, I must say that the Philippine islands belong to the Philippines people."[70]

Joseph Pulitzer, editor of the *New York World*, accused McKinley of acting like an emperor and Congress of abdicating its authority over foreign policy. Addressing the president, South Dakota's Senator Pettigrew charged, "Your effort to subjugate these people by force, is the international crime of the century," and demanded that McKinley discharge all troops from his state in the Philippines whose term of service was up. The country's most revered literary personality, Mark Twain, bitterly attacked the "bandit's work" being done in the Philippines, and regarded the talk of bringing the "blessings of civilization" as thin cover for the goal of capturing "a good commercial property."[71]

Veteran abolitionist New Englanders like Hoar and newspaper publisher Samuel Bowles Jr. made the link between the worsening racial climate in the South "and our lynching of a people in the Philippines." Blacks, like other Americans, remained split over expansion—some identifying with it or seeking to affirm their right to citizenship by offering support; others, such as Howard University mathematics professor Kelly Miller, thought that imperialism abroad contributed to racial violence at home, and backed Filipino self-determination. A meeting of black Bostonians at Fanueil Hall during summer 1899 resolved: "The duty of the president and country is to reform the crying domestic wrongs and not to attempt the civilization of alien peoples." The black-owned *Indianapolis World* noted that "the administration can field armies to suppress the Filipinos . . . but no troops are sent to New Orleans to suppress the riotous murders or to North Carolina to check the red shirts."[72]

Critics also seized upon the mounting toll of American casualties (by war's end, of 126,000 soldiers who had served in the Philippines, 4,200 were dead and 2,800 had been wounded). They decried the impact of military life in the Philippines, with its tropical fevers and binge drinking and whoring in Manila's ubiquitous saloons and brothels, on the physical and moral well-being of American soldiers. The sight of troop ships filled with men wracked by typhoid and other diseases, and held in military brig, caused *Harper's Bazaar* to editorialize: "Do women think these sacrifices are worth it?"[73]

Ultimately, the anti-imperialists, while retaining a degree of support on college campuses such as Stanford, the University of Chicago, and Harvard, in certain churches, and among some trade unionists, were unable to build a broadly based political movement capable of challenging administration policy. Perhaps the closest they came was a January 6, 1900, meeting at Manhattan's Plaza Hotel where Andrew Carnegie huddled with Carl Schurz,

Franklin Giddings, and other luminaries, and offered to donate $15,000 to start a party opposed to the war and match fund-raising dollar for dollar.

The proposed political organization, however, never materialized. Given the disinterest and apathy of the American people and their momentary infatuation with expansion, organizing them into a political force was improbable. Moreover, the sheer diversity of the anti-imperialists, who counted New England reformers, southern racists, black intellectuals, and Populists in their ranks, meant unbridgeable disagreements on other issues.[74]

What further undermined the movement to oppose imperialism was the ambivalence of the anti-imperialists themselves about expansionism. Most never disengaged from the romance of a global American destiny, and there were few among them who did not share McKinley's or Beveridge's sense of the American "civilizing mission" and the benefits of exporting the American dream and locating new overseas markets for surplus goods. Some contended that the United States could civilize "the lower races," and obtain needed new markets too, but that this could be done more efficiently through techniques of informal colonization. Too often, where they differed with the expansionists was over strategy, not principles.[75]

The consequence was to muddle the issue and undercut the movement's moral power. Prominent opponents of annexing the Philippines, like Carl Schurz, Andrew Carnegie, and Richard Olney, suddenly turned rabid colonizers when the subject of Cuba was raised. *Atlanta Constitution* editor Clark Howell and William Jennings Bryan advocated holding the Philippines in "trust." It was nonchalantly assumed that even after independence, coaling stations must continue to be available for the U.S. Navy.[76]

So the McKinley administration was able to frame the terms of the debate. Its line of argument was simple and forceful: No alternative existed to remaining in the Philippines. National self-respect and future prosperity demanded it. It was "Duty and Destiny." In a December 1899 message to Congress, McKinley stated that it was not possible to "withdraw our forces from the islands either with honor to ourselves or with safety to the inhabitants." A month later, Alfred Beveridge delivered a major address before an admiring gallery in the Senate. "The Philippines are ours forever," he said:

> We will not repudiate our duty in the archipelago. We will not abandon our opportunity in the Orient. We will not renounce our part in the mission of our race, trustee under God of the civilization of the world.[77]

There were dire warnings that to lose the Philippines and emerging markets meant sliding into "industrial strangulation at home . . . to sink backward into another long night like that of the dark ages." "Shall we go forward or stand still?" asked tall, thin Orville Platt, the immensely powerful senator from Connecticut. "If we would maintain ourselves in the front rank we must go forward."[78]

Right through the 1900 election campaign, the Administration hammered its message home. Presidential commissions were dispatched to the Philippines to ratify the work in progress, and McKinley gave comforting assurances of the war's imminent end. Prowar newspapers like *The New York Times* blamed the antiwar opposition for prolonging the fighting.

That opposition was about to have its last chance. William Jennings Bryan, certain to be the 1900 Democratic candidate for president, was touring the country making anti-imperialist speeches. Speaking to 25,000 people in Toledo, Ohio, in May, he assured them that the "Filipinos will demand the right of free government."[79]

Chapter 10

Of Trusts, Islands, Dinner Pails, and an Election

Never in human history anywhere on earth have security for life and property, unfettered opportunity for intelligence and energy, individual freedom, and the self-respect of manhood, attained a higher level than now marks the condition of this fortunate Republic.

—Secretary of War Elihu Root, October 1900

The issue presented in the campaign of 1900 is the issue between the dollar and the man.

—William Jennings Bryan, July 1900

For good government, good times and good money give us four more years of McKinley and good times.

—Fred J. Gould, salesman, St. Louis, to William McKinley, July 1900

We can sleep soundly tonight being assured that our believed fort is in your good hands.

—Mark Hanna to William McKinley, November 6, 1900

The election of 1900 was essentially a continuation of what had begun on the afternoon of July 9, 1896, when William Jennings Bryan, a sturdily built, former Nebraska congressman with a dimpled jaw and expressive face, mounted the platform of the Democratic National Convention to speak to the issue bitterly dividing the delegates: the free coinage of silver.

The thirty-six-year-old Bryan was a supremely gifted orator ("the most perfect voice I ever heard," thought a Texas congressman's wife) and this was his moment, one he had meticulously prepared for during the past months and years. If lacking in much substance, this speech, loaded with the melodrama and fiery Biblical images that fin de siécle audiences loved, was to number among the most political orations in American history.[1]

"From the first sentence the audience was with me" was how Bryan would later remember it. He challenged the supporters of the gold standard to expand their notion of "businessmen" to farmers, miners, and workers and insisted the people of the West were the equals of anyone. A crash of applause from the 20,000 people inside the Chicago Coliseum began to punctuate the ending of each sentence. Bryan's tone grew increasingly bold, prophetic, each point carefully driven home. "Burn down your cities and leave our farms, and our cities will grow up again," he declared. "But destroy our farms and the grass will grow in every city of the union."

To the speaker it seemed that "the audience seemed to rise and sit down as one man. At the close of a sentence it would rise and shout and when I began upon another sentence, the room was as still as a church." One reporter wrote of "cheers rising and falling like the noise of a tremendous storm." Ending his speech with "You shall not press down upon the brow of labor this crown of thorns and you shall not crucify mankind upon a cross of gold," Bryan spread his arms out to simulate a crucifixion. A moment of absolute silence ensued, then the convention hall was enveloped by wave after wave of mass hysteria. On the next day, Bryan was nominated as Democratic candidate for president.[2]

The Bryan phenomenon arose out of the multiple crises of the mid-nineties and the anarchy unleased by an uncontrolled and revolutionary market economy. "The economic world has literally jumped in the process of evolution," mused William Allen White, the noted Kansas newspaperman. An earlier cultural equilibrium was breaking down. Citizens numbed by bad times and traumatic changes, and helpless before international agricultural markets and industrial monopolies, were attracted by the evangelical free silver crusade's promise of a quick fix. What they desired was a return to a fairer, simpler world they might understand and have some control over. In Bryan, they had finally located an exemplary spokesman.

Since the Civil War, national politics had been essentially opportunistic and venal, about satisfying local interests and exploiting the spoils of office. Politicians were generally purchasable, and outright theft of the public domain the norm. National political conventions were usually manipulated by narrow men ignorant of national issues. Showmanship and political circus took precedence, and, once in office, parties were not expected to deliver on platforms. The sheer complexity, the weighty checks and balances of the political system, mitigated against popular reform. Outside the South, most states were fairly competitive between Democrats and Republicans, who might quibble on some issues, but agreed on essentials. Only third parties like the Populists and Socialists dared question the country's moral base and direction.[3]

But the transformations and dislocations of late nineteenth-century life had made issues once again vital. New voting constituencies were up for grabs. The sudden emergence of a major party candidate representing older American principles turned the 1896 election into something extraordinary. William Jennings Bryan was running on "a platform astonishingly radical for the age," and directed at those who saw themselves marginal to the harsh new American dream. If the main thrust was coining silver at 16:1, the Democrats also borrowed liberally from Populist notions of nationalizing railroads, neutralizing the power of federal courts, and ending court injunctions against strikes. The People's Party, in fact, was so impressed by the Democratic program, and desperate to locate a national audience, that it promptly endorsed Bryan for president—an act that, in retrospect, amounted to political suicide.[4]

The Bryan candidacy turned the 1896 election into nothing less than a referendum on whom the country belonged to and where it was going. It gave the lie to the mythic notion of a community of interest between big business and finance and workers and farmers. The country's rampaging inequalities were, he charged, ruining the American dream of liberty and opportunity. The plutocrats had rigged the economy against ordinary Americans, and, in the absence of dramatic changes, deliverance and abundance would not be forthcoming. For the first time in decades, a major-party presidential candidate was declaring the country's trajectory had to be changed.

The Bryanite vision was of a rebirth of the older Jeffersonian American dream. If muddled in conception and weak on concrete measures to right the wrongs, it envisioned government transformed from a creature of monopolies and the upper classes to the active ally of the ordinary farmer and worker. One secret of Bryan's "magnetism," wrote the perceptive William Allen White, was the people's "hope to see the state lay hold of the industrial system and untangle its many snarls." Federal powers would be used to restore the world existing before the rise of the mega-corporations.[5]

The Republicans and their candidate, Governor William McKinley of Ohio, never tried to disguise their vision of the American future. The nation would continue to march along the lines developed over the last generation, and the Grand Old Party would safeguard citizens' wealth and property. The best strategy to restore "the full dinner pail" was to maintain the gold standard, keep tariffs high and big business free from government regulation and able to penetrate overseas markets. Eventually, the new abundance would surely trickle down. Existing patterns of economic ownership and control were to be left alone, thank you.

Years of economic depression under Democrat Grover Cleveland had led Republican leaders to believe the White House was theirs for the taking in 1896. But Bryan's oratorical magic made them apprehensive. Under the capable, autocratic direction of the rough-hewn Cleveland industrialist Marcus Alonzo Hanna, a genius for detail who had astutely shepherded William McKinley's campaign for the presidential nomination, party strategy was hammered out. The campaign machinery Republicans constructed was really the forerunner of modern twentieth century political organizations. Hanna's men, working out of headquarters in Manhattan and Chicago, systematically took "donations" from a host of industrial and financial corporations, emerging with a massive political war chest of over $3 million. The country's "best people," feeling their advantages threatened as never before, had circled their wagons.[6]

The Republican focus was on mobilizing working- and lower middle-class voters, many of whom had initially been attracted to Bryanism. The propaganda blitz that summer and fall was unprecedented in size and scope. It included prepared newspaper columns, a 410–page *Republican Campaign Textbook* for party activists, and millions of pamphlets, fliers, and colorful McKinley posters. A stable of some fourteen hundred speakers traveled the country excoriating Bryan and free silver.

Indeed, no public indictment of Bryan, or the "Popocrats," was too harsh. The press lashed him as an "immature boy," an "anarchist," a "socialist," and hinted that he was hiding "Irish" origins. His sanity was questioned, as was the undue influence of his wife. The *New York Times* decried free silver as "a policy which might have been conceived in an asylum for lunatics." Professors and clergymen predicted a Bryan presidency would bring "industrial destruction and financial disaster." A million copies of William Allen White's scathing denunciation of the free silver movement, "What's the Matter with Kansas?" were circulated. Employers announced that Bryan's election meant layoffs.[7]

The two candidates were a study in contrast. "Major McKinley," suave and imperturbable, looking every inch presidential, remained in residence in Canton, Ohio, where he received large delegations of war veterans, industrial workers, and Republican clubsmen, who paraded from the railway station waving flags and beating drums right up to the yard of his house. These "front porch" affairs were as minutely scripted as modern television conventions. To great applause a beaming McKinley would emerge onto his porch, and, after a presentation by the delegation's leaders, thank his "fellow Americans" for the visit, utter a few platitudes about the dangers of Bryanism, and shake some hands. At its peak, sixteen delegations and 30,000 people arrived in a single day.[8]

Meanwhile, Bryan toured the country, traveling 18,000 miles, making dozens of speeches daily, wildly cheered by sizable crowds at railways, halls, and open air gatherings, campaigning to the point of physical and emotional breakdown. But in the end, he was simply overwhelmed by a superbly financed and efficient organization overseen by Hanna, which successfully crafted McKinley's image as "the advance agent of prosperity," by a media that demonized Bryanism, and by the albatross of silver.

If Bryan was the product of the silver panacea, he was equally its prisoner. Free silver dominated his campaign, and even the attacks on New York and London financiers woven into his speeches emphasized "the conspiracy to strike down silver." This made it easy for Republicans to ridicule him and sow fear among the voters. Small bank depositors were told that free silver meant a "fifty-three-cent dollar" that would shred savings. Artisans and laborers could expect the purchasing power of wages slashed. A "Gold Democrat" presidential ticket headed by a pair of Civil War generals split the Democratic party and ruined Bryan's hopes of carrying the critical states of the upper Midwest and border South.[9]

The silver obsession also made Bryan wholly alien in certain labor circles that might have been attracted by the Democratic platform. The Northeast remained, in Bryan's words, the "enemy's country." The prosperous farmers of the upper Midwest, a key group, distrusted cheap money and stayed Republican. In the end, he was isolated as a sectional candidate of the discontented agrarians from the South and West. Despite talking less silver and more class toward the campaign's end, Bryan never located the language or alternative program (if either existed) that would have united his wildly diverse and mutually suspicious potential constitutencies. So on election day, Bryan captured the deep South and a smattering of western silver states, and was beaten everywhere else.[10]

But the 1896 election had transformed William Jennings Bryan into a national political celebrity. He had garnered 6,500,000 votes, or a million more than any previous Democratic candidate, and was odds-on favorite to be the party's next presidential nominee. Among one segment of Americans, Bryan was now also virtually an icon, showered with adulation as he toured the country. As the "Great Commoner," personifying popular resistance to the values of business monopoly and modern culture, and reflecting in his graphic speeches the world they experienced and believed in, he inspired intense devotion among rural and small-town folk. Indeed, Bryan validated their struggles, presented them as they liked to think of themselves, gave voice to their aspirations, and never talked down to them. They understood that this kindly, unaffected man would never betray their trust.

If Bryan never quite grasped the nature of the complex forces driving the capitalist revolution, he did have "a keen intuitive understanding" of how they had "narrowed the scope of the American dream and excluded his people from its pursuit." Country people could identify him as someone who genuinely felt their pain and frustrations, a savior who, once ensconced in the White House, would act to protect them from hostile forces.[11]

Bryan also shared his supporters' provincialism, ignorance, and narrow biases. A small-town evangelical Christian who took the Bible as literal truth and saw life and political questions in terms of dualities between good and evil, his analysis of complex problems was often startlingly simplistic. He accepted the agrarian myth of the innate goodness of farm life and evil of the cities. His faith in the absolute will of "the people" as something akin to the will of God often made him susceptible to popular crackpot notions.[12]

And Bryan, like his followers, embraced the American dream and private property as sacred. He might denounce J.P. Morgan and "predatory wealth," but the self-made man who prospered in the Great Race was his hero, someone touched by godliness. Such insistence on the fundamental soundness of the structures of the private profit market economy turned Eugene Debs and the socialists against him. "I want a government that gives every poor boy the hope of being rich someday," Bryan said. "What I object to is a government that protects a few men in their robbery of the masses."[13]

Bryan's goal, then, was to use government as an instrument of public power to suppress these unfair advantages and restore the competitive economy of midcentury. Ultimately, his credo was to change the rules of the game so that every man had real opportunity to grab a piece of the dream pie.

Meaning every *white* man. Bryan's sense of the place of blacks and Asians in American society was in line with prevailing American wisdom on the subject. Lynching and terror were inappropriate (if sometimes understandable in cases of rape), but "one race must be dominant" and it must be the white. "Social inequality" was impossible, he thought, and blacks must learn not to "allow their violence and lusts to provoke hostility."[14]

The 1896 election had brought a remarkably gifted political figure to the national political stage. He would courageously challenge the relentless commodification of American life, the domination of giant capital, and the

onset of consumerism, and champion some of the visionary social and economic legislation that later became law in the New Deal and afterward. But
at a moment when America teetered between various paths, Bryan was mis-
cast as savior. He was, himself, much too deeply immersed in American
individualist dream ideology to be its critic, or to imagine the possibility of
an alternative vision. His program was, at best, flimsy. Nor could he hope to
unite the diverse strands of American malcontents into a dominant nationwide movement. What his presidential campaigns did do was to absorb much
of the energy and passion of those critical of where the nation was going, and
provide a channel of protest against the emergent corporate-consumer society.

Almost from the counting of the ballots in 1896, the compulsively political Bryan had been eagerly anticipating a rematch, speechmaking across the
country and writing columns for the Hearst and Pulitzer newspapers. He still
thought of his destiny as being entwined with the nation's. A little heavier
and sterner faced in 1900 than he had been four years earlier, his celebrated
voice a bit more metallic, Bryan was more the politician this time around,
seeking the support of Democratic state and city bosses. He would show
himself in this campaign to be an intriguing combination of political opportunist and idealistic reformer.

The year 1900 would have been difficult for any presidential challenger.
The sitting president was a patient, highly skilled politician cultivating the
aura of a devout clergyman and surrounded by a strong supporting cast. His
first term had witnessed the return of economic prosperity and a victorious
war that had added to U.S. world stature and power. McKinley had, with
some success, identified himself as a *national* leader, and was a past master
at creating a public image of being tolerant and inclusive. He was expanding
the prestige and responsibilities of the presidential office at a time when
most Americans welcomed these measures.[15]

Nonetheless, Democrats did have an opportunity to exploit both fin de
siécle America's unease with its new role in the world and the burgeoning
concentration of wealth and power. If Bryan shared the McKinley notion of
a divinely ordained overseas mission, he wanted it without colonies or violence. Colonialism was the devil's work and Bryan attacked it from the moment the Spanish-American war ended: U.S. troops "did not volunteer to
attempt to subjugate other peoples, or establish U.S. sovereignty elsewhere,"
he cabled McKinley.

The "forcible annexation" of the Philippines amounted to "criminal aggression." An American empire requiring a large standing army must pose a
direct danger to democratic institutions.[16]

Convinced that the American conscience could be awakened and grassroots
opposition to overseas adventures politicized, Bryan announced in 1899 that

imperialism would be the "paramount" issue of the campaign.

Yet for all its fire and brimstone, Bryan's Philippines policy was still predicated on the notion that the United States would continue to play a dominant role in that country's future. Washington should form a stable government and "protect" the Filipinos; independence would come when they were deemed ready for it. The United States would retain military bases for the long-term future. Of course, Senator Hoar and other anti-imperialists mocked this scheme as a simple variation on McKinley's general theme. But it made Bryan appealing to some easterners who had scorned him in '96.[17]

During the late nineties, Bryan, denouncing the "heavy hand of monopoly" and the control that a few men exerted over the nations' prices and wages, had made himself a high-profile critic of the trusts and their allied investment houses like J.P. Morgan, Kuhn, Loeb and Company, and Kidder Peabody. "A private monopoly is indefensible and intolerable," he declared at the September 1899 Chicago Anti-Trust Conference. Trusts were not God's but man's creation, and should be tamed by society. Once in the White House, he assured his audiences, his mission would be to array the powers of the government against the abuses that allowed them to thrive. Bryan advisor and former governor of Illinois John Peter Altgeld said bluntly: "We have declared that private monopoly . . . shall not exist in America."[18]

So trusts would be the second critical issue. Bryan would eloquently lash McKinley and Hanna's complicity with America Inc. The Democrats had reasonable expectations here: The merger mania was reaching unprecedented levels and a public falling out between Andrew Carnegie and Henry Clay Frick (Frick labeled Carnegie "a goddamned thief") over control of the Carnegie steel complex revealed how enormous the profits of corporations like Carnegie's had become.[19]

In condemning the trusts, Bryan also attacked the escalating concentration of wealth, and pledged to take the side of the beleaguered working man seeking a fair share of the fruits of the new economy. The election was no less than a contest of "plutocracy against democracy," a conflict between "the dollar and the man." The Democratic platform pledged to repeal court injunctions against labor organizing, and to seek fair arbitration of disputes. A labor department would be established at cabinet level.[20]

This meant that whatever flaws Bryan and the Democratic party of 1900 had, they were pledged to confront three of the nation's most critical issues —which made the election one with a great deal at stake and profound long-term consequences.

This was well understood by the man who would, as he had had four years earlier, mastermind the Republican offensive in 1900—Marcus Alonzo Hanna.

Hanna's enterprises included coal and iron ore mines, foundries and smelt-ers, transportation networks, a Cleveland streetcar system, and a newspaper. He was also U.S. senator from Ohio and William McKinley's special friend. Sixty-three years old in 1900, Hanna was in dubious health, severely rheu-matic, his face ashen white, leaning on a cane. Early in the year, citing ill-ness, and with relations between him and McKinley strained, he had declined to manage the Republican presidential campaign. But the president had urged him to reconsider and Hanna, who could never deny McKinley (whom he revered) anything, consented.[21]

Mark Hanna was one of the most reviled people in the country. Cartoons in Democratic, Populist, and Socialist newspapers portrayed him clad in dollar bills, a bloated monster drunk on power and trampling women and children. "Every man has his price and Hanna has the money," editorialized the *Nation*. "A campaign fund is all he asks; give him that and he will do all the rest." Yet Hanna was an American original, coming as close to the quintessential na-tional personality of his day as anyone. "A representative American" is what the always insightful William Allen White called him, "a walking breathing, living body of the American spirit."[22]

Hanna was a superb salesman in a country of salesmen, a consummate believer in an individual's powering his way to success. Like his country-men, he saw the world in black and white dualities. The best man at his wedding would later recall his having "a strong character, an awful force of character." Hanna was a brutally tough antagonist capable of using wads of money and thuggery to win elections, yet also a pragmatist who knew when to make compromises, a rough-hewn, laughing, swearing, generous man who loved Shakespeare and evening cards with friends and corned beef break-fasts and had a reputation for elegant entertaining in Washington.[23]

One of Hanna's political strengths was his acutely intuitive understand-ing of how profoundly citizens were attached to the American dream. In the midst of the mid-1990s depression, when other businessmen feared a revo-lution in the making, he had mocked their fears. "You're just a bunch of damned fools," he told them. Hanna, in fact, never trusted the narrow self-ishness of the business class he represented politically. He knew that in the absence of fairly general abundance and a respect for labor, capitalism could not be sustained, and as a businessman he tried to make that a mode of con-duct. "Well, boys, what is the trouble now?" he would greet delegations of employees coming into his Cleveland office.[24]

In July, when Mark Hanna entered the Republican National Convention in Philadephia's Continental Hall, the band played "Hail to the Chief." It was apropos. The convention had been designed by Hanna and associates as a well-organized, well-policed, business-like showpiece of party discipline and unity. Spontaneity was not on the agenda, and Hanna's orchestration of things extended to waving a palm leaf fan and a white handkerchief from the speakers platform to raise audience volume. The party's foremost orators were prominently displayed, McKinley unanimously renominated, and a platform approved stressing prosperity and promising that the peoples "brought under the American flag as a result of the Spanish war will enjoy such a degree of political liberty and material prosperity as they have never known before." To pacify concerns about the trusts, Hanna had even written a plank condemning "all conspiracies and combinations intended to restrict trade." What he had not anticipated, however, was the rapturous enthusiasm inspired by the presence of the governor of New York, sporting a provocative, wide-rimmed, cowboy-style black hat.[25]

The forty-two-year-old Theodore Roosevelt was the most exciting new personality in national politics, combining in one persona the Americas of the literary New York blueblood and the frontier cowboy. A charter member of the Imperial party and obsessed with fostering the cult of manliness and the "strenous life," he had resigned as assistant secretary of the navy at the outbreak of the war, organized the Rough Riders cavalry unit, and led them in a blood-curdling charge up a hill in eastern Cuba. San Juan Hill had caught the country's imagination and given him instant national celebrity.[26]

Narrowly elected governor of New York on his return, Roosevelt had for the past two years engaged in a complex political dance with that wily intriguer, Thomas "the Easy Boss" Platt, master of New York State's Republican Party. Roosevelt and Platt customarily met at the senator's suite on Sundays in the Fifth Avenue Hotel to negotiate over offices, patronage, and policy. "He wants to see his power secure against everyone," the governor wrote to a friend, and complained that Platt expected an obedience that he could not give. Ultimately, the Platt organization and its business allies such as the insurance industry, alarmed by Roosevelt's push for reforms, including a franchise tax on corporations, decided he had to be exiled from New York. McKinley's vice president having died in office, Platt led the effort to nominate Roosevelt at the convention.[27]

Realizing how ill-fitted by temperament he was for the office of vice president and thinking it a political dead end, Roosevelt was agonized by indecision. "The Vice Presidency has less and less attraction for me the more I think of it," he replied to friends who urged his candidacy. On their part, Hanna and McKinley were wary of the popular and impulsive Roosevelt, whom they did not regard as a "safe man," and preferred other running mates.[28]

At the convention, alarmed by the fervor for the New York governor,

Hanna extracted a Roosevelt pledge that he would make himself unavailable. It was too late. The draft-Roosevelt tide led by Republican state bosses like Platt and Quay and delegates from the West had too much momentum. Sensing the mood of the convention, the White House telephoned on June 17 to inform the reluctant Hanna that the "administration's close friend must not undertake to commit the adminstration to any candidate, it has no candidate. The convention must make the nomination." This aborted any last-ditch anti-Roosevelt effort. Roosevelt's nomination was an emotional high point in an otherwise deadly dull political affair. But a week later, still disturbed, Hanna sent the president a revealing message (whose fears eerily anticipated the September 1901 assasination that made Roosevelt president):

> Well it was a nice little scrap at Philadelphia, not exactly to my liking with my hands tied. However, we came out of it in good shape and the ticket is all right. Your *duty* to the country is to live for *four* years from next March.[29]

Roosevelt, for his part, was determined to minimize the friction with the "Ohio gang" and make every effort to promote the ticket. "I want you to appear everywhere as the champion of the president," his close political confidant Henry Cabot Lodge advised. "Fortunately, his policies on the great questions are our own policies. He is doing admirably as I can see in all directions."[30]

Theodore Roosevelt's energies and enthusiasms were always outsized. But during the campaign of 1900 he was also driven by an eastern aristocrat's fierce loathing of Bryan ("the most infamous scoundrel in America today," he told an English friend) and all he represented. The Bryan Democrats were, he wrote other correspondents, "traitors to the country"; they "stand for lawlessness, and disorder, for dishonesty and dishonor." Informing Hanna that "I wish in this campaign to do whatever you think wise and advisible. . . . I am as strong as a bull-moose and you can use me to the limit," Roosevelt vowed to carry the GOP message to the country. Raspy-voiced, flashing his teeth, and making a fist to make a point, he lashed Bryan across 20,000 miles and twenty-four states, rousing the curious, friendly audiences who came to see him.[31]

The Democratic Party convention opened in the sweltering heat of the hottest Kansas City July in recorded history. Into this wide open town whose ragtime saloons, gambling halls, and brothels were the stuff of legend came Bryan delegates, riding in from the plains on trains and covered wagons. They were fully in control from the beginning, and the convention platform, such as the call for "an unceasing warfare against private monopoly in any form," directly culled from Bryan's speeches and ideas. Something of the cult of personality reigned and mere mention of the Bryan name evoked

166

hysterical cheering on the convention floor and the frenetic waving of thousands of U.S. flags.[32]

But there was serious opposition to including a free-silver plank in the platform, especially from eastern Democrats. Bryan himself understood that the mining of new sources of gold and recent economic expansion had reduced the saliency of the silver issue, and had received considerable advice from prominent Democrats to jettison it. But he had spent years uniting all the silverites behind him and was loath politically and psychologically to abandon his most fervent supporters. There was also the matter of principle; silver, to him, was a "righteous cause," the symbol of the "producer classes" he was fighting for. He wanted to run on the *entire* Democratic platform of '96. So Bryan not only refused, but virtually blackmailed the convention by telephone from his Nebraska home into (very narrowly) adopting free silver once again.[33]

To win in 1900, Bryan had to carry the states he had won in '96, while capturing key swing states like Indiana and New York from McKinley. Free silver made this especially tough. The free-silver plank badly alienated some voters favorably disposed to the Democratic stance on trusts and monopolies. It revived the old specter of economic anarchy under a Bryan presidency. Once again, the silver demon had left Bryan vulnerable to Republican attack. Which is why one-eyed Ben Tillman, reading the platform to the convention, strode up and down the rostrum shouting that imperialism was "paramount," until his audience began gyrating in a wild, bellowing demonstration.[34]

On the "Bryan Special" to Indianapolis in early August to receive formal notification of the nomination, Bryan was accorded a tumultuous welcome at every train station en route. Standing before a densely packed 40,000 people in Military Park, slightly flushed but calm, in his trademark black sack coat and white necktie, he spoke for an hour, his powerful voice reaching the farthest reaches of the crowd. Bryan was at his political peak, and testing the impact of his campaign themes on his audience.

Imperialism and the trusts were clearly primary. "We insist that liberty is not the gift of human government, but is the gift of God himself," Bryan told his audience, and there were loud cheers when he said: "Tell them you are not willing to trade one American boy for the trade of the Orient." He insisted that the "eight or ten million Asiatics, so different from us in race and history" could not be integrated. If elected, he would call Congress into special session and establish "a stable form of government in the Philippines," give the country independence, and "protect" them "while they work out their destiny." The United States must influence the world through moral and political suasion, not military means.[35]

Denouncing monopoly, Bryan challenged the Republican party "to meet us on the trust question." He charged that the concentration of wealth among the upper classes stemmed from the exploitation of farmers and workers:

> No one has the right to expect from society more than a fair compensation for the service which he renders to society. If he secures more, it is at the expense of someone else.[36]

Bryan spent the first six weeks of the campaign consolidating his base in Nebraska and making some speeches in Ohio and Illinois. However, by early autumn, he realized the necessity for an all-out campaign in the key states of the Midwest and East, and launched a typically frenzied Bryanesque offensive.

Unlike 1896, many Republicans found it difficult to take the Bryan threat seriously. That summer, affluent Americans were filling up the hotels in London's Westminster area, visiting the Paris Exposition, watering at Dieppe, and attending the New York Yacht competition and national tennis championships at Newport. The Republican National Committee struggled to overcome apathy and to whip up the enthusiasm of the bankers, railroad moguls, and manufacturers who were McKinley's big financial donors. Hanna played up the dangers of Bryanism, and, opening the New York headquarters, announced: "We have all got the hardest kind of work before us." There *was* some genuine anxiety about key voting blocs such as the anti-imperialist Irish and Germans transferring their allegiance to Bryan. Would voters blame administration policy for the trust boom? McKinley, in accepting the Republican nomination on his porch in Canton, was careful to declare that trusts were "dangerous conspiracies against the public good" and laws were needed. To charges of fostering empire, speakers like Roosevelt retorted that expansionism was simply "duty and destiny."[37]

The Grand Old Party retained critical advantages. The funds that eventually poured in from corporate donors (amounting to $5 million, or ten times Democratic monies) were used to spread the word about an administration that had given Americans back the "full dinner pail." An army of speakers, pointing to high prices for cotton, wheat, hogs, beef, and tobacco, and industry running at near capacity, emphasized the risk of tampering with prosperity. Elihu Root, the secretary of war, in a major campaign speech, boasted of the accessibility of the American dream "to every boy who thumbs his primer in the common school."[38]

What the Republicans did most effectively was to bash Bryan. They focused attention on his pro-silver policies and twisted his statement favoring an amendment to the constitution giving "Congress a power to destroy every trust in the country" into the intent to destroy *all* business. The ferociously negative political campaigns of the 1990s had nothing on the election of 1900.[39]

But the potent Republican claims of "prosperity at home and prestige abroad" were suddenly challenged that summer and fall by unexpected events. The first occurred in a China ruled by a decrepit Manchu dynasty unable to protect the country from humiliation by Westerners intent on carving out spheres of influence. The Russians were encroaching on Manchuria, the French on southern China, the British were in the Yangtze Valley. But it was in German-dominated Shantung, where the foreign intrusion was disrupting traditional society, that a cult wearing red ribbons and claiming magical protection, known as Fists of Righteous Harmony (Boxers), had begun attacking Christian missionaries and other foreigners. Queried as to what he was fighting for (by a *St. Louis Globe Democrat* reporter), one Boxer, Wong Ta, replied, "Partly because we hate you. Partly because the foreign devils have stolen so much of our country."[40]

Throughout the early months of 1900, the Boxers were expanding the scope and intensity of their activities across northern China while receiving covert support from the court in Peking. In March, U.S. Ambassador Edwin H. Conger was advising Washington that serious trouble lay ahead. By late May, a U.S. Marine detachment was sent to help the legation in Peking in case of trouble. Within a month, foreigners were fleeing to the legations for protection, and on June 16 a siege began with heavily armed Boxers nightly attacking the foreigners and Chinese encamped in the British legation.[41]

At the end of June, word of the siege reached Washington. A telegram from Conger to McKinley conveyed the urgency: "For one month we have been besieged in British legation. Quick relief only can prevent massacre." In comparison to the hysterical spirit of revenge unleashed in Berlin and other capitals, McKinley, determined the United States should continue to occupy the high moral ground it had assumed in the Hay "Open Door" Notes of the previous year, adopted a low-key moderate approach. The Americans were also wary of the Japanese and Russians using the crisis to grab Chinese territory.

Two thousand soldiers and Marines from the Philippines were dispatched to join a 25,000–man international relief force marching ninety miles across a ruined landscape from Tientsin to Peking. Despite colossal blundering and internal conflict, this expedition finally relieved the foreign settlements in early August. Throughout the crisis, Washington remained calm, although the president returned to the White House on August 2 in order to monitor the situation. With the Boxers defeated, U.S. troops paraded through the gate of the Forbidden Palace. Meanwhile, McKinley continued to insist that Chinese independence be respected, and, fearing the outbreak of war between the allies themselves over spoils, speedily disengaged.[42]

The relief expedition was popular with an American public riveted on the fate of the missionaries and legations. Its success and U.S. magnanimity toward the Chinese added to the credibility of McKinley's globalism. Having supported the relief of Peking, Bryan was unable to exploit the situation politically, while, in campaign speeches, Teddy Roosevelt drew parallels between the bloodthirsty Boxers and the Filipino resistance. Only occasional public voices like that of clergyman Henry C. Potter cut through the maze of self-congratulation to ask why it was any "surprise" that "the Chinese should hate Americans, who having shut the American door in their faces, have now turned around to force open the Chinese doors."[43]

Throughout the election campaign numerous strikes and workplace stoppages erupted as Minnesota wood workers, building trades workers in Chicago and Philadelphia, Cincinnati iron workers and plumbers all walked off the job. The most violent strike occurred in St. Louis, where 3,300 trolley conductors and motormen demanded the establishment of a union shop and grievance and arbitration procedures. Newspaper headlines nationwide screamed of mob rule in the city as fourteen people were killed and seventy wounded, strikers shot, female trolley riders attacked and stripped of their clothes, scabs hauled off of trolleys, and cars dynamited. Ultimately the mayor deputized and armed several thousand middle-class citizens to police the streets.[44]

No workers were more discontent than the anthracite miners of eastern Pennsylvania, whose grievances extended from wages ($2.50–$3.50 for digging nine tons of coal per day) to the exhorbitant cost of powder supplied by the mining companies. In a massive and surprising show of solidarity, in early September, 140,000 miners, both native born and immigrant, struck under the leadership of the boyish twenty-nine-year-old United Mine Workers President John Mitchell, a veteran of recent strikes in soft coal country. Demands were for a slate of changes including a 20 percent increase in wages. Strike leaders preached ethnic solidarity and nonviolence, and neither shootings by sheriffs nor destitution broke the strikers' spirit. The coal companies, intent on maintaining absolute control over the mines, simply refused to negotiate. The strike dragged on into October threatening to cause coal shortages in the cities and raise prices in northern cities. Worse from a Republican point of view, images of ragged, hungry mine families in their shanties mocked the much-ballyhooed "full dinner pail." Bryan, meanwhile, cognizant of industrial workers' grievances, was campaigning vigorously for their votes. In a Labor Day speech in Chicago, he denounced "government by injunction" and assured the unions that as president he would not put down strikes.[45]

Conscious of the dangers, Mark Hanna interceded, cajoling the mine owners, and finally utilizing the formidable powers of J.P. Morgan to pressure them into an agreement. The president was informed, "I am working hard in this strike matter and don't want to leave for a moment until I acomplish something or fail." A settlement was cobbled together giving the miners a 10 percent increase, but leaving other issues unresolved. On October 29, a week before the election, the workers went back into the mines. A tenuous agreement (soon to be sabotaged by the mine owners), it nonetheless was a victory for worker solidarity over ethnic division and a premonition of the industrial unionism of the 1930s.[46]

Bryan took his campaign into frenetic gear in October and the last five and a half weeks before the election would see him travel 16,000 miles making countless speeches in the course of grueling 13– to 16–hour days. While he continued to emphasize the dangers to liberties at home of denying the Filipinos constitutional rights and governing them as subjects, the trusts and corporate wealth and power had clearly become his primary focus: Big business, he said, would "close the door of opportunity against young men" and make them supplicants for jobs. Bryan pledged that as president he would curb trusts by vigorously enforcing existing laws and proposing new ones. Monopoly corporations would be denied federal licenses to do interstate business, and their products lose tariff protections.[47]

The appreciative audiences were there. Miners and factory workers laid down their tools and showed up en masse when Bryan arrived in the neighborhood. The rural crossroads and small towns still belonged to him. But observers noted that the rousing enthusiasm and electric excitement of 1896 had diminished. The crowds seemed more interested in Bryan the national celebrity and the country's most famous voice than his issues. Neither free silver, nor anti-imperialism, nor the trusts, generated a great response.[48]

What Bryan needed to build was a broad-tented coalition of farmers, labor, ethnic groups and northern blacks akin to what Franklin Roosevelt would construct the New Deal around three decades later. But his issues divided his constituencies. Gold Democrats disliked the free-silver plank and Bryan's talk of class. Silverites were put off by his anti-imperialism. And fears of Bryan's silver policies undermined his hopes of utilizing the support of Carl Schurz and major German newspapers to detach the key Midwest German voting bloc from the Republicans.

Likewise, Bryan's approaches to northern black voters disenchanted by McKinley had some success, but were largely sabotaged by his identification as the candidate of the party of the white supremacist South and the prominence of people like Ben Tillman in his campaign. Moreover, Bryan refused to address the racial crisis, deflecting questions about disenfranchisement of southern blacks by talking about injustices in the Philippines.[49]

Then there were the costly gaffes. Tammany boss Richard Croker, under challenge in New York City and needful of national Democratic support, warmed to Bryan as the campaign progressed. He even called the Nebraskan "one of the greatest men America has produced." Bryan, in turn, desperate for the votes Croker's machine controlled in the contest to capture New York State, seized upon him as an ally. In October, when Bryan made a campaign appearance in New York City, Tammany provided a lavish reception. During an October 13 speech at Cooper Union, the grateful Bryan impulsively held his hand over Croker's head and intoned, "Great is Tammany and Croker is its prophet." It was an action that discredited him among some of the political independents he needed in his corner.[50]

As the campaign ran down, the sheer Republican advantage in organization and money began to tell. Having been abandoned by their own major financial angels (for example, financier August Belmont), the Democrats had no funds for speakers and little for literature at a time when the country was awash with pamphlets, posters, and newspaper supplements featuring McKinley and his platform. Republicans such as Secretary of the Treasury Lyman Gage skillfully manipulated public fears about free silver.[51]

One of the most effective administration stump speakers turned out to be none other than Mark Hanna, who made a four-state speaking tour giving eighty-two speeches. On October 16, Hanna's two-train contingent had left Chicago and proceeded north to Madison, Wisconsin, where he predicted that Bryan would destroy prosperity by removing tariffs. At Mankato, Minnesota, Hanna further developed his theme that a Bryan presidency spelled disaster:

> I prophesize that if Mr. Bryan should be elected we will have within thirty days the worst panic, the worst depression of prices we have ever known in this country and we won't get over it in ten years.[52]

As the trip progressed, it became obvious that Mark Hanna was a tremendous attraction, if only because of his notoriety. Even Populists and Democrats came out to see the hated "Dollar Mark." But Hanna's rough and direct, folksy speaking style struck a chord everywhere he went. At a train stop, he would lean over the rail of his car and ask the crowd, "What has Bryan done for the workingman?," hesitate a moment, and say, "Confidentially, now, not a damned thing." Then he would hold up a fifty-cent silver coin to illustrate what would happen to the dollar in a Bryan presidency. Crowds liked the way he replied to hecklers and his indignant denials that he was a "labor crusher." Hanna showed flashes of humor and humility: "I am the engineer of the Republican party," he said, posing with the engineer of his train. "You are the engineer of this train. I run the party and you run me."[53]

In South Dakota and Nebraska, where large crowds greeted Hanna amid fireworks and torchlight parades (there was even a well-attended meeting in the opera house at Bryan's home town of Lincoln), he warned that Bryan wanted to destroy business in general and his presidency would paralyze the economy.

Exhausted by the end of the tour, his hands swollen, Hanna had scored a personal triumph. Folk in the hinterland had recognized in this earthy businessman-politician one of them, only the Success Ethic writ big, a personification of their beloved American dream. All four states wound up in the McKinley column in November.

During the early fall, there were some Republican anxieties. McKinley confided to his secretary that even if he lost the election, he would leave sufficient forces in the Philippines so that Bryan could not easily withdraw. But around mid-October reports began filtering into Republican National Committee headquarters that toss-up states like West Virginia and Kansas were moving strongly toward McKinley. Hanna noted that "just now a tidal wave is sweeping in our favor," while one committee official predicted "that the bottom will drop out of the Bryan camp." Wall Street betting odds reached 4:1 and 5:1 for McKinley with few takers. Returning from his trip, Hanna wired Theodore Roosevelt congratulations on Roosevelt's own western campaign swing, adding, "I feel the time for anxiety has passed."[54]

William Jennings Bryan never (at least publicly) lost his optimism, and insisted until the end that working people had not been fooled by talk of the "full dinner pail." Nonetheless, to many Americans, the beaming, stolid, optimistic McKinley, the man with the pink carnation in his buttonhole, seemed reassuring and competent in a way that Bryan was not. At least one ex-Populist advised a friend, "Common sense will compel us to vote for Republican gold in preference to Democratic agitation and hard times. Everybody is employed now." Ultimately, neither an Asian war nor the dangers of empire really alienated the American people from McKinley. "In my judgment," acknowledged Elwood S. Corser, Bryan's campaign manager, sadly, "we have failed to awaken the lethargic American conscience."[55]

The last week of the campaign saw Bryan in an orgy of nonstop speechmaking before huge crowds in Denver and Chicago, while Republicans 1896 déjà vu did their best to generate fears of a business depression following hard on a Bryan victory. Business contracts were signed on the proviso that Bryan be defeated. On election night, a large, cheery crowd gathered at Manhattan's Herald Square as pictures of McKinley were illuminated on the wall of a building. Before midnight, Bryan, at home in Lincoln with his family, realized that he had lost again; the popular vote eventually being 7,207,923 votes to 6,358,135. Outside the South, Bryan had won only four western states, losing even Nebraska. In the wake of the victory and the largest plurality in thirty years, Republican spokesmen and the conservative media claimed a clear mandate to govern for McKinley, who boasted that he was "now president of the whole people."[56]

But against overwhelming odds, Bryan had made a quite respectable showing. Indeed, McKinley's share of the popular vote had only increased 1 percent over 1896. Moreover, on Bryan's left, the socialist Eugene Debs—running on a Social Democratic Party platform supporting workers' control over industry, national labor laws, women's suffrage, public works for the unemployed, and drawing hugely enthusiastic crowds among coal miners and railroad workers—had garnered 97,000 votes. White women and the great majority of people of color were unable to vote, but a substantial number of those who could had reservations about the Republican party–American business project for the new century.[57]

In a post-mortem on the election, Bryan would attribute his defeat to Republican money, the victorious war, and "better times." He also cited "the fear of change." Indeed, all were critical factors. McKinley and Bryan had in 1900 presented two varying approaches to delivering up a not terribly dissimilar American dream. But the economic, territorial, and psychic expansion of the years between 1897 and 1900, the technological and consumer breakthroughs, had fortified public confidence in the Republican–business design for organizing society, and rendered Bryan's ideas archaic. The values of the corporate state had become the nation's.[58]

Bryan, the candidate, proved something of a liability to his cause. Despite his progressive, vanguard positions in many areas of public policy, he remained very much a man of the mid-nineteenth century, trying to revive an American order based on a vanishing economy and communities. As the promoter of an archaic American dream Jeffersonian style, he was prisoner of an idealized past that could not hope to triumph against those riding the crest of a dynamic, pulsating American future—which meant that at the end of the day, Bryan could not offer a compelling alternative narrative to McKinley's version of deliverance, could not persuade the American people that their Constitution and institutions were at risk.[59]

Bryan's real chance had been four years earlier in the midst of what one historian has called "the strange democratic interlude" of the nineties. By 1900, the world had changed and his time had already passed. The election of 1896, called by Walter Dean Burnham "a fundamental turning point in the course of American electoral politics," marked one of the really decisive political shifts in U.S. history. A "critical realignment" of national and local political forces had occurred: Bryan's call for economic reform and corporate accountability had driven the horrified business and professional classes north of the Mason-Dixon line into the Republican party, putting formerly competitive states like Pennsylvania firmly in the Republican column and tilting presidential elections and congressional power to the GOP.[60]

The election of 1900 sealed what had been done in 1896. The tone of American politics had been set until 1932. Republicans would dominate national politics: the Democrats, the great cities and the South. The ongoing debate about the country's future was settled in favor of the financial/industrial elites and their allies. The poor, the lower, working classes, and racial minorities would nearly cease to be represented at all. Big Business would be shielded from public control, ideology and issues replaced by interest group politics. Corporate capitalism, individualism, and the American dream had been soldered together, one and inseparable.[61]

On the day following the 1900 election, William McKinley received a telegram from a thoroughly exhausted Mark Hanna: "The continued confidence of the American people as expressed at the polls yesterday is a tribute to your personality and matchless administration." But Elizabeth Bury Gamble, writing to The *Nation* from Detroit, saw it quite differently. "The result of the last election," she wrote, "was exactly what might have been expected in an age in which greed constitutes the motive force in human action."[62]

Business was ecstatic about the election results: "With financial interests on a sound basis," said John D. Rockefeller, "the next few years ought to accomplish much for the American people." Stock prices on Wall Street immediately boomed. The party celebrating the close of the year at the New York Stock Exchange featured music by the Seventh Regiment Band and a wildly applauded four-round boxing match between two black boxers, Young Walcott and Sam Boland (dressed as bear and bull), as ragments of paper poured down.[63]

McKinley's December message to Congress was careful to make the distinction between "useful" and evil trusts. Convinced that industrial combinations could now continue without fear of government interference, investment bankers and merger lawyers moved aggressively. Rumors that Andrew Carnegie might diversify into finished steel production and Rockefeller make a massive foray into steel were causing J.P. Morgan deep anxiety about the fate of his own steel interests. In December, he began making overtures to Carnegie about buying him out in order to form what a few months later became the world's first billion-dollar company: the United States Steel Corporation. On New Year's Day 1901, an equally momentous event occured: The Spindletop well near Beaumont, Texas, hit oil and gushed

100,000 barrels a day before being capped. The era of plentiful, cheap oil had arrived.[64]

The McKinley victory was promoted by Republicans as something it was not, a positive mandate for imperialism to continue. The president's reelection became the signal for an all-out attack on Filipino resistance fighters already demoralized by the failure of Bryan's campaign. Pressure on various war fronts was intensified, and Aguinaldo was captured early in 1901.

It was a soldiers' war awash with bountiful promotions of junior officers and, in the words of Secretary Root, "characterized by humanity and kindness to the prisoner and noncombatant." In reality, the U.S. had adopted a scorched earth-depopulation policy: The troops of Brigadier General Jacob Smith were under orders to turn Samar into a "howling wilderness," while General Franklin Bell, in Batangas, forced villagers into concentration camps, burnt crops, and turned areas outside U.S. control into free-fire zones. Torture and summary executions were followed by legal exonerations of officers indicted for crimes. News reports about these atrocities (the *Philadelphia Ledger* editorializing: "Our men have killed to exterminate men, women and children.") caused a brief, useless congressional inquiry. Ultimately, between 200,000 and 600,000 Filipinos died in the war. In 1902, as President Theodore Roosevelt was officially declaring the fighting ended, George Hoar rebuked him on the Senate floor for the huge sacrifice of lives and treasure. "We cannot get rid of this one fact . . . ," Hoar said. "You chose war instead of peace." But by then the war was over and the Philippines no longer a political issue.[65]

Of course, the unanswerable question is what William Jennings Bryan might have achieved as president to alter the trendlines of American history. Radicals like John Peter Altgeld and Henry Demarest Lloyd supported Bryan in 1900 because they believed a Bryan presidency could lead to the reform and democratization of the fundamental structures of capitalism. One suspects, however, that, given the circumstances, his accomplishments would have been minimal. Conservative forces held virtually every other bastion of power in the country. Confronted by a hostile Congress and press and the power of business to paralyze the economy, Bryan would have been either forced into accommodation (and thus discredited among his own supporters) or quickly isolated.

Yet the campaign of 1900 deserves some honor. Bryan was really the last American presidential candidate who in the name of ordinary folks and great principles, would really challenge the power of corporate elites to shape the country. Ultimately, his fight was to control and democratize the onrushing capitalist revolution, something clearly understood by Marcus Alonzo Hanna, who rallied a New Jersey campaign audience, with the lines, "the fate of Bryanism is in the balance. If it is killed now, it is killed forever."[66]

Epilogue
Back to the Future: 1900 and 2000

How many of these victories over material things benefit all Americans; and how many benefit one or a few at the expense of all the rest?

—Charles Johnston, 1900

The Negro comes to us from yesterday's wrong and he generates beings who are carrying into tomorrow the birthmarks of to-day's evils.

—Simon Patten, *The New Basis of Civilization*, 1900

The United States is about to enter the 21st century much the same way it left the 19th century; with a two-class society—a nation of "have mores" and "have lesses."

—Donald L. Bartlett and James B. Steele, *Who Stole the Dream*, 1996

Free markets have clear dangers and limits.

—Bishop William Skylstad, 1996

The America of 2000 first became distinctly visible a century ago. Of course, nobody back then could really imagine what the country would be like a hundred years hence. The still primitive automobile gave no hint that it would one day reconstruct both the American landscape and dating mores, the monumental role of radio and television, airplanes, the microchip, and so on, in transforming the daily lives of the nation's citizens had yet to be revealed. Nonetheless, the *trendlines* were there to see in the revolutionizing of productive processes, transportation, communications, and corporate organization, the defining of virtually everything in purely market terms. Americans, then as now, looked to economic growth through technological innovation as the great, unquestioned panacea for all national ills, economic and otherwise.

In the voracious Christmas shoppers of 1900 or 1901 crowding the aisles at Macy's and Jordan Marsh, and the flourishing new advertising industry and mail order houses, we see the harbinger of the coming age of American consumerism—defined by one journalist in 1998 as "the right to pursue happiness by getting and spending faster than any other civilization in the history of the planet." Likewise, in the the gaggle of female fans waiting outside the theater stage door when the matinee idol Henry Montague was playing, or the manner in which newspapers and magazines worshipfully followed the travels of the magnate William Vanderbilt, we glimpse the making of a "rich and famous" celebrity culture.[1]

The popularity of amusement parks like Coney Island and summer vacations to the mountains and abroad prefigured the present-day theme parks and preoccupation with leisure "fun" and travel. And don't we see antecedents of the Super Bowl, "March Madness," and the annual major league home run derby in the hysteria that swept Pittsburgh and Brooklyn during the final stretch of the torrid 1900 National League baseball race (game reports receiving more newspaper print than the Boxer rebellion).

In business and politics, the continuities between 1900 and 2000 are also striking. Recent mergers between such behemoths as America Online–Time Warner, Mobil–Exxon, Chrysler–Daimler Benz and Viacom–CBS and the globalization of production and markets mark the latest stage in a process only taking off in the 1890s. We can speculate that Marcus Alonzo Hanna, grand maestro of the McKinley for President political campaigns, would find today's lavishly financed, supermedia-hyped political extravaganzas and the quid pro quo of business dollars for political protection quite congenial. One imagines him being deeply impressed by the intense professionalization of political party managers and consultants and the astronomical funds (i.e., George W. Bush's pot of $70 million *in advance* of the start of the 2000 presidential campaign) and space-age technologies available to them to promote candidates.

Even the medicated regime many Americans live under today has its foundations in the earlier era: Aspirin was first marketed in 1900 to deal with increasingly stressful work and noisy city environments. And contemporary suburban complaints about long commutes and absentee fathers began to be heard a century ago when the construction of inter-city trolley lines led to newly developed white-collar suburbs.

The gift of a century of hindsight also allows us to understand that the revolution occurring in America circa 1900 was at the vanguard of a global socioeconomic upheaval that would gather force throughout the twentieth century: Washington political insider Charles Conant was already hailing the rise of a "world market" in which it was "possible to transfer goods at small cost from the place of production to the remote corners of the world." What was being incubated in the United States—a consumer culture predicated on new forms of production, delivery of goods, and mass markets— would by 2000 have achieved global dimensions.[2]

But nothing is inevitable. While the transformations of the twentieth century have been capital and technology driven, the element of human *agency* has been critical. The policies that Americans circa 1900 were choosing, consciously, or by default, became powerful and complex legacies *setting the tone for how the nation would develop throughout the century.* Here we return to the trio of core questions with which this study began. The first:

How should the nation address the logic of markets in concentrating increasing wealth and economic power in the corporate elites and big business, while marginalizing vast numbers of working and poor people? In brief, could the society be democratized to provide opportunity for the majority of Americans?

The Americans of 1900 never really came to grips with this one. Since the vested interests of local and national elites lay in maintaining the social status quo, ingenious mechanisms were developed for keeping such a dangerous question off the national political agenda. Ultimately, perhaps the most potent weapon possessed by the upper classes was the ability to sustain the hegemony of an ideology built around the American dream. Good dream believers that they were, most Americans continued to have faith in the possibilities of abundance in "God's country."

Those citizens who wanted to mobilize political constitutencies to confront elite power and democratize society, namely, Bryanites, socialists, and Populists, remained divided and fragmented, suffered repression, and were mostly ineffectual. Meanwhile, the sheer force and rapidity of change, the disconnect of the present from the past, and the frightening lack of precedents to go by, encouraged passivity. As H.G. Wells commented at the time, "The plain fact is that in the face of the tearing situation of today America does not know what to do." The forces of reform that were successful, most

notably the Progressives, were content to affirm existing dreams and hierarchies. Filling the vacuum and hyping confidence in the future was the new
cornucopia of consumer goods and entertainments. "Markets can take care
of themselves as long as they take care of us" sums up the guiding orthodoxy
both in 1900 and 2000.[3]

Consequently, restrictions would not be placed on the wealth and economic power that individuals and families might accumulate and exercise.
The lack of government intervention around 1900 to either dismantle or effectively regulate corporate oligopolies meant that as their indispensability
to satisfying American dreams grew, they would become untouchable. Markets and private compartments would be allowed to continue to allocate rewards. The Rockefellers, Mellons, Morgans, and Harrimans, or rather the
professional managers who increasingly ran the corporations they had
founded, continued secure in their control, joined over the years by newcomers riding the crest of lucrative new industries.

The parameters for future policy had been set. Apart from some showy,
but superficial, federal antitrust activity during the presidencies of the two
Roosevelts, Wilson, and Taft, large corporations would be permitted to
dominate industrial and financial life. Politics continued to be mainly the
domain of private interests. Business administrations rolled back public con-
trols. Both world wars strengthened the role of big capitals in the U.S.
economy and superbly positioned them to take advantage of the post–1945
economic boom.

Spurred by new technologies, the quest for global reach and greater economies of scale, the late 1990s became a decade of corporate combinations.
The "merger boom" year of 1996 witnessed 10,000 deals worth $650 bil-
lion. Showcased among the 12,086 mergers and acquisitions in 1998, the
first trillion-dollar ($1.6 trillion) merger year, were the joining of Mobil and
Exxon, Bell Atlantic and GTE, and Nations Bank and the Bank of America.
Industries as varied as airlines, pharmaceuticals, banking, automobiles, the
media, and meatpacking have become more concentrated. The year 2000
began with a series of monster mergers headlined by the $166 billion America
Online–Time Warner combination[4]

The Great Depression of the 1930s and World War II had hugely expanded
the federal government's responsibilities in maintaining social and economic
peace and equilibrium, guaranteeing corporate profitability and U.S. global
leadership. A modest welfare state and a limited apparatus to regulate corporate activities had been carved out. The acute contradictions generated by
performance of these roles within the context of a business culture limited
governmental effectiveness and made Washington the fall guy when the postwar economic miracle gave way to a series of harsh recessions and eco-

nomic shocks between 1973 and 1992. Strident business/neoconservative "free market" forces emerged to demand a diminished "mixed economy" and curtailing of federal regulation of business. This discourse found powerful bipartisan support in a Congress increasingly in thrall to corporate dollars. Presidents from Ronald Reagan, whose policy of tax reduction and military buildup saddled the federal government with vast new debts, to "New Democrat" President Bill Clinton (gleefully announcing "the end of big government") gladly collaborated. The effectiveness of federal regulatory agencies was allowed to wither, and rules preventing companies from dominating local media markets were overturned. American healthcare was virtually handed over to insurance companies and health maintenance organizations.

The lack of federal vigilance or meaningful debate about the boundary between public and private interests is resulting in the monopolization by giants like Microsoft and Dell of the knowledge frontier: "From medical research to software design, entrepreneurs are trying to significantly tighten their control over knowledge to create new monopolies." Vital intellectual resources are now being commandered in much the same way Rockefeller once controlled petroleum supplies, and Carnegie, iron ore.[5]

Between 1980 and 2000, thanks to a new corporate reward structure, along with the slashing of top federal income tax rates and windfall profits from the huge stock price inflation, the wealthiest American families experienced exceptionally strong after-tax growth in income and wealth. Not only did the rich and super rich capture the lion's share of economic growth, but they were ingesting what formerly belonged to those below. "U.S. wealth concentration in 1989," argued economics professor Edward Wolff, "was more extreme than that of any time since 1929." During the nineties, the trend continued: Between 1988 and 1993, the top one-fifth of households increased their share of total household income by about 2 percent. America's top-earning 5 percent of families now have more income than the bottom 40 percent. The richest 1 percent of the population (or 2.5 million people) own over 40 percent of total national wealth. The 2.7 million highest-earning households have as much income as the bottom $100 million—Microsoft's Bill Gates's fortune alone (nearly $85 billion dollars in 1999) surpasses the combined holdings of tens of millions of Americans.[6]

The land that enshrined that legendary being, the millionaire, as a demigod, has considerably more of them now than ever before. These days, of course, having really big money means billions, the United States boasting more billion-plus fortunes than any other two countries combined. Old-line families have been surpassed by upstart entrepreneurs such as Microsoft's Gates and Paul Allen, the Waltons of Walmart, speculators Warren Buffet, Carl Icahn, and Ronald Perlman, newcomers who cashed in on the monies to be made in techonological breakthroughs, financial manipulations, the inflation of stock securities, and new services.

The "bitch goddess success" damned by William James a century ago still reigns unchallenged. It is still what one can get away with that separates the "big winners" from everybody else. Forced into bankruptcy by a series of illegal deals, the celebrated Wall Street house of Drexel-Burnham-Lambert lavished $350 million on its top executives. Junk bond king Michael Milken emerged from prison as one of America's wealthiest men, got a cool $50 million for mediating the sale of Turner Broadcasting to Time Warner, and became a major player in the booming private education business. Huge fortunes are instantaneous. Take the newly minted Internet billionaires, or Jim Jannard, founder of sunglasses maker Oakley Inc., whose net worth zoomed to $750 million when his company went public.

In what is reminicent of the 1900 era, people dependent on paychecks are getting less and less of the American pie compared to those who draw dividends and investments. The rewards of the productivity revolution flow upward. At the top of the corporate and legal hierarchies, "compensation," given the tendency of companies to award top executives millions in annual stock options, tends towards the astronomical: Disney's Michael Eisner leading the 1998 sweepstakes with $589 million. Differentials within companies have escalated wildly. In 1980 the typical major corporation CEO was making 42 times the wages of the average factory worker. Eighteen years later, the figure was *419* times.[7] The United States now has the severest income inequality in the industrialized world.

Affluence extends well beyond the super rich to others within those top 20 percent of households controlling over 80 percent of the nation's personal wealth. Included here are the upper managers, management analysts, architects, physicians, lawyers, and engineers whose incomes have remained buoyant and who have prospered mightily with the upsurge in stocks and the value of technology-based businesses. Adjusted gross incomes above $200,000 are sharply up on federal tax returns reports. Since skills have become synonymous with education, returns on educational investments are greater than ever. Some college men and women able to parlay educations, personal connections, and resources into lucrative professional careers have done especially well. Good Americans dreamers, folks like these increasingly tend to build castle-like structures behind guarded gates and walls. As former labor secretary Robert Reich puts it, they have "pooled their resources for the exclusive benefit of themselves."

At the beginning of the twentieth century, most Americans hovered around or below the poverty line. By the century's end, economic growth, unions, and political struggles to create a welfare state had lifted the great majority to a considerably higher material plateau. Americans in the middle of the income structure now routinely have houses, automobilies, televisions, CD players, VCRs, and microwaves.

Yet, economic and psychic security have always been elusive, and the same capitalist revolution that has been recently throwing up so many millionaires and billionaires has been causing trauma for the those at the bottom and middle rungs of the income hierarchy. Commentators as diverse as political columnist Kevin Philips and former Secretary of Labor Robert Reich agree that "different people seem to be living in different economies." Which economy a person lives in often depends upon how insulated one is from the ongoing revolution in capital markets, structures, and technologies.

A wide spectrum of Americans clearly are not insulated. Not only have the bottom 60 percent of households been losing economic ground relative to the top 40 percent, but the lowest one-fifth of families, the "others" of 2000, were experiencing (until the late nineties boom) an absolute erosion in income. One of five children is in poverty. The so-called "middle Americans," the historically stable working and lower-middle classes occupying the next two-fifths, have been income stagnant or gained only marginally. Indeed, median family incomes (even given the massive entrance of women into the labor force) have hardly budged since 1973. Despite the productivity bonanza and tighter labor markets of 1995–2000, working-class incomes have barely recovered the losses of the early nineties, those without college educations being especially hard hit. Jobs are abundant, but not living wage ones. One critical factor here is the continuing stagnation (despite heroic efforts to reverse a long and steep decline) of trade union membership.[8]

So a vast number of Americans remain acutely vulnerable. What the abrupt rise in bankruptcies and foreclosures during the economic turmoil of the early nineties revealed was how fragile the finances of working lower middle-class people are. Any major change in life circumstances—loss of job, divorce, illness (since over 40 million Americans lack medical insurance) —becomes a possible scenario for a sudden descent into the economic abyss. In *Falling from Grace*, Katherine Newman concluded that "downward mobility has become a major feature of the economic landscape . . . as hundreds of thousands of middle-class families plunge down America's social ladder every year." Among these are white collars and professionals formerly sheltered from market storms. A substantial proportion of the workers laid off during the Reagan, Bush, and Clinton years have been forced into lower-skill, lower-paying employment.[9]

Insecurity is accentuated by the radical reconfiguration of the workplace generated by the merger mania and intense pressures from financial markets for high quarterly returns. Top executives, driven by balance sheets and revoutionary technologies, dare resist this imperative at their own peril—thus the managerial drive (bordering on the pathological) to reduce costs and raise profits. Minimalist corporate strategies are focused upon driving down costs of labor, production, and inventory to rock bottom. Headquarters staff and middle-management are slashed mercilessly, whole divisions erased, vital services outsourced from independent contractors.

All of this has made the workplace more hostile for workers. In 1900, the critics of monopoly and corporate bigness made dire predictions about the destruction of the autonomy and independence of the American worker. What is happening today largely confirms those fears. Corporate culture continues to prize hierarchy, subordination, and executive egomania. In the obsessive grab for ever greater "flexibility" and control, downsizings and "rightsizings" become routine. Millions have been riffed, the survivors shaken by uncertainty and encumbered by increased workloads.

"Human capital" strategies, rather than being directed at liberation and creativity, are used to enhance management control and worker discipline. A whole slew of new office and shop-floor technologies—electronic surveillance systems, computer chips in name badges, and searches of voice mail and computer files—have been developed as much to control workers as for efficiency. Other new technologies such as laptops, faxes, and mobile phones, bind the worker more tightly to the workplace, even during free time. Numerous employee polls reveal declining job satisfaction, feelings of lack of self-expression and isolation, and the stress of hypercompetitiveness. Veteran workers, cognizant of the threat posed to their jobs by younger (and cheaper) workers, feel shaky. Younger workers see career ladders and the opportunity for creativity disappearing and feel betrayed by their employers. Across the country there is massive employee cynicism and a definite lack of trust.[10]

Thus the paradox: In the midst of the "Goldilocks" high-growth, low inflation/low unemployment economy with which the United States entered 2000 were tens of millions of citizens who fear a future in which they can no longer protect themselves, or their children, economically, physically, or emotionally. Reasonable opportunity and meritocracy seem artifacts of the past. A recent Pew Research Center survey, *America Past, Present, Future,* found widespread fears of rising healthcare costs making decent healthcare inaccessible. After a comprehensive study of labor conditions, two *Philadelphia Inquirer* writers concluded:

> . . . 100 million Americans, mostly blue-collar, white collar and professional, are being treated as expendable. The American Dream . . . has been revoked.[11]

There are places where the worlds of 1900 and 2000 fuse. One is in Silicon Valley, whose ten top executives pulled in $422 million in 1998, while $10–an-hour gardners, nannies, and laborers take care of their children and estates. "We see unprecedented prosperity, millionaires being minted on the hour," remarks a spokesman from the local labor council. "But on the other hand we see hundreds of thousands of people simply being left behind." Here, as in 1900, there is the stark divide between those who control revolutionary technologies and others who do not. There is the scene at Manhattan's Madison Avenue and Thirty-sixth Street, where an elderly woman in a porkpie hat and sneakers begs for coins across from the J. Pierpont Morgan Library, a peerless collection of paintings by Rembrandt and Seurat, Mesopotamian tables and Mozart's handwritten scores put together by the legendary "Jupiter."[12]

The second question:

Would Americans accept and draw strength from what they really were— a great experiment in ethnic/racial diversity—and create pluralistic ideas and institutions—or hunker down and seek to remain a "White Man's Country"?

The United States in 2000 would seem to have broken with its horrific past as a White Man's Country. For one thing, because of immigration, the country has more color than ever before, the Latino and Asian populations growing more quickly than any other. California, to take our most important state, is predicted to have a nonwhite majority by 2020. While Asian entrepreneurs in Silicon Valley are being hailed as epitomes of the "model minority," Latinos have become established political-power centers in south Florida and the Southwest. Something of a Native American resurgence has occurred around the financial resources provided by gaming casinos. There now exists a huge black professional middle-class occupying a range of positions undreamed of in Booker T. Washington's time, a Black Congressional Caucus numbering forty members watches over black interests, and the current American pantheon of celebrities includes Michael Jordan, Colin Powell, and Oprah Winfrey.

This seems a far cry indeed from 1900 when white Americans were opting by vote, rope, gun, or mainly by passive silence to maintain the United States as a racial dictatorship in which they were dominant and the economic, political, and cultural opportunities of Native Americans, Asians, and Hispanics were strictly curtailed. Yet, despite these dramatic changes, the failure during the late nineteenth century to incorporate people of color into

"We the People" continues to impact them in ways that resonate powerfully unto 2000. If prejudice and discrimination, a myriad of glass ceilings in education and the workplace, still exist to limit Latino and Asian chances, it is black Americans, because of both their numbers and their historic relationship to whites, who still bear the greatest burdens of the years of racial dictatorship.

The failure to incorporate African-Americans as equal citizens put them radically at risk in an industrialized, mechanized new century. Standing in 1900, their long-term prospects for achieving parity in U.S. society were dismal. Just one-half of southern blacks were literate; only half of black young people between the ages of ten and fourteen were attending school. In Georgia, 200,000 black children had no schools, and 100,000 were in school for a few weeks a year. Those schools often lacked blackboards or desks and had classes averaging sixty students or more per teacher. Assuming that "Negro education is a failure," the southern trend was to upgrade white schools by taking tax dollars from black ones. A dual white/black educational trajectory was cemented: Of those born in 1900, whites would have over double the rate of black high school graduation. The dearth of nonmenial jobs for high school and college graduates further acted to discourage black education.[13]

Meanwhile, the black family circa 1900 was coming under intense economic and social pressures as men wandered the South looking for employment and women became the major breadwinners. One Georgia white woman thought that the "Negroes need . . . fathers and mothers, homes, they are a fatherless, motherless, homeless race." This problem invariably was attributed to a combination of faulty genes and culture. The connection between family disintegration and racial and labor market discrimination almost never was made.[14]

Oppression in the South and the attractiveness of the North and West would ignite a vast black migration starting in earnest around World War I. A rural southern population would become primarily urban and northern. But racial traditions of discrimination and segregation remained dominant in the North, too, and the "Promised Land" often proved illusory. The persistence of racial ideology and structures made it terribly difficult for blacks to enter mainstream American life even well after World War II.

The civil rights revolution, beginning in the 1950s and culminating during the mid-1960s, saw stupendous victories and the overthrow of officially sanctioned white supremacy. There was access to the vote and political office for those long excluded. Black workers moved into both stable industrial jobs and the professional-managerial-technical ranks;

women left domestic service for clerical and professional work. Through the mid-1970s, black middle-class growth was strong and theories of race "convergence" popular.

But in 2000, it is clear that the grand transformations which the civil rights revolution aimed to achieve remain terribly incomplete. In retrospect, what has occurred is a *partial* victory for equality. Although racial attitudes and meanings have definitely shifted from what they were fifty or one hundred years ago, race (as Michael Omi and Howard Winant adroitly observe) continues to be "a fundamental organizing principal" of our society.[15]

White identity is still linked to differences with the "other." Negative and abusive stereotypes remain deeply infused into the rituals, language, humor, and habits of everyday life. The "tragic limitation of the white racial imagination" so apparent in the 1900 era is still much in evidence. If the bulk of white Americans have, in the wake of civil rights, readjusted their racial lenses, if denial of the full humanity and citizenship of people of color is no longer part of mainstream culture, then denial about the consequences of the nation's historical legacy of race continues to be a fact of American life— thus the dominant racial discourse of our time, which reduces black disadvantage to the problems of any American *ethnic group* bootstrapping it up the ladder.[16]

A presidential commission on race reporting in September 1998 concluded that whites do not understand how they benefit from "white privilege." As in 1900, a rapidly transformed economy and society are undermining the traditional sources of white male identity and self-esteem, and placing social roles, economic skills, and "manhood" on the line. White backlash (although taking more subtle forms than in 1900) is driven by a complex interweave of economic interest, identity crisis, and lack of viable channels of expression. It flows out of traditional stereotypes and animositites toward minorities, threatened grassroots American dreams, and economic structures fostering intergroup competition. Defensive ethnicity and claims to the status of a victimized "minority" are logical responses as whites lay their difficulties to the "advantages" Americans of color allegedly possess. Affirmative action policies thus become the inevitable battlegrounds in school and job sites across the country.[17]

And just as racism circa 1900 was manipulated by Democratic politicos of the ilk of Tillman and Vardaman, the "New Racism" has been massaged by such Republican stalwarts as Ronald Reagan, Jesse Helms, Trent Lott, and the Bushes, whose attraction for southern working-class whites demonstrate the continuing sway of race over class as the "important line of conflict in American politics." Racial scapegoating and the "southern strategy" were crucial to GOP domination of the presidency between 1980 and 1992 and congressional control afterward, and have critically affected the shape of national social welfare policy.[18]

Meanwhile, despite the dominant national mythology of a "level playing field" existing for all, black Americans remain severely disadvantaged by historical processes, contemporary market dynamics, and a resilient, highly flexible racism mutating into new forms. The dual labor market of the 1900 era remains alive and well. At most levels, black and white workers have different entry ports into the economy, and different pay and promotion possibilities. The late entry of blacks into the industrial sector made them especially vulnerable to the economic recessions and massive corporate economic restructuring of the seventies and eighties. The shrinking of smokestack America meant diminished economic opportunity for young people who were either displaced or never hired. Central-city black youth entered labor markets just as manufacturing was giving way to information processing and business services. In the face of auomation and export of work to suburbs or abroad, inadequate job networks, a lack of good schooling and skills, they have become dependent upon low-wage service jobs, or else simply superfluous.[19]

Thus, we find a black social class structure sharply splintered into a professional middle-class/stable working-class group and the others. Urban poverty among African-Americans remains deeply rooted. Desperate to get some "paper" and the respect it buys, young street-wise blacks have fabricated a drug/criminal culture parodying the corporate culture outside. Studying Philadelphia street youth, sociologist Elijah Anderson notes: "There's also a sense in which the opportunity to be anything but the way they are is not there." The fact that a quarter of young black males are in the coils of the legal justice system (half of the 1.2 million inmates of U.S. prisons are black) recalls black newspaper editor T. Thomas Fortune's 1900 comment, "It is vastly cheaper to build school houses than to build jails." The astronomical homicide rate for young black males is one of a number of reasons black men live, on average, seven years less than white men.[20]

Single parenthood and poverty have become a way of life for vast numbers of women and their children. A look at black unemployment, poverty, single parenthood, and infant mortality shows that perhaps 40 percent of the black population remain at or near the bottom of the American economic structure. While this is a distinct improvement on the 90–plus percent of 1900, it is still abysmal.

The workplace remains racially contested terrain. Middle-class blacks see the continued resilience of workplace discrimination as a source of frustration and despair. Notwithstanding lip service to "diversity," traditional stereotypes often remain dominant. The 1995 Glass Ceiling Commission Report found stereotyping and prejudice rife in corporate life. School and residential integration have stagnated and majorities of whites and blacks (and Latinos) live in virtual isolation. Nowhere is this separation clearer than in the nation's capital with its two-thirds black population: Affluent and heavily white Northwest Washington exists worlds away from the broken, violent black neighborhoods across Rock Creek Park. Anacostia, located east of the Potomac, resembles an American urban "war zone."

Experiencing the United States as two separate and unequal societies, African-Americans have adopted their own stance of "defensive ethnicity." Large majorities agree that "America owes us a better chance," view white Americans as uninterested in dialogue on racial inequality, and see the United States moving toward a separate and unequal society. The same identity politics that speaks to the powerful alienation of whites speaks to blacks also. Integration has always taken a psychic toll, and now, across the spectrum of black society, there is increased cynicism about the entire project, a cynicism reinforced by routine harassments and hate crimes emanating from what researchers Jack Levin and Jack McDevitt call "the growing culture of hate."[21]

Separatism, once a tactic in the struggle for integration, has emerged as an end in itself. "It's a black thing. You wouldn't understand" read T-shirts worn by black college students choosing to segregate themselves. The percentage of blacks approving of interracial marriage has declined. Paranoia easily floats into this vortex of distrust. A Rashomon-like racial chasm is apparent in the radically differing takes that blacks and whites have on events such as the O.J. Simpson trial verdicts and the Million Man March.

These days, of course, balkanization extends far beyond the black/white split into intraminority struggles for jobs, political power, and so on. It is as prevalent in municipal police forces as in high school lunchrooms. The Los Angeles upheaval of 1992 and ferocious political/economic struggles in cities like Dallas, Miami, New York, and Houston illustrate a crazy-quilt pattern of antagonisms and distrust between blacks, Asians, and Latinos. Much of this derives from the acute black perception that newcomers to America—even people of color—will always be accorded more favorable life chances than they themselves.

In 1900, white Americans, lacking the vision, courage, and moral resources to accord citizens of color an equal place within the nation, chose to retain racial dictatorship to control and limit them. In 2000, these official structures of racism may have been dismantled, and we appear at least superficially to have accepted the notion that as a society everyone should be accorded equality. Yet, diversity remains highly suspect and the legacy of the past is present

189

in our stereotypes, our mutual distrust, and in the structures of inequality and repression that remain intact from another era.

This is highlighted in incidents such as the 1999 execution-like killing of unarmed West Indian immigrant Amadou Diallo at the hands of New York City police. The reaction of one citizen to the Diallo incident—"There's no way a young black man can live in this city and not have a run-in with the police"—recalls the lament of black New Yorkers during the long hot summer of 1900. In February 2000, the acquital of the four police officers involved in the killing left blacks angry and convinced that a double standard of justice still prevailed. "He was black and they decided to have some target practice," commented a retired merchant seaman. Meanwhile, the individual and societal changes that need to be made are stalled. In this chasm between promise and reality lies great peril for the future.[22]

The third question:

How was the nation to fulfill its new role as a world power and balance its moral and economic objectives abroad?

"America is on the tongue of everybody you meet," wrote the Rev. F.B. Henson, pastor of the First Baptist Church of Chicago, when he returned from Europe in the fall of 1900. "All seem to realize that the United States is destined to become the nation of the world." Certainly, few Americans, in the aftermath of the war with Spain, had doubts about this. To the spanking new role of world power, they brought the assumptions and myths one might expect of a nation that deemed itself "the city on the hill." The messianic "Americanize the globe" spirit of Albert Beveridge, Josiah Strong, and Teddy Roosevelt fused together the belief in a special Anglo-Saxon destiny with the objective of locating vigorous new psychic and economic frontiers overseas. In brief, the United States was to become benevolent leader and mentor to other nations, the "indispensable" nation.[23]

So Americans came to world power harboring a "strategic innocence" about their own innate benevolence and the universality of American-style democracy, freedom, and dreams. Even Roosevelt, Root, Hanna, and Lodge, cynical masters of realpolitik though they were, fervently believed in a community of interests linking the United States and those foreigners whom it touched. This legitimized the incorporation of Hawaii, Puerto Rico, and Guam, the cramming of the Platt Amendment down Cuban gullets, and the genocidal suppression of the Filipino war for independence. That the majority of Hawaiians, Cubans, or Filipinos might pass on the opportunity to become an appendage of the North American colossus merely affirmed their unfitness for self-rule.

American policy-makers never denied the element of self-interest: In bestowing salvation upon the world, the nation might also locate the resources to guarantee economic abundance and prevent the country from imploding upon itself. This would allow the United States to escape the fate of other great civilizations that had exhausted their frontiers, and decayed and disintegrated—and also evade (as historian William A. Williams has suggested) confronting its own internal contradictions and dysfunctions.

So attention would be paid to organizing the twentieth century to suit American needs and tastes. The globalistic stance the nation had begun assuming around 1900 was curiously similar to the one it would still be maintaining a century later. The first order was to keep the world open and safe for global capitalism and United States trade and investments. The second involved keeping the lid on social movements for self-determination that might threaten its prerogatives and system stability. In a dangerous world, the nation's military had to be ready to fight wars on several fronts simultaneously.[24]

After World War II, when the United States bestrode the world stage like a colossus and "internationalism" was the official mantra, this was translated into reorganizing a new global economy along dollar lines and (in the name of anticommunism) constructing a national security state of unprecedented dimensions. There was support for an array of dictator-led client governments, and sponsorship of coups and counterinsurgency in countries like Iran, Guatemala, Indonesia, Chile, and Nicaragua. During the sixties, United States policy-makers, convinced that they could intervene massively and with impunity in the Third World, would be drawn into a disastrous war in Indo-China.

Some historians have argued that a fairly direct line runs between the decisions American policy-makers made in 1900: for example, the suppression of the Filipino independence movement, and what subsequently happened in Korea, Vietnam, and so on. Thus, the Philippines emerges as a model for American intervention and domination in Asia-Pacific, and Cuba in Latin America. Historical realities, however, tend to be less linear and more messy; on-the-spot options and decisons are never as inevitable as they appear in hindsight. What appears more likely is that the triumph of the party of expansion and empire circa 1900 set the United States on a *general course* toward the diplomatic and military roles it plays today, and has provided the historical foundation for projecting direct American power throughout the globe.[25]

Where the direct legacy of 1900 foreign policy can be seen most clearly today is in the evolution of the Spanish colonies commandeered by the United States in the wake of the "splendid little war." The McKinley adminstration's decision to transform Cuba into a de facto colony unleashed forces that ultimately brought Fidel Castro and the Cuban Communist Party to power, resulting in a forty-year United States economic and political offensive against the island. In October 1962, a crisis over the implantation of Soviet missiles on the island nearly led to nuclear war. And in the post-Castro era to come, we may expect the relationship of Cuba and the United States to be deeply affected by the neocolonial past. Then, there is Cuba's near neighbor, Puerto Rico, that remains designated as a United States "commonwealth," a kind of political limbo that leaves its quest for "political dignity" unfulfilled. Puerto Ricans find themselves conflicted in terms of cultural identity and paralyzed politically by internal conflicts over future status. Unemployment, poverty, and welfare dependency are at epidemic levels. The legacy of the decision to colonize the Philippines is a high degree of continuing American political, economic, and cultural influence, which, decades after official independence, still inhibits full Filipino sovereignty and national identity. The dictator Ferdinand Marcos governed in intimate partnership with Washington until ousted in 1986 and spent his last years in Hawaiian exile. And in Hawaii itself, when "reconciliation" talks between federal officials and native Hawaiians were held in December 1999, native Hawaiian speakers demanded "restoration" of the Hawaiian nation.[26]

Immigrants from neocolonies will quite naturally gravitate to the mother country. By 2000, a massive inflow of refugee Cubans had transformed southern Florida's demographics, culture, and politics; large Puerto Rican communities were established in New York, New Jersey, Chicago, and other areas, while Filipino-Americans constitute one of the most rapidly growing communities in the United States.

Between 1899 and 1902, the movement opposing United States expansionism initiated a critical debate about the uses and proper objectives of American military power overseas. Defeat of Bryan and then the Filipinos squashed that dialogue and it has appeared only fitfully (usually to be monopolized by elite foreign policy circles) ever since. During the 1947–1989 Cold War, such a debate was closed off by anticommunist hysteria. Following the collapse of the Soviet Union, it was regarded as superfluous.

Meanwhile, as the century ended, in the skies above Iraq, Serbia, and the Sudan, the United States was, like an old-time Hollywood gunfighter, shooting first and asking questions later. Ultimate policy objectives remained ambiguous at best, and there was no real public debate on where and how the United States should use its awesome military power, or what was realistic in terms of security. Meanwhile the use of that power (even behind the mask of NATO) was alienating Russia and China and preparing the psychological ground for future conflicts. U.S. policy toward both allies and "rogue states" remains muddled. The dominant year 2000 spirit, at least in Congress and the Pentagon, was to seal North America off from the chaos of the world by means of antimissile shields and such, while preserving the American prerogative to strike "surgically" anyplace, anytime—a policy, incidentally, of which Theodore Roosevelt and friends would undoubtedly have approved.

William Jennings Bryan's 1900 warnings that empire would require a "large standing army" and "rapid growth of a military establishment" have proved prophetic. Over the last half-century, the Pentagon (and its budget) have become insulated from public dialogue or oversight. The highly professionalized American military (which Secretary of War Elihu Root had begun building in 1900–1901) has, in conjunction with an industrial establishment wedded to military contracts, become a state within a state. The military's hold on the national treasury ($270 billion in 1999) has scarcely diminished (the Soviet Union had barely collapsed when the security establishment was already locating new demons to be neutralized!), and a major increase in funding is planned with bipartisan political support for the 2000–2007 period. The opportunity costs of this are cited by the distinguished economist John Kennth Galbraith:

> The military power continues to control for its own purposes the resources that, if used for basic income support, job creation, and housing, and drug counseling, would ease the crisis in the inner cities.[27]

Ironically, the century-old American obsession with international security may not only constitute a major destabilizing force in the world today, but it may also be depriving the nation of the internal resources it needs to begin to resolve domestic issues of racism, poverty, and individual insecurity.

Sixty years ago, on the eve of the United States' entry into World War II, media tycoon Henry Luce declared the twentieth century to be the "American Century." Looking back from 2000, few people would contest this. The United States remains unique today—the sole global economic/military/cultural superpower.

Yet, the many celebrants of the "American Century" never get around to totaling up its costs to ourselves and others. Nor do they confront the century's *failures*: how critical areas of American life have stagnated and decayed. Our crucial decision-making processes seem as chaotic and unenlightened today as in 1900 and just as profoundly undemocratic. If anything, Americans feel *more* powerless and manipulated politically and have less democratic space than they did then. They seem more alienated from local communities and the larger world. There is a radical disconnect between glitzy new technologies and the mountain of material goods flooding our shelves and human well-being and spirit. Linkages between the world of today and that of the recent past (or near future) are broken. Life scripts seem obsolete. People find immense difficulty in making sense of the changes around them. This moral crisis is especially intense for young people: Witness the omnipresent shopping mall youth, the violence at places like Columbine High, and adolescent sex rings in Georgia suburbs.[28]

Ultimately, the great connecting rod and legacy of the 1900 era for us in 2000 is the flourishing American dream. It, too, has not escaped transformation, being less inner-directed than a century ago, and more oriented toward the notion that "the only rights that really matter are those that indulge the self." Yet, the dream remains, as always, an ethic grounded in anarchic individualism, dynamic enterprise, and compartmentalized realities, and the illusion that Americans control their own destinies. Which explains why observations from the 1900 era such as, "Nothing except the dollar is believed to be worthy of the attention of a serious man," or "Our national fantasy is that we can be whatever we want to be," and "These days we Americans are in the greatest haste to be rich of any people on earth" seem so utterly contemporary. Indeed, when Texas governor and presidential candidate George W. Bush in an October 1999 speech intoned, "And the purpose of our prosperity is to see to it that the Great American Dream touches every willing heart," he could have been taking a leaf from a William McKinley or Theodore Roosevelt speechbook.[29]

But in 2000, the existing American dream has become a barrier to understanding who we are and what we would be and to creating viable alternatives for the future. What does it have to tell us about how we can begin to confront the wrenching moral crises of our time, or how to act beyond our own narrow self-interests? What kind of deliverance can be expected from more "stuff" in the malls, or "virtual communities" operating in the hollowness of cyberspace?[30]

Historians tell us that every civilization must "prune" its excesses in order to survive and flourish. Pruning time in the United States may be long overdue for an American Dream that isolates us from each other and is increasingly out of sync with basic human needs. It is high time to ask what national ends are worth working toward, time to embrace a mythomoteur dipped in the best traditions of the American people, which takes devotion to place as a point of departure and provides new ideals and points of reference to sustain us.

If looking back at the world of 1900 teaches us anything, it is that the future is being constructed in the present moment. So we had best pay attention and attend to the potential long-term consequences of our actions right *now*. Because *history does matter*, and the crucial decisions we are making at the beginning of this new century will surely resonate down through 2100 and beyond. May we take to heart the words penned by an anonymous writer in June 1900:

> The time has come when we should pull ourselves together and see what can be done to redeem our age in the eyes of posterity, or what is even more important, to save posterity from the evil results of our own actions.[31]

Notes

Chapter 1

1. All of the above events are taken from newspapers of January 2, 1998, including *New York Times*, the *Houston Post*, the *Milwaukee Journal*, and the *Rocky Mountain Post*.

2. Weibe, *The Search for Order 1877–1920*, 105.

3. Kasson, *Amusing the Million; Coney Island at the Turn of the Century*, 6.

4. Turner, "The Problem of the West," 259–290.

5. Ibid.

6. Noble, *The End of American History*, 10–13.

7. Wrobel, *The End of American Exceptionalism*, 53–63. In an illuminating message Roosevelt wrote to a friend: "In strict confidence . . . I should welcome almost any war, for I think this country needs one." Roosevelt to Francis Greene, September 23, 1897 (Theodore Roosevelt Papers, Library of Congress).

8. Pollack, *The Populist Mind*, 161. See Argersinger, *The Limits of Agrarian Radicalism*; *Western Populism and American Politics*; and Goodwyn, *Democratic Promise; The Populist Movement in American History*.

9. Pollack, *The Populist Mind*, xi, 89, 201. In Pollack's words (xx): "They sought to build a society, in sum, where the individual fulfills himself not at the expense of others but as a social being, and in so doing attains a higher form of individuality."

10. Ibid., xix; Argersinger, *The Limits of Agrarian Radicalism*, 38–75.

11. Hoffman, *The Depression of the Nineties: An Economic History*, 262; Pollack, 330–342.

12. Grant, *Self-Help in the 1890s*, 10; Sproat, *The Best Men: Liberal Reformers in the Gilded Age*, 238.

13. Pollack, *The Populist Mind*, 342–347; LaFeber, *The New Empire: An Interpretation of American Expansionism 1860–1898*, 149; Marcus, *The Grand Old Party: Political Structure in the Gilded Age*, 256.

14. Trachtenberg, *The Incorporation of America: Culture and Society in the Gilded Age*, 25.

15. Higham, *Strangers in the Land Patterns of American Nativism*, 73–82.

16. Ibid., 103–105.

17. Hofstadter, "Manifest Destiny and the Philippines," 172–200.

18. Leech, *In the Days of McKinley*, 180; see Wrobel, *The End of American Exceptionalism*, chapter 1.

19. Schreiner, "The Woman Question" *Cosmopolitan*; Wrobel, *The End of American Exceptionalism*, 29–41.

20. Ziff, *The American 1890s: Life and Times of a Lost Generation*, 89; John Graham Brooks, in his 1908 book, *As Others See Us*, asked perceptively, "Is it because at heart the inhabitants of the States really doubt their greatness that they so clamorously insist upon it?"

21. Hough, "The West and Certain Literary Discourses"; Wrobel, *The End of American Exceptionalism*, 66.

22. *Harper's Weekly*, editor's note. Dewey's popularity was such that he was actively promoted for the presidency in 1900, until some of his public comments (e.g. "It is easy enough to be President, all you have to do, I see, is to take orders from Congress and I have been obeying orders all my life") made him something of a laughingstock.

23. Traxel, *1898: The Birth of the American Century*, xi.

Chapter 2

1. Weibe sums it up well in *The Search for Order*, 40; "In a time of confusion they responded with a quantitative ethic that became the hallmark of their crisis in values. Men defined issues by how much, how many, how far."

2. Chandler, *The Visible Hand: The Managerial Revolution in American Business*, 80, 212; Nelson, *Managers and Workers: Origins of the New Factory System in the United States, 1880–1920*, 11–33.

3. Ibid.

4. Ibid. and Trachtenberg, *The Incorporation of America*, 56.

5. "The Skyscrapers of New York City," *Collier's*; Baker, "The Modern Skyscraper."

6. Chandler, *The Visible Hand*, 498–500; Twelfth Census of the U.S. 1900.

7. Emory, "Our Commerical Expansion," 537; *Saturday Evening Post*, September 15, 1900; Hearings Before the U.S. Industrial Commission, Preliminary Report testimony of John W. Gates, 1900, 1015; Baker, "The Barometer of Business."

8. Emory, "Our Commercial Expansion"; *Seattle Post-Intelligencer*, January 2, 1900; Vanderlip, "Our New Prosperity," 422.

9. May, *Imperial Democracy: The Emergence of America as a Great Power*, 229; *Harper's Weekly*, April 21, 1900.

10. Chernow, *Titan: The Life of John D. Rockefeller Jr.*, 379: James Hill to D.S. Clamont, January 27, 1900. James Hill Papers, Library of Congress.

11. Baker, "The Barometer of Business" *Collier's*, December 1, 1900; Cande, "Oklahoma"; Baker, "The New Prosperity," 86.

12. *Seattle Post-Intelligencer*, December 30, 1899.

13. William McKinley's annual message to Congress, December 3, 1899; Photograph Archive, Warshaw collection, Smithsonian Institution; *Harper's Bazaar*, December 15, 1900.

14. Trachtenberg, *The Incorporation of America*, 131; Wright, "The Department Store in the East; Chandler, *The Visible Hand*, 289; Cross, *Time and Money: The Making of Consumer Culture*.

15. Lears, *The Culture of Consumption: Critical Essays in American History, 1880–1980*; Strasser, *Satisfaction Guaranteed*; xii–9.

16. *Harper's Weekly*, editor's note, July 1, 1899, December, 22, 1899; Lears, *The Culture of Consumption*, 16; Trachtenberg, *The Incorporation of America*, 131; Strasser, *Satisfaction Guaranteed*, 148. *Harper's Bazaar*, December 15, 1899.

17. *Oregonian*, July 25, 1899; *Lesley's Weekly*, November 3, 1899; Woodward, *The Origins of the New South*, 294.

18. Chandler, *The Visible Hand*, 229–235.

19. Hayden, *Redesigning the American Dream*, 17; Thompson, "Life in a Milltown"; *Lesley's Weekly*, November 3, 1899; *Harper's Weekly*, April 1900.

20. Kasson, *Amusing the Million*, 38–46.

21. Trachtenberg, *The Incorporation of America*, 123–128; *Police Gazette*, February 1900; Banner, *American Beauty*, 170–187.

22. Trachtenberg, *The Incorporation of America*, 165, 38; Polanyi, *The Great Transformation*, 249.

23. Armstrong, *Nations Before Nationalism*, 3. Armstrong explains: "The mythomoteur is what sustains a policy and enables it to create an identity beyond that which can be imposed by force or pushed by peace and prosperity."

Chapter 3

1. James Truslow Adams, who originated the term "American Dream," described it quite succinctly: "It is not a dream of motor cars and high wages merely, but a dream of a social order in which each man and each woman shall be able to attain to the fullest stature of which they are innately capable, and be recognized by others for what they are, regardless of the fortuitous circumstances of birth or position." Adams, *The Epic of America*.

2. Weibe, *The Search for Order.*

3. Bellah et al., *Habits of the Heart: Individualism and Commitment in American Life.*

4. de Tocqueville, *Democracy in America*, 35–142.

5. Wyllie, *The Self-Made Man in America*, 4.

6. Ibid, 12–136.

7. Lasch, *The Culture of Narcissism: American Life in an Age of Diminishing Expectations*, n.p.

8. Grant, *Self-Help in the 1890s*, 65–118.

9. Diner, *A Very Different Age: Americans of the Progressive Era*, 101.

10. Hamsun, *The Cultural Life of Modern America*, 19.

11. The most readable source for this process still remains Matthew Josephson, *The Robber Barons: The Great American Capitalists, 1861–1901.*

12. Wells, *The Future in America*, 116.

13. Conwell, *Acres of Diamonds*; Huber, *The American Idea of Success*, 55–61.

14. Huber, ibid., 124–180.

15. Mathews, "Men of Pluck," 388.

16. *Saturday Evening Post*, January 27, 1900, September 12, 1900, January 5, 1901.

17. *Lesley's Weekly*, September 1, 1900, Josephson, *The Robber Barons*, 78–91, 178, 191.

18. Keller and Davie, eds., *Essays of William Graham Sumner.*

19. Graves, "The College Man's Game," *Saturday Evening Post*, October 28, 1899.

20. Tebbel, *From Rags to Riches: Horatio Alger Jr. and the American Dream*, 8.

21. Wyllie, *The Self-Made Man*, 32, 145–146; Thernstrom in *Towards a New Past*, ed. Barton Bernstein, 266.

22. Thernstrom, *The Other Bostonians*; *Poverty and Progress in the American Metropolis, 1880–1970*, 99–124; *The Forum*, February 1900.

23. W.A. Clugston to Joseph Pew, September 26, 1900. Joseph Pew Papers. Located in Hagley Museum, Series #15.

24. *McClure's*, June 1900, 130–137; Adney, "The Summer Rush to Cape Nome."

25. McCullough, *Truman*, 74.

26. Banner, *Women in Modern America: A Brief History*, 1–15; Banner, *American Beauty*, 187.

27. London, "Housekeeping in the Klondike."

28. Wells, *The Future in America*, 61.

29. Trachtenberg, *The Incorporation of America*, 141. William James, with his usual insight and eloquence, remarked on "that American condition by which everybody remains outside everybody's sight . . . with one-half of our fellow countrymen . . . entirely blind to the significance of the lives of the other half."

30. *Saturday Evening Post* series on "Why Young Men Fail," October 1, 1899; October 28, 1899; November 18, 1899.

31. *Saturday Evening Post* series on "Why Young Men Fail," January 27, 1900; Brooks, *As Others See Us*, 53; Rugoff, *The Gilded Age: Intimate Portraits from an Era of Extravagance and Change*, 180–187; Banner, *Women in Modern America*, 24; Eidmann, "The Divorce Evil," 88.

32. Lewis, *The Culture of Inequality*.

33. Nally, "Why Young Men Fail"; Ogen, "Getting and Keeping a Business Position."

34. Beveridge, "The World and the Young Man."

35. *Saturday Evening Post*, February 15, 1900.

36. *Saturday Evening Post*, May 26, 1900.

37. Sumner, *What Social Classes Owe Each Other*, 46.

38. Kirkland, *Dream and Thought in the Business Community, 1860–1900*, 110–115.

39. Commager, ed., *Lester Ward and the Welfare State*.

40. Grever, ed., *Lester Frank Ward*, 24; Clark, *America's Gilded Age: An Eyewitness History*, 150.

41. Leech, *In the Days of McKinley*, 162.

42. Sproat, *The Best Men*, 145–155.

43. Wells, *The Future in America*, 61.

44. Harrison, "The New Rich Element in New York Society," 941.

45. Brooks, *The Conflict Between Private Monopoly and Good Citizenship*, 4.

46. *Harper's Weekly*, December 1899.

47. Flynt, "In the World of Graff."

48. An insightful analysis of Croker as Tammany overlord is William Allen White's "Croker" in *McClure's*, February 1901, 324.

49. Chernow, *Titan*, 153.

50. *The Nation*, February 8, 1900.

51. *The Sporting News*, March 24, 1900; Thatcher, "The Rise of Amateur Athletics in the Middle West."

52. Chapman. *Selected Writings of John Jay Chapman*, 243; Chapman, "Social Results of Commercialism" *New York Times*; Chapman, "Between Elections"; Chapman, *Causes and Consequences*.

53. Bremner, *From the Depths: The Discovery of Poverty*, 84; Painter, *Standing at Armageddon: The United States 1877–1919*, 101–105.

54. Johnston, "The American Psychic Atmosphere," 173.

Chapter 4

1. On social classes in nineteenth-century America, see Pessen, *Three Centuries of Social Mobility in America*, 59–189.

2. Josephson, *The Robber Barons*; Trachtenberg, *The Incorporation of America*, 100; Painter, *Standing at Armageddon Life in the United States, 1877–1919*, xvii; Spahr, *The Present Distribution of Wealth*, 53–69.

3. Flower, "A Pilgrimage and a Vision"; Kirkland, *Dream and Thought in the Business Community, 1860–1900*, 37.

4. Indeed, at least in some cities such as New York (estimated to have 100,000 paupers), the rate in the increase of paupers was outpacing that of the general population (Spahr, *The Present Distribution of Wealth*); Ziff, *The American 1890s*, 54.

5. Diner, *A Very Different Age*, 154.

6. *Saturday Evening Post*, October 7, 1900; Harrison, "Society Women in Business," 8.

7. Carnegie, "The Duty of the Men of Wealth."

8. Rugoff, *America's Gilded Age*, 62–80.

9. *New York Times*, December 3, 1899.

10. Harrison, "The New Rich Element in New York Society"; *Harper's Weekly*, September 29, 1900.

11. Rensselaer, "The Barons of New York Society."

12. *New York Times*, January 1 and December 3, 1899; Auchincloss, *The Vanderbilt Era: Profiles of a Gilded Age*; De Novo, *The Gilded Age and After*, 20; Beebe, *The Big Spenders*.

13. Veblen, *The Theory of the Leisure Class*. Lester Ward's remark about *The Theory*—''The trouble with this book is that it contains too much truth" (*American Journal of Sociology*, May 5, 1900, 829–873)—was on the mark.

14. *The Nation*, October 19, 26, 1899; *Munsey's*, April 1900; Karp, *History of the Jews in America*, 155; Higham, *Send These to Me: Jews and Other Immigrants in Urban America*, 148.

15. Davis, "Magnificent Newport," 473–475.

16. Banner, *American Beauty*, 260–269.

17. Josephson, *The Robber Barons*, 105–106; Schreiner, *Henry Clay Frick: The Gospel of Greed*, 32.

18. Stewart, "Club and Club Life in New York,"122; Sangster, "From a Woman's Viewpoint," 16.

19. Fox, *The Discovery of Abundance: Simon N. Patten and the Transformation of Social Theory*, 149. Patten, *The New Basis of Civilization*, 31.

20. Casson, "The Suicidal Methods of Trusts,"*Arena*.

21. John Graham Brooks (in *The Conflict Between Private Monopoly and Good Citizenship*) remarks: "We don't ask you how to succeed—enough you succeed."

22. Ramirez, *When Workers Fight Back: The Politics of Industrial Relations in the Progressive Era, 1898–1916*, 39.

23. *The Sporting News*, January 20, 1900.

24. Montgomery, *Workers Control in America: Studies in the History of Work, Technology, and Labor Struggles*, 4–7; Brooks, *The Social Unrest*, 184.

25. Nelson, *Managers and Workers*, 45; Tolman, "What More than Wages?" 258.

26. Chernow, *Titan*, n.p.

27. Nelson, *Managers and Workers*, 106–130.

28. Ibid.

29. Ibid.

30. Tolman, "What More than Wages?" 258.

31. Traxel, *A Very Different Age*, 44.

32. Ford, "The Vanderbilts and the Vanderbilt Millions"; Chernow, *Titan*, 336.

33. *Munsey's*, May 1900, 302; *Harper's Weekly*, October 13, 1900.

34. Davis, "Magnificent Newport."

35. Clark, *The Saturday Evening Post*, October 7, 1900, 252.

36. Ibid.

37. Lyman Gage to William Trotten, July 9, 1900, Gage Papers, Library of Congress; *Cosmopolitan*, July 1900.

38. Ely, *Monopolies and Trusts*, 137.

Chapter 5

1. Collier, *The Trust*, 115–119; Josephson, *The Robber Barons*, 375–403; Naomi Lamoreaux, *The Great Merger Movement in American Business 1895–1904*, 1–31.

2. Lamoureux, ibid.; Chandler, *The Visible Hand*, 265–288.

3. Nation, December 21, 1899.

4. Chandler, *The Visible Hand*, 190; Collier, *The Trust*, 7–15. Gould, *The Presidency of William McKinley*, 160–161; Lamoureaux, *The Great Merger Movement*, 87.

5. Collier, *The Trust*, 1–20.

6. Peck, *Twenty Years of the Republic: 1885–1905*, 138–141.

7. Gates' testimony before U.S. Industrial Commission, *Preliminary Report on Trust and Industrial Combinations*; Schreiner, Henry Clay Frick, 200.

8. Traxel, *A Very Different Age*.

9. Chandler, *The Visible Hand*, 285–314; Conant, "Recent Economic Tendencies."

10. U.S. Industrial Commission, *Preliminary Report*, 253.

11. Kirkland, *Business in the Gilded Age*, 25; Chandler, *The Visible Hand*, 285; Cook. *The Corporation Problem*.

12. Collier, *The Trust*, 16–32, 337; Dorfman, *The Economic Mind in American Civilization*, 215.

13. Clark, *The Problem of Monopoly*, 6.

14. Ibid.

15. Collier, *The Trust*, 15–50; Selz, "How Trusts Affect Trade."

16. Dowe's testimony is in the United States Industrial Commission Preliminary Report on Trusts, 1900, 26; Montgomery, *Workers Control in America*, 102. Jenks and Clark, *The Trust Problem*, 69.

17. Jenks and Clark, ibid., 139.

18. Traxel, *A Very Different Age*, 54

19. Miller, "The Trust Question: Its Development in America," 40–50.

20. McEwen, "The Trust as a Step in the March of Civilization"; Kipnis, *The American Socialist Movement, 1897–1902*, 63.

21. Reed, "Monopolies."

22. McEwen, "The Trust as a Step in the March of Civilization."

23. *U.S. Industrial Comission Preliminary Report on Trusts*, 129–132.

24. Ibid.

25. Reed, "Monopolies."

26. Collier, *The Trust*, 188.

27. U.S. Industrial Commission, *Preliminary Report*; Collier, *The Trust*, 188–190.

28. London, "The Class Struggle," *Independent*.

29. Ripley, "The Making of a Railroad Man"; Stuart M. Blumin, *The Emergence of the Middle Class Social Experience in the American City 1760–1900*, 295.

30. Chernow, *Titan*, 548; Miller, "The Trust Question,"*Arena*, January 1900.

31. John Jay Chapman had a typically insightful take on this "We have escaped an age of tyrants because the eyes of the bosses and their masters were fixed on money." *Selected Writings of John Jay Chapman*.

32. McChesney and Shughart, *A Statistical Study of Antitrust Enforcement*, 11.

33. Ely, *Monopolies and Trusts*, 271.

34. *Oregonian*, September 13, 1899; *Harper's Weekly*, October 1899.

35. *Oregonian*, ibid.

36. Hofstadter, *The Age of Reform: From Bryan to Franklin Delano Roosevelt;* see Painter, *Standing at Armaggedon*.

37. Collier, *The Trust*, 8; *Oregonian*, September 13, 1900.

38. Diner, *A Very Different Age*, 264.
39. *Saturday Evening Post*, October 14, 1899, 276.
40. Weibe, *The Search for Order 1877–1920*, 166–195; Hofstadter, *The Age of Reform*, 214–215.
41. Ely, *Monopolies and Trusts*, 260.
42. *Nation*, May 10 1900; Weibe, *The Search for Order*, 182–183.
43. *Seattle Post-Intelligencer*, January 3, 1900.
44. *New York Times*, December 4, 1899.

Chapter 6

1. Clark. *America's Gilded Age*, 94–96; *The Oregonian*, November 27, 1899.
2. *Saturday Evening Post*, January 27, 1900; Patten, *The New Basis of Civilization*, 70–96; Garanty, *The Transformation of American Society, 1870–90*.
3. Cohen, *Out of the Shadows: A Russian Jewish Girlhood on the Lower East Side*, 205.
4. *Forum*, April 1900, 446; Painter, *Standing at Armageddon*.
5. Patten, *The New Basis of Civilization*, 70–85; Robert Hunter, *Poverty*, 70; Dubnoff, "A Method of Estimating the Economic Welfare of American Families of Any Composition, 1860–1901," 137; Trachtenberg, *The Incorporation of America*, 90. The contemporary analyst Charles Spahr surmised that one-half the families in the country were "very poor" and another 38 percent "poor." Morton Keller, in *Affairs of State*, provides the figure of 60–88 percent for poverty.
6. Painter, *Standing at Armageddon*, xxii; Hunter, *Poverty*, 4; *Forum*, April 1900, 446. See Spargo, *Capitalist and Laborer, Modern Socialism*.
7. Clark, *America's Gilded Age*, 118; *Oregonian*, November 24, 1899; Patten, *The New Basis of Civilization*, 70; Hunter, *Poverty*, 54, 60–65; Trachtenberg, *The Incorporation of America*, 22.
8. Hunter, *Poverty*, 70–75; Spargo, *Americas Working People*; Brooks, *The Social Unrest*, 92.
9. *Arena*, September 1900, 239; Hunter, *Poverty*, 70–75.
10. *Oregonian*, July 27, 1899; Thompson, "Life in a Southern Mill Town," *Political Science Quarterly* (March 1900): 3.
11. David Montgomery, *Workers Control in America*, 34–60.
12. U.S. Industrial Commission on Agriculture and Agricultural Labor, *Report No. 10, 1901*, 69, 445.
13. *Saturday Evening Post*, September 11, 1900, and November 25, 1899.
14. *North American Review*, October 1900; *Saturday Evening Post*, September 15, 1900. Two thousand railroad men were killed in 1899 and 30,000 injured. Hunter, *Poverty*, 60–62, 190.
15. Hunter, 37, 60–62; Daniel Nelson, *Manager and Workers*; John Graham Brooks noted that "no civilized nation can match our hot pace and careless disregard of human life." (*The Social Unrest*, 215). Even comparatively well-paid skilled workers put in excruciatingly long hours. That railroad aristocrat, the engineer, made decent wages ($140–175 per month) but worked seventy-hour weeks, often without a day off.
16. *Saturday Evening Post*, April 28, 1900; Riis, "Reform by Human Touch," 745.
17. Brooks, *The Social Unrest*, 201–203; Hunter, *Poverty*, 37.
18. Ibid.
19. Garanty, *The Transformation of American Society*; Brooks, *The Social Unrest*, 215, Hunter, *Poverty*, 367–382.
20. *Harper's Bazaar*, August 11, 1900.
21. Banner, *Women in Modern America*, 62–95; Meredith, "The Feminine Factor," *Arena*, March 1900. Hunter, *Poverty*, 60–62.

22. John Spargo, *The Bitter Cry of the Children*. The 1900 census showed 1.7 million children working in agriculture, 44,000 in cottonmills, 24,000 in mines, 284,000 in manufacturing, 138,000 as servants and waiters.

23. Hunter, *Poverty*, 229.

24. DeGraffenreid, "Georgia Cracker and the Cotton Mill," 487–88; Hunter, *Poverty*, 229, 367.

25. Dreiser, *Sister Carrie*, 15.

26. "Women's Wages in Manual Work," *Political Science Quarterly* (November 1900); Hunter, *Poverty*, 203; Stewart, "Service Reform in Boston." Van Woodward, *The Origins of the New South*, 175–180; Cameron. *Laboring Women in Lawrence Massachussetts 1860–1912*, 99; Riis, "The Battle with the Slum," 626.

27. Spargo, *The Bitter Cry of the Children*; Hunter, *Poverty*, 257; Riis, "The Battle with the Slum"; *New York Times*, December 31, 1899.

28. *Harper's Bazaar*, September 8, 1900; Bremner, *From the Depths*, 3; Hunter, *Poverty*, 257.

29. Deforest and Veiller, eds., *The Tenement House Problem*.

30. Cohen, *Out of the Shadows*, 305.

31. Hunter, *Poverty*, 170–185.

32. Ibid, 148–185; Spargo, *The Bitter Cry of the Children*, 144–160.

33. Hunter, *Poverty*, 4; Brooks, *The Social Unrest*, 3–14; *Lesley's Weekly*, February 17, 1900; Clark, *America's Gilded Age*, 167.

34. Riis, "The Genesis of the Gang," *Oregonian*, August 3, 1899; Hunter, *Poverty*, 120–134, 191; *Harper's Weekly*, October 13, 1900.

35. Hunter, *Poverty*, 72.

36. Diner, *A Very Different Age*, 79; Ramirez, *When Workers Fight Back*, 91–124.

37. Diner, *A Very Different Age*, 72–169; Trachtenberg, *The Incorporation of America*. The slogan emblazoned on the walls of the Heinz Factory in Pittsburgh (rather ironic, in view of the prevailing burnout) was "Energy brings bread; indolence brings want."

38. Thernstrom, *The Other Bostonians*, 60–103.

39. Brooks, *The Social Unrest*, 188.

40. Moody and Kessler-Harris. *Perspectives of American Labor History: The Problem of Synthesis*; *New York Sun*, August 29, 1899; Foner, *History of the Labor Movement in the United States*.

41. *American Federationist*, December 1899; Foster, "Trade Unionism and Social Reform," 22.

42. Brooks, *The Social Unrest*, 188.

43. *Oregonian*, August 3, 1899.

44. *Harper's Weekly*, May 20, 1899; author's visit to musuems in the Wardner, Idaho, area; *American Federationist*, September 1899.

45. *Harper's Weekly*, July 1, 1899; *Oregonian*, July 27, and August 3, 1899.

46. Spahr, *America's Working People*, vii; Ramires, *When Workers Fight Back*, 9; Painter, *Standing at Armageddon*, 175; *Oregonian*, September 25, 1899; Trachtenberg, *The Incorporation of America*, 100.

47. Montgomery, *Workers Control in America*, 20; *American Federationist*, December 1899; Ramirez, *When Workers Fight Back*, 9.

48. Karson, *American Labor Unions and Politics, 1900–18*, 135.

49. Saxton, *Indispensable Enemy: Labor and the Anti-Chinese Movement in California*, 228; Wrobel, *American Exceptionalism*, 202; Moody and Kessler-Harris, *Perspectives of American Labor History*, 152; Ramirez, *When Workers Fight Back*, 91; Foner, *Organized Labor and the Black Worker 1619–1973*, 64–86; AFL, *Report of the Proceedings of the 20th Annual Convention of the American Federation of Labor*, 22–23; Karson, 137.

50. *American Federationist*, September 1899; Jentz, "Chicago's Furniture Industry and Its Work Force from 1880 to 1910," 292.

51. Foner, *History of the Labor Movement*, 400–405; *AFL, Report of the Proceedings of the 20th Annual Convention of the American Federation of Labor*, 12.

52. AFL, ibid. Philip Foner, *History of the Labor Movement in the United States*, 400–414; Montgomery, *Workers Control in America*, 48.

53. Ramirez, *When Workers Fight Back*, 94–104; Montgomery, *Workers Control in America*, 82.

Chapter 7

1. *Nation*, November 2, 1899, 332.

2. Lewis, *The Culture of Inequality*, 46.

3. Kovel, *White Racism*, 180.

4. Roediger, *Toward the Abolition of Whiteness*, 16.

5. Fredrickson, *The Black Image in the White Mind*, 18. James Baldwin put this in context in his 1963 book, *The Fire Next Time*. "White people in this country will have quite enough to do in learning how to accept and love themselves and each other. When they have achieved this, the Negro problem will no longer exist, for it will no longer be needed."

6. Riis, 153; Hunter, *Poverty*, 256–280; *U.S. Census 1900 Population*. volume 1.

7. Shelton, *Reformers in Search of Yesterday: Buffalo in the 1890s*, 15–20.

8. Higham, *Strangers in the Land*, 80–82, 103–108; W.J.H. Traynor, "Policy and Power of the American Protective Association," 666.

9. *Harper's Bazaar*, September 22, 1900; *Nation*, February 1, 1900; Beck, *The Case Against Immigration*, 243; Higham, *Strangers in the Land*, 112–115.

10. Ibid.; Higham and Beck, *Collier's*, December 1, 1900. See Saxton, *The Indispensable Enemy*.

11. Higham, *Strangers in the Land*, 40–43, 95–102; Higham, *Send These to Me*, 40–43.

12. Ibid., Higham, *Strangers in the Land*, 149; *Nation*, October 12, 1899.

13. *Nation*, October 12, 1899, and December 28, 1899.

14. DeKay, "Painting Racial Types," 169.

15. Higham, *Strangers in the Land*, 56; Wrobel, *The End of American Exceptionalism*, 192.

16. Roediger, *Towards the Abolition of Whiteness*, 186; Peck, *Twenty Years of the Republic 1885–1905*; Chan, *Peoples of Color in the American West*, 270–271, 329; Wrobel, *The End of American Exceptionalism*, 202–207.

17. Strong, *The New Era or the Coming Kingdom*, 79–80; Wrobel, *The End of American Exceptionalism*, 48, 76. Advocate for the poor Robert Hunter argued that immigration was causing a "low standard of American manhood."

18. Painter, *Standing at Armageddon*, xxii–xxxv.

19. Hunter, *Poverty*, 282. See O'Grady, *How the Irish Became American*; Painter, *Standing at Armageddon*, xxxv.

20. Theodore Roosevelt to Ernest Brunncken, June 28, 1900, Roosevelt Papers, Library of Congress.

21. Ringer, *'We the People' And Others: Duality and America's Treatment of its Racial Minorities*.

22. Cleghorn, "New Immigrants," 535.

23. Theodore Roosevelt to Mr. Strachey, January 27, 1900, Roosevelt Papers, Library of Congress; Dyer, *Theodore Roosevelt and the Idea of Race*, 17–19.

24. *Saturday Evening Post*, March 24, 1900.

25. McCullough, *Truman*, 89.

26. DeKay, "Painting Racial Types," 169.

27. Borden and Graham, *Speculations on American History*, 94; Fred Hoxie, *A Final Promise: The Campaign to Assimilate the Indians 1880–1920*, 1–15.

28. Hoxie, *A Final Promise*, 46–110.

29. Borden and Graham, *Speculations on American History*, 90–97.

30. *Rocky Mountain Daily News*, November 16, 1900.

31. Hoxie, *A Final Promise*, 12–20.

32. Frissell, "What Is the Relation of the Indian of the Present Decade to the Indian of the Future?"*Arena*, 470.

33. *Nation*, November 16, 1899, 310; Hoxie, *A Final Promise*, 150–154; *Harper's Weekly*, May 4 and November 18, 1899; Trachtenberg, *The Incorporation of America*, 34; Traxel, *A Very Different Age*, 239–244.

34. Ibid., *Nation*, November 16, 1899, 52–57; *Harper's Weekly*, November 18, 1899, 239–244.

35. *Nation*, May 10, 1900.

36. Traxel, *A Very Different Age*, 244.

37. Gardner, *The Image of the Chinese in the United States 1885–1915*, 45.

38. Saxton, *The Indispensable Enemy*; Cheng Tsu-Wu, "Chink," 146–7; Chan and Wong, *Claiming America: Constructing Chinese American Identity During the Exclusion Era*, 9, 57; Gardner, *The Image of the Chinese in the United States*, 175.

39. Lim, *The Chinese American Experience*, 31; Chan, *Peoples of Color*, 11–19; Diner, *A Very Different Era*, 101; Ten Broek, Barnhart, and Matson, Prejudice, *War and the Constitution*, 18–25; Gardner, *The Image of the Chinese in the United States*, 77.

40. Saxton, *The Indispensable Enemy*, 200–240; Gardner, *The Image of the Chinese in the United States*, 77, 149.

41. Ibid., 200–250; McWilliams, *Prejudice; Japanese Americans: Symbol of Racial Intolerance*, 14–21.

42. *Organized Labor*, March 10, 1900.

43. Diner, *A Very Different Age*, 101; Sinkler, *The Racial Attitudes of American Presidents from Abraham Lincoln to Theodore Roosevelt*, 289; *Harper's Bazaar*, October 13, 1900, 537.

44. McWilliams, *Prejudice; Japanese-Americans*, 16.

45. Girdner and Loftis, *The Great Betrayal: The Evacuation of the Japanese During World War II*, 33–53.

46. McWilliams, *Prejudice; Japanese-Americans*, 12–17; Daniels, *The Politics of Prejudice*, 21.

47. Ringer, *"We the People" and Others*, 686–690; McWilliams, *Prejudice Japanese-Americans*, 16–17.

Chapter 8

1. Newby, The Development of Segregationist Thought, 4; Newby, Jim Crow's Defense: Anti-Negro Thought in America, 1900–1930, 3–16; Williamson. The Crucible of Race: Black/White Relations in the American South Since Emancipation, 120–130; Fredrickson, *The Black Image in the White Mind*, 90–98; Shaler, "The Negro Since the Civil War," 149; Dyer, Theodore Roosevelt and the Idea of Race, 90.

2. Atkinson, "The Atlanta Exposition."

3. Fredrickson, *The Black Image in the White Mind*, 259; Bingham, *An Ex-Slaveholder's View of the Negro Question*.

4. Fredrickson, *The Black Image in the White Mind*, 272–278; Thomas, *The Ameri-*

can Negro, What He Was, What He Is, and What He May Become; Newby, *Jim Crow's Defense*; Carroll, *The Negro: A Beast or in the Image of God.*

5. *Twelfth Census of the U.S. 1900*, vol. 3, pt. 1, vital stats ix–x; Williamson, *The Crucible of Race*, 443.

6. Stratton, "Will Education Solve the Race Problem?" 786–794.

7. Woodward, Jim Crow, 79; Roediger, *Toward the Abolition of Whiteness.*

8. Dyer, *Theodore Roosevelt and the Idea of Race*; Newby, *The Development of Segregationist Thought*, 3–50.

9. Woodward, *The Origins of the New South*, 111–133; Ringer, *"We the People" and Others*, 209.

10. Ibid., 111.

11. Woodward, *The Strange Career of Jim Crow*, 45; Woodward, *Tom Watson: Agrarian Rebel*, 120–160, 220–239; Kirwan, *Revolt of the Rednecks: Mississippi Politics 1875–1925*, 47.

12. Woodward, *Tom Watson: Agrarian Rebel*, 120–160, 220–239; Woodward, *The Strange Career of Jim Crow*, 42–46; Woodward, *The Origins of the New South*, 249.

13. Woodward, *The Origins of the New South*, 249–356; Woodward, *The Burden of Southern History*, 141–159.

14. Spahr, *America's Working People*, 106.

15. Simkins, *Pitchfork Ben Tillman, South Carolinian*, 402.

16. Ringer, *"We the People" and Others*, 224.

17. *Seattle Post Intelligencer*, December 30, 1899.

18. *Harper's Weekly*, May 28, 1899; Dunning, *Essays on the Civil War and Reconstruction and Related Topics*, 250; Sproat, *Liberal Reformers in the Gilded Age*, 70.

19. *Saturday Evening Post*, February 3, 1900, 690–694; Williamson, *The Crucible of Race*, 320; Brown, *In the Golden Nineties*; Fredrickson, *The Black Image in the White Mind*, 86–95; Baker, *Following the Color Line*, 183–185.

20. William McKinley to Mark Hanna, February 26, 1895, William McKinley Papers, vol. 87, no. 89, Library of Congress; Gould *The Presidency of William McKinley*, 25–28; Sinkler, *The Racial Attitudes of American Presidents*, 47, 289; Morgan, *William McKinley and His America*, 141; *New York Times*, January 1, 1899.

21. William McKinley to Dr. C. Stewart, June 12, 1899, William McKinley Papers, vol. 87, no. 132, Library of Congress; Sinkler, *The Racial Attitudes of American Presidents*, 289–307.

22. Prather, *We Have Taken a City*; Gould, *The Presidency of William McKinley*, 157.

23. *Cleveland Gazette*, August 11, 1900; *Indianapolis World*, August 18, 1900.

24. *Oregonian*, September 2, 1899; Gould, *The Presidency of William McKinley*, 156–158.

25. Merrill, *The Republican Command 1897–1913*; Morris, *The Rise of Theodore Roosevelt*, 13–15.

26. Theodore Roosevelt to Albert Tourgee, November 11, 1900, Theodore Roosevelt Papers, Library of Congress; Dyer, *Theodore Roosevelt and the Idea of Race*, 100.

27. *Lesley's Illlustrated Weekly*, May 19, 1900; Tillman, "The Race Question," 439–446.

28. Spahr, *America's Working People*, 112–115.

29. Baldwin, *The Fire Next Time*, 22.

30. *Cleveland Gazette*, January 27 and April 21, 1900; Williamson, *The Crucible of Race*, 181–184.

31. Williamson, ibid., 181–184; *Nation*, December 14, 1899.

32. Newby, *Jim Crow's Defense*, 103; Hair, *Carnival of Fury: Robert Charles and the New Orleans Race Riot of 1900*, 107.

33. *Harper's Weekly*, December 23, 1899; Oregonian, Dec. 7, 1899; Williamson, *The Crucible of Race*, 181–184.

34. Williamson, ibid.; Woodward, *Origins of the New South*, 211.

35. *Oregonian*, July 24, 1899.

36. *New York Times*, December 1, 1899.

37. Newby, *The Development of Segregationist Thought*, 130.

38. Prather, *We Have Taken a City*, 79.

39. Copeland, ed., *Democracy in the Old South: Essays of Fletcher Melvin Green*; Mandle, *Not Slave, Not Free*, 8.

40. Diner, *A Very Different Era*, 125–127; Dunbar, "Negro Life in Washington."

41. Lynch, *The Black Urban Condition*, 7–8.

42. Baker, *Following the Color Line*, 6, 155–175.

43. Smock, *Booker T. Washington in Perspective*, 17–164; *New York Times*, December 2, 1899.

44. Smock, ibid., 103–111; Gould, *The Presidency of William McKinley*, 28.

45. *Harper's Weekly*, October 27, 1900.

46. Washington, "The Case of the Negro," 55; Smock, *Booker T. Washington in Perspective*, 112; *Harper's Weekly*, October 23 and December 11, 1898.

47. Washington, "Education Will Solve the Race Problem," and "Signs of Progress Among the Negroes," 472–477; Dixon, *The Leopard's Spots*, 61.

48. Spahr, *America's Working People*, 106.

49. Mandle, *Not Slave, Not Free*, 8–19; Kuzirian, *Taking Sides*, 37; Baker, *Following the Color Line*, 191.

50. Diner, *A Very Different Era*, 137, 148–192; *Atlanta Journal*, August 1–15, 1900.

51. Grossman, *Land of Hope: Chicago, Black Southerners and the Great Migration*, 16, 165; *New York Times*, March 21, 1900.

52. Slemons, "The Industrial Color-Line of the North"; Ringer, *"We the People" and Others*, 265; Thernstrom, *The Other Bostonians*, 182–193.

53. Sholty, "Colored People in Baltimore, Maryland," 519–529; Foner, *Organized Labor and the Black Worker, 1619–1973*, 64–74, 118–120; Grossman, *Land of Hope*.

54. Sholty, "Colored People in Baltimore, Maryland"; *New York Times*, December 3, 1899.

55. Baker, *Following the Color Line*, 125; *New York Times*, December 3, 1899; *Sporting News*, February 17, 1900.

56. *Harper's Weekly*, May 29, 1900.

57. *Atlanta Journal*, May 5, 1900; *Nation*, June 14, 1900; *Cleveland Gazette*, May 19, 1900.

58. *Atlanta Journal*, May 9–11, 1900.

59. *Raleigh News and Observer*, July 2–August 5, August 19, 1900; *Harper's Bazaar*, November 25, 1900.

60. Hair, *Carnival of Fury*, 1–98; *New Orleans Times and Democrat*, July 25–27, 1900; *New Orleans Daily Picayune*, July 25– 27, 1900.

61. Hair, *Carnival of Fury*, ibid.

62. Ibid.

63. Ibid.; *Cleveland Gazette*, August 4, 1900.

64. *New York Times*, August 16 and 17, 1900; *Nation*, August 23, 1900.

65. *New York Times*, ibid.

66. *New York Times*, August 27, 1900; *Cleveland Plain Dealer*, August 27, 1900; *Nation*, August 23, 1900.

67. *Cleveland Plain Dealer*, August 23–25, 1900.

68. *Cleveland Gazette*, November 17, 1900.

69. *Atlanta Journal*, August 31, 1900; Benjamin Tillman, "Causes of Southern Opposition to U.S. Imperialism."

70. *New York Times*, August 10, 1900; Diner, *A Very Different Era*, 148, 199; *Atlanta Journal*, August 18, 1900; *Nation*, August 10, 1900.

71. Cable, *A Southerner Looks at Negro Discrimination*, 11.

72. Diner, *A Very Different Era*, 101; *Report of the Commissioner of Education for the Year, 1900–1901*, Washington, 1902 1, xxxx; Williamson, *The Crucible of Race*, 397–415; *Nation*, April 26, 1900.

73. Cash, *The Mind of the South*.

74. Winant, *Racial Conditions: Politics, Theory, Comparisons*, 11.

75. Williamson, *The Crucible of Race*, 286–306.

76. Diner, *A Very Different Era*, 137–138; Grossman, *Land of Hope*, 25–26.

Chapter 9

1. *London Times*, May 12, 1898; May, *Imperial Democracy*, 229.

2. May, 228–230; 268; Corry, *1898: Prelude to a Century*, 120. Healy, *The United States in Cuba 1898–1902*, 32.

3. LaFeber, *The New Empire*, 81–102, 360; Stead, *The Americanization of the World, or the Trend of the Twentieth Century*; *Lesley's Illustrated Weekly*, March 17, 1900.

4. *Nation*, November 8, 1900; LaFeber, *The New Empire*, 176–185, 412; Conant, "Can New Openings Be Found for Capital?"

5. May, *Imperial Democracy*, 187; Rosenberg, *Spreading the American Dream: American Economic and Cultural Expansion 1890–1945*, 21.

6. LaFeber, *The New Empire*, 301; Healy, *The United States in Cuba*, 64.

7. LaFeber, ibid., 167; Pratt, *Expansionists of 1898: The Acquisition of Hawaii and the Spanish Islands*, 237–257; *New York Chamber of Commerce Bulletin*, June 17, 1898; Healy, *The United States in Cuba*, 192–200.

8. LaFeber, *The New Empire*, 325.

9. Rosenberg, *Spreading the American Dream*, 28; Healy, *The United States in Cuba*, 135.

10. "The Influence of the Western World on China," *Century*, September 1900. Ironically, it fell to John Barrett, a former U.S. ambassador to Siam and one of the leading boosters of trade with China, to remind his countrymen that "Christianity and civilization in their forward movement appeal to us in this crisis even more than commercialism and trade conquest." In "What America Has at Stake in China," *Harper's Weekly*, August 11, 1900. See also Strong, *Expansion Under New World Conditions*.

11. *Congregationalist*, August 18, 1898; Rosenberg, *Spreading the American Dream*, 7.

12. Beveridge, "The American Army Officer in Action."

13. *Saturday Evening Post*, June 12, 1900, and March 24, 1900.

14. Ibid.

15. Post, "Guam and Its Governor."

16. *Collier's*, August 18, 1900.

17. McGregor, *1898–1998: Rethinking the United States in Paradise*; Charles Allen to William McKinley, August 26, 1899, McKinley Papers, Library of Congress; Williams, "The Outlook in Cuba."

18. *Nation*, April 1, 1901, 38.

19. Hodgson, *The Colonel: The Life and Times of Henry Stimson 1867–1950*, 1990, 51; Elihu Root to William McKinley, August 17, 1899, William McKinley Papers, vol. 31, no. 7057–58; Foner, *The Spanish-Cuban-American War and the Birth of American*

Imperialism, 1895–1902, 417. William A. Williams, in *The Contours of American History*, eloquently discusses the nineteenth-century U.S. concept of "destiny."

20. William James, in a letter to the *Boston Herald*, February 1900, in *The Philippines Reader*; Schirmer; Clark, *America's Gilded Age*, 175; Hodgson, *The Colonel*, 151.

20a. Morgan. *William McKinley and His America*, 295; McKinley told U.S. Senator George Hoar of Massachusetts, "Japan has her eye on the islands. Her people are crowding in them."

21. Nevins, *Grover Cleveland*, 194; Morgan, *William McKinley and His America*, 296; Pratt, *Expansionists of 1898*; Welch, *Response to Imperialism*; *The United States and the Philippine-American War, 1899–1902*, 54–55.

22. Foner, *The Spanish-Cuban-American War*, 417–420; Ziff, *The American 1890s*, 24; Healy, *The United States in Cuba*, 241–247; Welch, *Response to Imperialism*, 49–51.

23. *Harper's Weekly*, February 1898; Pratt, *Expansionists of 1898*, 289; *Nation*, March 8, 1900.

24. Tillman, "Bryan or McKinley: Causes of Southern Opposition to Imperialism," 439–446.

25. Welch, *Response to Imperialism*, 61–62, 77–78; Schurz, "Peculiar Institutions"; Andrew Carnegie, "Americanism Versus Imperialism," 1–13.

26. Foner, *The Spanish-Cuban-American War*, 428; *American Federationist*, October 5, 1898, 92.

27. Rosenberg, *Spreading the American Dream*; Clark, *America's Gilded Age*, 172; Morgan, *William McKinley and His America*, 405–440.

28. Morgan, ibid., 403.

29. Pratt, *Expansionists of 1898*, 231; LaFeber, *The New Empire*, 301–332; Gould, *The Presidency of William McKinley*, 243–244.

30. Leech, *In the Days of McKinley*, 184; Morgan, *William McKinley and His America*, 435–445; Gould, Ibid.

31. Ibid., 237; McKinley, Annual Message to Congress, December 3, 1899; *New York Times*, December 4, 1899; Rosenberg, *Spreading the American Dream*, 27.

32. *Saturday Evening Post*, September 30, 1899. William McKinley, in a message to General Otis and Admiral Dewey, dated January 8, 1899, wrote, "Our obligation as guardian was not lightly assumed."

33. William McKinley, Annual Message to Congress, December 8, 1899, McKinley Papers, Library of Congress, *New York Times*, December 4, 1899; Koenig, *A Political Biography of William Jennings Bryan*, 207, 300; 123; Ashby, *William Jennings Bryan: A Champion of Democracy*, 80–84.

34. Louis A. Perez Jr. quoted in "New Wave of Research Changes Views of Cuba," *Chronicle of Higher Education*, January 8, 1999; Perez, *Cuba Between Two Empires, 1878–1902*, 212–227.

35. Leech, *In the Days of McKinley*, 190–200; Healey, *The United States in Cuba*, 8, 53; Foner, *The Spanish-Cuban-American War*, 417–422; Gould, *The Presidency of William McKinley*, 442; *Saturday Evening Post*, April 19, 1900.

36. Foner, *The Spanish-Cuban-American War*, 339. War correspondent Stephen Crane sent this dispatch to the *New York World*, July 14, 1899: "Both officers and privates have the most lively contempt for the Cubans. They despise them." *Nation*, November 23, 1899.

37. Foner, ibid., 396; Thomas, *Cuba: The Pursuit of Freedom*, 455–470; *Nation*, December 3, 1900; Pepper, *Literary Digest*, 1900, 96; Perez., *Cuba and the United States: Ties of Singular Intimacy*, 94–100. Healy, *The United States in Cuba*, 82.

38. *McClure's*, February 1900; Perez, *Cuba Between Two Empires*, 281, 301–306.

39. Foner, *The Spanish-Cuban-American War*, 450–475; Leonard Wood to Orville Platt, December 6, 1900, Wood Papers, Library of Congress.

40. Leonard Wood to William McKinley, February 6, 1900, Root Papers, Manuscript Division, Library of Congress.

41. *Nation*, June 21, 1900.

42. *Collier's*, December 1, 1900; Foner, *The Spanish-Cuban-American War*, 526.

43. Perez, *Cuba and the United States: Ties of Singular Intimacy*, 103–107; Thomas, *Cuba*, 470; *Nation*, December 3, 1900; Foner, *The Spanish-Cuban-American War*, 540–545; Leopold. *Elihu Root and the Conservative Tradition*, 3–12.

44. Foner, *The Spanish-Cuban-American War*, 540–546, 560.

45. Paterson, *Contesting Castro: The United States and the Triumph of the Cuban Revolution*, 5.

46. Perez, *Cuba and the United States*, 180–201; Thomas, *Cuba*, 470; Paterson, *Contesting Castro*, 549.

47. Paterson, ibid., 230.

48. Gould, *The Presidency of William McKinley*, 243; May, *Imperial Democracy*, 252.

49. Traxel, *A Very Different Age*, 283; May, *Imperial Democracy*, 255.

50. Gould, *The Presidency of William McKinley*, 182; May, ibid.; Riccards, *The Ferocious Engine of Democracy: A History of the American Presidency*, 359.

51. Gould, *The Presidency of William McKinley*, 146.

52. Ibid., 214; *Nation*, February 16 and March 8, 1900; Traxel, *A Very Different Age*, 283; *Harper's Weekly*, July 1, 1899; Annual Message to Congress, December 3, 1899; Foner, *The Spanish-Cuban-American War*, 33, 420–425; *Oregonian*, August 30, 1899; Healy, *The United States in Cuba*, 226.

53. May, *Imperial Democracy*, 261.

54. Morgan, *William McKinley and His America*, 432; Schirmer, *Republic or Empire: American Resistance to the Philippine War*, 125–132; *Oregonian*, August 30, 1899.

55. Schirmer, ibid., 112–115; Welch, *Response to Imperialism*, 14–19.

56. *Harper's Weekly*, February 25, 1899.

57. *Nation*, December 28, 1899.

58. Storey and Lichauco, *The Conquest of the Philippines by the United States, 1898–1925*, 104–105.

59. *Lesley's Illustrated Weekly*, March 17 and 31, 1900; Leopold, *Elihu Root and the Conservative Tradition*; *Nation*, April 26 and August 16, 1900; *Oregonian*, September 2, 1899.

60. *Oregonian*, July 25, 1899; Arthur MacArthur to U.S. Adjutant General, August 30, 1900, William McKinley Papers, Library of Congress; Elihu Root, *The Military and Colonial Policy of the United States*. This is a reprint of the Root speech of March 2, 1900, at Canton, Ohio.

61. *Harper's Bazaar*, September 1, 1900.

62. Gould, *The Presidency of William McKinley*, 141–146; Painter, *Standing at Armageddon*, 46, 389; Constantino, *Historical Myth and Reality*, 31.

63. *Harper's Weekly*, February 4, 1900; Root speech, February 4, 1900.

64. *Lesley's Illustrated Weekly*, June 1900.

65. *Lesley's Illustrated Weekly*, September 1, 1900; Hillyer, "They Died," *Harper's Weekly*, June 17, 1900.

66. Schirmer, *The Philippines Reader*, 112.

67. Elihu Root, *The Military and Colonial Policy of the United States*. This is a reprint of the Root speech of October 1899 at the Marguette Club in Chicago.

68. *Harper's Weekly*, July 1, 1999.

69. John H. Parker to Theodore Roosevelt, October 15, 1899, Theodore Roosevelt Papers, Library of Congress.

70. *Harper's Weekly*, July 1, 1899.

71. *Atlanta Journal*, May 2, 1900; Mark Twain, "To the Person Sitting in the Dark"; *Nation*, July 20, 1900.

72. *Boston Post*, July 18, 1899; *Indianapolis World*, August 18, 1900.

73. *Harper's Bazaar*, July 17, 1900; Painter, *Standing at Armageddon*, 146.

74. *Nation*, October 25, 1900; *Atlanta Journal*, May 2, 1900; *North American Review*, February 1900; Welch, *Response to Imperialism*, 43–57.

75. Welch, ibid.; *Nation*, October 25, 1899; Gould, *The Presidency of William McKinley*, 156.

76. Welch, *Response to Imperialism*, 43–56; Rosenberg, *Spreading the American Dream*, 42–49.

77. Rosenberg, ibid.; Schirmer, *The Philippines Reader*, 25; *Oregonian*, December 6, 1899.

78. *Forum*, July 1900; Constantino, *Historic Myths and Reality*, 7–12; Morgan, *William McKinley and His America*, 404.

79. *Atlanta Journal*, May 4, 1900.

Chapter 10

1. Sladen, *Washington Wife: Journal of Ellen Maury Sladen 1897 to 1919*.

2. New York Times, July 10, 1896; William Jennings Bryan, *The Memoirs of William Jennings Bryan*, 115.

3. Woodruff, *Political Science Quarterly*, 260.

4. Argersinger, *The Limits of Agrarian Radicalism*, 132; Pollack, *Populist Response to Industrial America*, 101–114; Marcus, *The Grand Old Party*.

5. Marcus, ibid., 256; White, "Bryan," McClure's, July 1900; Leech, *In the Days of McKinley*, 86

7. Harper's Weekly, October 13, 1896; Morgan, *William McKinley and His America*, 228–229; Leech, *In the Days of McKinley*, 86.

8. Morgan, *William McKinley and His America*, 230–231.

9. Ashby, *William Jennings Bryan*, 64–71.

10. Ashby, ibid.

11. Ibid.; *Harper's Weekly*, October 3, 1896.

12. Ginger, ed., *William Jennings Bryan Selections*, vi–xvi.

13. *Nation*, August 24, 1900.

14. Glad, *William Jennings Bryan and His Democracy*, 52. Loomis, "The Political Horizon," *Atlantic Monthly*, April 1900; Ginger, ed., *William Jennings Bryan*, xi–xxxii; Bryan, "The Race Problem," *Commoner*, August 2, 1903, 1–2.

15. Gould, *The Presidency of William McKinley*, 48–52, 165.

16. Koenig, *A Political Biography of William Jennings Bryan*, 288.

17. Ashby, *William Jennings Bryan*; Koenig, *William Jennings Bryan*, 288, 329; *Atlanta Journal*, January 5, 1899.

18. *New York Times*, August 2, 1900.

19. Schreiner, *Henry Clay Frick*, 145.

20. Bryan, "The Issues of the Campaign." *Collier's*, July 14, 1900; *New York Times*, January, 8, 1899, and August 2, 1900.

21. White, "Hanna."

22. Ibid.

23. *Nation*, February 1900; Morgan, *William McKinley and His America*, 300–335; Herbert Croly manuscript on Hanna in Hanna Papers, Library of Congress.

24. Marcus, *Grand Old Party*, 251; Rhodes, *The McKinley and Roosevelt Administra-*

tions, 1897–1909, 1–30, 279–288; *Harper's Weekly*, July 27 and August 11, 1900; *Nation*, February 1, 1900; White, "Hanna."

25. *Harper's Weekly*, June 27, 1900; Collier's, July 17, 1900.

26. Morris, *The Rise of Theodore Roosevelt*, 665.

27. Ibid., 679–712.

28. Morgan, *William McKinley and His America*, 403; Morris, *The Rise of Theodore Roosevelt*, 729–730; Rhodes, *The McKinley and Roosevelt Administrations*, 133.

29. Hanna to McKinley, June 25, 1900, McKinley Papers, Library of Congress; Dawes, *A Journal of the McKinley Years*, 2.

30. Henry Cabot Lodge to Theodore Roosevelt, June 29, 1900, Theodore Roosevelt Papers, Library of Congress.

31. Theodore Roosevelt to Mark Hanna, June 27, 1900, Theodore Roosevelt to Edward North Buxton, November 9, 1900, Theodore Roosevelt to J.M. Palmer, August 9, 1900, Theodore Roosevelt Papers, Library of Congress; Morris, *The Rise of Theodore Roosevelt*, 729–730.

32. Ashby, *William Jennings Bryan*, 78–85.

33. *Atlanta Journal*, July 3, 1900.

34. *Collier's*, July 14 and July 21, 1900; *Harper's Weekly*, August 18, 1900; Bryan, *Memoirs*, 123.

35. Ashby, *William Jennings Bryan*, 75–90.

36. *New York Times*, August 9, 1900.

37. Gould, *The Presidency of William McKinley*, 225.

38. *Harper's Weekly*, October, 21, 1900; *Nation*, August, 23, 1900.

39. Ashby, *William Jennings Bryan*, 90–92; *Saturday Evening Post*, July 21, 1900.

40. Gould, *The Presidency of William McKinley*, 225–226.

41. Ibid., 218; O'Connor, *The Spirit Soldiers*, 1–30; *Nation*, September 27, 1900.

42. Gould, *The Presidency of William McKinley*, 223–224; *Harper's Weekly*, November 10, 1900.

43. Potter, "Chinese Traits and Western Blunders," *Century*, October 1900, 929; John Berdan Gardner, *The Image of the Chinese in the United States*, 163; Koenig, *A Political Biography of William Jennings Bryan*, 329.

44. *Atlanta Journal*, May 8, 1900; Koenig, *A Political Biography of William Jennings Bryan*, 334; *Harper's Weekly*, June 27, 1900; *Nation*, June 14, 1900; *Harper's Weekly*, July 21, 1900.

45. Gluck, *John Mitchell, Miner*; Ramirez, *When Workers Fight Back*, 28.

46. Mark Hanna to William McKinley, July 27, 1900, William McKinley Papers.

47. *Nation*, September 6, 1900; *Oregonian*, September 25, 1899.

48. *Nation*, October 25, 1900.

49. Merrill, *The Republican Command*, 77; *Nation*, November 15, 1900.

50. Koenig, *William Jennings Bryan*, 334.

51. *Nation*, August 10, 1900; *Harper's Weekly*, October 22, 1900.

52. Gould, *The Presidency of William McKinley*, 225–229; Koenig, *William Jennings Bryan*, 309; *Collier's*, November 17, 1900; *Lesley's Weekly*, October 1900.

52. *Chicago Record*, October 16, 1900.

53. *Sioux Falls Daily Press* and *Cleveland Plain Dealer*, October 17–19, 1900.

54. Mark Hanna to Theodore Roosevelt, October 24, 1900, Roosevelt Papers, Library of Congress; *Harper's Weekly*, October 22, 1900; Heath, "The Lessons of the Campaign," 392.

55. George Cortelyou Papers, Library of Congress, September 7, 1900; Bailey, "Was the Presidential Election of 1900 a Mandate on Imperialism?," 47–51.

56. Koenig, *A Political Biography of William Jennings Bryan*, 343; *Harper's Weekly*, October 20, 1900; Lewis Gould, *The Presidency of William McKinley*, 230.

57. Central Committee of the Socialist Party, *Eugene Victor Debs, The Centennial Year*, 199; Kipnis, *The Socialist Movement in America 1890–1912*, 99; Shannon, *The Socialist Party in America*.

58. Bryan, "The Election of 1900," 789–798.

59. Bryan, ibid.; Gould, *The Presidency of William McKinley*, 230; *Saturday Evening Post*, July 7, 1900.

60. Marcus, *The Grand Old Party*, 257.

61. Burnham, *Critical Presidential Elections and the Mainsprings of American Politics*.

62. *Nation*, December 1900; Mark Hanna to William McKinley, November 6, 12:48 p.m., McKinley Papers, Library of Congress.

63. *Saturday Evening Post*, January 5, 1901.

64. Ibid.; Chernow, *Titan*, 432; Laidler, *Concentration in America*, 37.

65. *Nation*, December 6, 1900; George Cortelyou Papers, Library of Congress; *Philadelphia Ledger*, November 11, 1901; Constantino, *History, Myths and Reality*, 62; Schirmer, 225–259; Hoar's May 22, 1902 speech is in Storey and Lichuaco, *The Conquest of the Philippines*, 151.

66. Hanna speech, Asbury Park, New Jersey, *Harper's Weekly*, September 1900.

Epilogue

1. Thompson, "Consumed."

2. Conant, "Recent Economic Tendencies."

3. Wells, *The Future in America*, 128, 248; "The New American Consciousness," *New York Times Magazine*, November 1, 1998.

4. *New York Times*, March 9, 1997; Yergin and Stanislaw, *The Commanding Heights*, 6; *Wall Street Journal*, February 26, 1997; "Corporate Dreams Converge in One Idea: It's Time to Do a Deal," *Wall Street Journal*, February 26, 1997; *Honolulu Advertiser*, January 2, 1999; "Frenzy of Merger Buyouts Has Shaken Up the U.S. Economy," *Honolulu Advertiser*, June 6, 1999.

5. Shulman, *Owning the Future*.

6. Bradsher, "Rich Get Richer"; *Honolulu Advertiser*, September 4, 1999; Borger, "Money Makes the Polls Go Round."

7. *Honolulu Advertiser*, September 6, 1999; "Workers Losing American Struggle for Prosperity," *Honolulu Star Bulletin*, June 2, 1995; "Is It a New Economy for Working America?" *Economic Policy Institute Journal* (winter 1999): 1–3. It is also germane to note that one-tenth of American households own 82 percent of all stocks: *Economic Policy Institute Journal* (spring 1999): 1.

8. *Honolulu Advertiser*, January 10, 1999; Economic Policy Institute economist Jared Bernstein argues: "Middle and low wage workers have been losing ground in this economy for two decades, with the exception of the last couple of years." *EPI Journal* (spring 1999): 7; Herbert, "More Poor Children: Shameful U.S. Statistic."

9. Newman, *Falling from Grace*.

10. Elliott, "Ease Up Before the Workers Crack Up"; "Young Workers Want to Advance," *Washington Post*, September 1999.

11. Bartlett and Steele, *America: What Went Wrong?*

12. *Honolulu Advertiser*, September 19, 1999.

13. Baker, *Following the Color Line*, 49; *Harper's Weekly*, February 10, 1900.

14. *Saturday Evening Post*, 1900, n.d.

15. Omi and Winant, *Racial Formation in the United States*, 114–136.

16. Ibid.; Fredrickson, *The Black Image in the White Mind*, xiii.

17. " 'White Privilege Builds Tensions,' Race Panel Says," *Honolulu Advertiser*, September 18, 1998, A3; King, "Fear and Hatred Here at Home"; Kent, "To Polarize a Nation: Racism, Labor Markets, and the State in the U.S. Political Economy, 1965–1986," 55–68.

18. Kent, ibid; Huckfeldt and Weitzel. *Race and the Decline of Class in America.*

19. Kent, "To Polarize a Nation."

20. Gates and West, *The Future of the Race*, viii; "More in U.S. Are in Prisons, Report Says," *New York Times*, May 5, 1999; Fortune, *Harper's Weekly*, February 10, 1900.

21. Levin and McDevitt, *Hate Crimes: The Rising Tide of Hate*; Marable, "Ethnic Identity in America."

22. *Washington Post*, February 26, 2000.

23. The Henson document is dated October 15, 1900, and is found in the McKinley Papers at the Library of Congress.

24. Rosenberg, *Spreading the American Dream*, 37.

25. Schirmer, *Republic or Empire*, 3; Welch, *Response to Imperialism*, 152–153; Williams, *The Tragedy of American Diplomacy*, 35–38.

26. Rosenfeld, "Standing Watch on Imperium."

27. Galbraith, *The Good Society: The Humane Agenda*, 102.

28. Maier, "Democracy and Its Discontents; A Moral Crisis," 48–64. In one poll two-thirds of Americans agreed, "The government is pretty much run by a few big interests looking after themselves." ("Is There a Crisis?" *Economist*, July 1999).

29. *New York Times*, Nov. 1, 1999, "The New American Consensus," *New York Times*, May 1, 1998. John Jay Chapman, 98.

30. Norman Birnbaum, *The Radical Renewal: The Politics of Ideas in Modern America*, 109; Harrington, *The Dream of Deliverance in American Politics*, 15–25.

31. *Harper's Weekly*, June 16, 1900.

Bibliography

Adams, James Truslow. *The Epic of America*. Boston: Little, Brown, 1931.

Adney, Tappen. "The Summer Rush to Nome." *Collier's*, July 21, 1900.

American Federation of Labor. *Report of the Proceedings of the 20th Annual Convention of the American Federation of Labor*. Louisville, KY, December 6–15, 1900, Washington, DC: 1900.

Argersinger, Peter. *The Limits of Agrarian Radicalism: Western Populism and American Politics*. Lawrence: University of Kansas Press, 1991.

Armstrong, John A. *Nations Before Nationalism*. Chapel Hill: University of North Carolina Press, 1982.

Ashby, Leroy. *William Jennings Bryan: A Champion of Democracy*. New York: Twaiyne, 1987.

Atkinson, W.T. "The Atlanta Exposition." *North American Review*, October 1895.

Auchincloss, Louis. *The Vanderbilt Era: Profiles of a Gilded Age*. New York: Scribners, 1989.

Bailey, Thomas A. "Was the Presidential Election of 1900 a Mandate on Imperialism?" *Mississippi Valley Historical Review* 4 (June 1937): 47–51.

Baker, Ray Stannard. "The Barometer of Business." *Harper's Weekly*, April 21, 1900.

———. "The New Prosperity." *McClure's*, May 1900, 86.

———. *Following the Color Line*. New York: Harper and Row, 1906.

Baldwin, James. *The Fire Next Time*. New York: Dial, 1963.

Banner, Lois W. *American Beauty*. New York: Knopf, 1983.

———. *Women in Modern America: A Brief History*. New York: Harcourt Brace College Publishers, 1995.

Barraclough, Geoffrey. *An Introduction to Contemporary History*. Middlesex, UK: Penguin, 1967.

Barrett, John. "What America Has at Stake in China." *Harper's Weekly*, August 11, 1900.

Bartlett, Ronald, and James B. Steele. *America: What Went Wrong?* Kansas City: Andrews and McMeel, 1992.

Beck, Roy. *The Case Against Immigration*. New York: W.W. Norton, 1995.

Beebe, Lucius. *The Big Spenders*. Garden City, NY: Doubleday, 1966.

Beisner, Robert, *Twelve Against Empire: The Anti-Imperialist 1898–1903*. New York: McGraw-Hill, 1968.

Bellah, Robert N.; Richard Madsen; William M. Sullivan; Ann Swidler; and Steven M. Tipton. *Habits of the Heart: Individualism and Commitment in American Life*. New York: Harper and Row, 1986.

Beveridge, Albert. "The American Army Officer in Action." *Saturday Evening Post*, April 21, 1900.

———. "The World and the Young Man." *Saturday Evening Post*, September 3, 1900.

Bingham, Robert. *An Ex-Slaveholder's View of the Negro Question*. Theodore Roosevelt Papers, Library of Congress, July 1900.

Birnbaum, Norman. *The Radical Renewal: The Politics of Ideas in Modern America*. New York: Pantheon, 1988.

Blumin, Stuart M. *The Emergence of the Middle Class Social Experience in the American City, 1760–1900*. New York: Cambridge University Press, 1989.

Borden, Morton, and Otis L. Graham Jr. *Speculations on American History*. Lexington MA: D.C. Heath, 1977.

Borger, Julian. "Money Makes the Polls Go Round." *Guardian Weekly*, August 5–11, 1999.

Bradsher, Keith. "Rich Get Richer." *Honolulu Star-Bulletin*, April 17, 1995.

Bremner, Robert H. *From the Depths: The Discovery of Poverty*. New York: New York University Press, 1956.

Brooks, John Graham. *The Conflict Between Private Monopoly and Good Citizenship*, New York: Houghton-Mifflin, 1900.

———. *As Others See Us: Studies in Labor and Socialist Movements*. New York: Macmillan & Co., 1907.

———. *The Social Unrest: Studies in Labor and Socialist Movements*. New York: Houghton-Mifflin, 1907.

Brown, Henry C. *In the Golden Nineties*. Hastings-on-Hudson: Valentine's Manual, 1927.

Bryan, William Jennings. "The Issues of the Campaign." *North American Review*, June 1900.

———. "The Election of 1900." *North American Review*, December 1900, 789–798.

———. "The Race Problem." *Commoner*, August 2, 1903.

———. *Memoirs of William Jennings Bryan*. Philadelphia: John C. Winston, 1925.

Burnham, Walter Dean. *Critical Presidential Elections and the Mainsprings of American Politics*. New York: W.W. Norton, 1970.

———. *The Current Crisis in American Politics*. New York: Oxford University Press, 1982.

Cable, George W. *A Southerner Looks at Negro Discrimination*. (First published in 1888 as "The Negro Question.") New York: International, 1946.

Cameron, Ardis. *Laboring Women in Lawrence, Massachusetts, 1860–1912*. Urbana: University of Illinois Press, 1993.

Cande, Helen Churchill. "Oklahoma." *Atlantic Monthly*, September 1900.

Carnegie, Andrew. "Americanism Versus Imperialism." *North American Review*, March 1899, 1–13.

———. "The Duty of the Men of Wealth." *North American Review*, June 1889, 657–662.

Carroll, Charles. *The Negro: A Beast or in the Image of God*. New York: American Book and Bible House, 1900.

Cash, W.A. *The Mind of the South*. Chapel Hill: University of North Carolina, 1940.

Cashman, Sean Dennis. *America in the Gilded Age*. New York: New York University Press, 1993.

Casson, Herbert. *Arena*, January 1900.

Central Committee of the Socialist Party. *Eugene Victor Debs, The Centennial Year*. 1956.

Chan, Suecheng. *Peoples of Color in the American West*. Lexington, MA: D.C. Heath, 1994.

Chan, Suecheng and Scott Wong. *Claiming America: Constructing Chinese American Identity During the Exclusion Era*. Philadelphia: Temple University Press, 1998.

Chandler Jr., Alfred. *The Visible Hand: The Managerial Revolution in American Business*. Cambridge: Harvard University Press, 1977.

Chapman, John Jay. *Causes and Consequences*. New York: Charles Scribner and Sons, 1898.

————. "Social Results of Commercialism" *New York Times*, February 20 and 27, 1898.

————. "Between Elections." *Atlantic Monthly*, January 1900.

————. *Selected Writings of John Jay Chapman*. New York: Farrar, Straus, Cudahay, 1957.

Cheng, Tsu-Wu. "Chink." New York: World, January 1972.

Chernow, Ron. *Titan: The Life of John D. Rockefeller Jr.* New York: Random House, 1998.

Clark, John Bates. *The Problem of Monopoly*. New York: Columbia University Press, 1904.

————. *Political Science Quarterly*. March, 1900.

————. *Saturday Evening Post*, October 7, 1900.

Clark, Judith Freeman. *America's Gilded Age: An Eyewitness History*. New York: Oxford University Press, 1992.

Cohen, Rose. *Out of the Shadows: A Russian Jewish Girlhood on the Lower East Side*. Ithaca: Cornell University Press, 1995.

Cleghorn, Kate Holladay. "New Immigrants." *Atlantic Monthly*, October 1900, 535.

Collier, William Miller. *The Trust*. New York: Baker and Taylor, 1900.

Commager, Henry Steele, ed. *Lester Ward and the Welfare State*. Indianapolis: Bobbs-Merrill, 1962.

Conant, Charles A. "Can New Openings Be Found for Capital?" *Atlantic Monthly*, November 1899.

————. "Recent Economic Tendencies." *Atlantic Monthly*, June 1900.

Constantino, Renato. *History, Myths and Reality*. Quezon City, Philippines: Kammel, 1995.

Conwell, Russell. *Acres of Diamonds*. New York: Harper and Row, 1915.

Cook, William A. *The Corporation Problem*. Krauss, 1891.

Copeland, J. Isaac, ed. *Democracy in the Old South: Essays of Fletcher Melvin Green*. Nashville: Vanderbilt University Press, 1969.

————. "Corporate Dreams Converge in One Ideal: 'It's Time to do a Deal.'" *Wall Street Journal*, February 26, 1997.

Corry, John A. *1898: Prelude to a Century*. New York:, 1998.

Courtelyou, George. Papers, Library of Congress.

Croly, Herbert. Manuscript in the Hanna Papers, Library of Congress.

Cross, Gary. *Time and Money The Making of a Consumer Culture*. London: Routledge, 1993.

Daniels, Roger. *The Politics of Prejudice*. New York: Atheneum, 1962.

Davis, Hartley. "Magnificent Newport." *Munsey's*, July 1900, 475–488.

Dawes, Charles. *A Journal of the McKinley Years*. Chicago: Lakeside Press, 1950.

De Forest, Robert W., and Lawrence Veiller. *The Tenement House Problem*. New York: New York State Tenant House Commission, 1900.

De Graffenreid, Claire. "Georgia Cracker in the Cotton Mill." *Century*, 19, (1896): 487–488.

DeKay, M. Charles. "Painting Racial Types." *Century*, 60, no. 2 (June 1900), 169.

De Novo, John. *The Gilded Age and After.* New York: Charles Scribner & Sons, 1985.

de Tocqueville, Alexis. *Democracy in America*. Vol. 2, chap. 8, 35–142. New York: Knopf, 1940.

Diner, Steven. *A Very Different Age: Americans of the Progressive Era*. New York: Hill and Wang, 1997.

Dixon Jr., Thomas. *The Leopard's Spots*. New York: Doubleday, 1903.

Dobson, John M. *Politics in the Gilded Age*. New York: Pralger, 1972.

Dorfman, Joseph. *The Economic Mind in American Civilization*. Vol. 3. New York: A.M. Kelley, 1966.

Dreiser, Theodore. *Sister Carrie*. Cleveland: World, 1927.

Dubnoff, Steven. "A Method of Estimating the Economic Welfare of American Families of Any Composition, 1860–1901." *Historical Methods* 13, no. 3 (summer 1980): 137.

Dunbar, P.L. "Negro Life in Washington." *Harper's Weekly*, January 11, 1900.

Dunning, William. *Essays on the Civil War and Reconstruction and Related Topics*. Gloucester, MA: P. Smith, 1969.

Dyer, Thomas G. *Theodore Roosevelt and the Idea of Race*. Baton Rouge: Louisiana State University Press, 1980.

Economic Policy Institute. "Is It a New Economy for Working America?" *EPI Journal* (winter 1999).

Eidmann, Andrew E. "The Divorce Evil." *Arena*, January 1900.

Elliott, Larry. "Ease Up Before the Workers Crack Up." *Guardian Weekly*, August 28–September 6, 1999.

Ely, Richard T. *Monopolies and Trusts*. New York: Macmillan, 1900.

Emory, Frank. "Our Commercial Expansion." *Munsey's*, January 1900, 537.

Flint, Charles R. "How Business Success Will Be Won in the Twentieth Century." *Saturday Evening Post*, November 17, 1899.

Flower, Benjamin Orange. "A Pilgrimage and a Vision." In *Thought and Writing in the 1890's*, ed. Donald Pizer. Boston: Houghton-Mifflin, 1972.

Flynt, Josiah. "In the World of Graft." *McClure's*, February 1901.

Foner, Philip S. *History of the Labor Movement in the United States*. Vol. 3. New York: International, 1955.

———. *The Spanish-Cuban-American War and the Birth of American Imperialism, 1895–1902*. Vol. 2. New York: Monthly Review Press, 1972.

———. *Organized Labor and the Black Worker 1619–1973*. New York: International, 1974.

Ford, Frank Lewis. "The Vanderbilts and the Vanderbilt Millions." *Munsey's*, January 1900.

Foster, Frank. "Trade Unionism and Social Reform." *American Federationist*, March 10, 1900.

Fox, Daniel M. *The Discovery of Abundance: Simon N. Patten and the Transformation of Social Theory*. Ithaca: Cornell University Press, 1967.

Fredrickson, George. *The Black Image in the White Mind*. New York: Harper and Row, 1971.

Frissell, Hollis. "What Is the Relation of the Indian of the Present Decade to the Indian of the Future?": ARICA, 1900, (also in Frederick Hoxie p. 193).

Gage, Lyman. Papers, Library of Congress.

Galbraith, John Kenneth. *The Good Society: The Humane Agenda*. Boston: Houghton-Mifflin, 1996.

Garanty, John. *The Transformation of American Society 1870–90*. Columbia: University of South Carolina Press, 1968.

Gardner, John Berdan. *The Image of the Chinese in the United States, 1885–1915*. Ann Arbor: University Microfilms, 1961.

Gates, Henry Lewis, and Cornel West. *The Future of the Race*, New York: Knopf, 1996.

Ginger, Ray, ed. *William Jennings Bryan Selections*. Indianapolis: Bobbs-Merrill, 1967.

Girdner, Audrie, and Anne Loftis. *The Great Betrayal: The Evacuation of the Japanese-Americans During World War II*. London: Macmillan, 1969.

Glad, Paul W. *William Jennings Bryan and His Democracy*. Lincoln: University of Nebraska Press.

Gluck, Elsie. *John Mitchell, Miner*. New York: Greenwood Press, 1969.

Goodwyn, Lawrence. *Democratic Promise: The Populist Movement in American History*. New York: Oxford University Press, 1976.

Gould, Lewis L. *The Presidency of William McKinley*. Lawrence: University Press of Kansas, 1980.

Grant, H. Roger. *Self-Help in the 1890s*. Ames: Iowa State University Press, 1983.

Graves, Harmon S. "The College Man's Game." *Saturday Evening Post*, October 28, 1899.

Grever, Israel, ed. *Lester Frank Ward*. New York: Thomas Y. Crowell, 1963.

Grossman, James R. *Land of Hope: Chicago, Black Southerners and the Great Migration*. Chicago: University of Chicago Press, 1989.

Hair, William Ivy. *Carnival of Fury: Robert Charles and the New Orleans Race Riot of 1900*. Baton Rouge: Louisiana State University Press, 1976.

Hamsun, Knut. *The Cultural Life of Modern America*. Cambridge: Harvard University Press, 1969.

Harrington, Mona. *The Dream of Deliverance in American Politics*. New York: Knopf, 1986.

Harrison, Mrs. Burton. "The New Rich Element in New York Society." *Saturday Evening Post*, April 14, 1900.

———. "Society Women in Business." *Saturday Evening Post*, December 15, 1900.

Hayden, Dolores. *Redesigning the American Dream*. New York: W.W. Norton, 1984.

Healy, Donald F. *The United States in Cuba, 1898–1902*. Madison: University of Wisconsin Press, 1983.

Heath, Percy S. "The Lessons of the Campaign." *Forum*, December 1900.

Herbert, Bob. "More Poor Children: Shameful U.S. Statistic." *New York Times*, December 17, 1996.

Higham, John. *Strangers in the Land: Patterns of American Nativism*. New Brunswick, NJ: Rutgers University Press, 1955.

———. *Send These to Me: Jews and Other Immigrants in Urban America*. New York: Atheneum, 1975.

Hill, James. Letter to D.S. Clamont, January 27, 1900. James Hill Papers, Library of Congress.

Hillyer, George. "They Died." *Harper's Weekly*, June 17, 1900.

Hodgson, Godfrey. *The Colonel: The Life and Times of Henry Stimson, 1867–1950*. New York: Knopf, 1990.

Hoffman, Charles. *The Depression of the Nineties: An Economic History*. Westport, CT: Greenwood, 1970.

Hofstadter, Richard. "Manifest Destiny and the Philippines." In *America in Crisis*, ed. Daniel Aron. New York: Alfred A. Knopf, 1952, 172–200.

———. *The Age of Reform: From Bryan to Franklin Delano Roosevelt*. New York: Alfred A. Knopf, 1963.

Hough, E. "The West and Certain Literary Discourses." February 1900.

Hoxie, Fred. *A Final Promise: The Campaign to Assimilate the Indians, 1880–1920*. Lincoln: University of Nebraska Press, 1984.

Huber, Richard. *The American Idea of Success*. New York: McGraw-Hill, 1971.

Huckfeldt, Robert R., and Carol Weitzel. *Race and the Decline of Class in American Politics*. Urbana: University of Illinois Press, 1989.

Hunter, Robert. *Poverty*. New York: MacMillan, 1904.

"The Influence of the Western World on China." *Century*, September 1900.

Jenks, Jeremiah W., and Walter E. Clark. *The Trust Problem*. New York: Doubleday, Doran, 1903.

Johnston, Charles. "The American Psychic Atmosphere." *Arena*, August 1900.

Josephson, Matthew. *The Robber Barons: The Great American Capitalists, 1861–1901*. New York: Harcourt Brace, 1962.

Jenz, Jon B. "Chicago's Furniture Industry and Its Work Force from 1880 to 1910." In *Impressions of a Gilded Age*, ed. Chenetier, et al.

Karp, Abraham. Haven and Home. *The History of the Jews in America*. Northside, NJ: Jason Aronson, 1985.

Karson, Marc. *American Labor Unions and Politics, 1900–18*. Carbondale, IL: Southern Illinois University Press, 1958.

Kasson, John F. *Amusing the Million: Coney Island at the Turn of the Century*. New York: Hill and Wang, 1978.

Keller, Albert Galloway, and Maurice Davie. *Essays of William Graham Sumner*. New York: Archon Books, 1969.

Keller, Morton. *Affairs of State: Public Life in the Late Nineteenth Century in America*. Cambridge: Harvard University Press, 1977.

Kent, Noel J. "To Polarize a Nation: Racism, Labor Markets, and the State in the U.S. Political Economy, 1965–1986." In *The Rising Tide of Cultural Pluralism*, ed. Crawford Young. Madison: University of Wisconsin Press, 1993, 55–68.

King, Colbert I. "Fear and Hatred Here at Home." *Washington Post*, December 26, 1998.

Kipnis, Ira. *The American Socialist Movement, 1897–1902*. Westport, CT: Greenwood Press, 1968.

Kirkland, Edward Chase. *Dream and Thought in the Business Community, 1860–1900*. Ithaca: Cornell University Press, 1956.

———. *Business in the Gilded Age*. 1952.

Kirwan, Albert Dennis. *Revolt of the Rednecks: Mississippi Politics, 1875–1925*. Gloucester, MA: Peter Smith, 1969.

Koenig, Louis. *A Political Biography of William Jennings Bryan*. New York: Putnam, 1971.

Kovel, Joel. *White Racism*. New York: Random House, 1970.

Kurzian, Eugene, and Larry Madaria. *Taking Sides: Clashing Views on Controversial Issues in American History*. 1988.

LaFeber, Walter. *The New Empire: An Interpretation of American Expansion 1860–1898*. Ithaca: Cornell University Press, 1963.

Laidler, Harry. *Concentration of Control in American Industry*. New York: James Y. Crowell, 1931.

Lamoureaux, Naomi. *The Great Merger Movement in American Business, 1895–1904*. New York: Cambridge University Press, 1985.

Lampton, William J. "The Cape Nome Goldfields," McClure's, June 1900, 130–137.

Lasch, Christopher. *The Culture of Narcissism: American Life in an Age of Diminishing Expectations*. New York: W.W. Norton, 1978.

Lears, T. Jackson. *The Culture of Consumption: Critical Essays in American History, 1880–1980*. New York: Pantheon, 1983.

Leech, Margaret. *In the Days of McKinley*. New York: Harper and Row, 1959.

Leopold, Richard W. *Elihu Root and the Conservative Tradition*. Boston: Little, Brown, 1954.

Levin, Jack, and Jack McDevitt. *Hate Crimes: The Rising Tide of Bigotry and Bloodshed*. New York: Plenum, 1993.

Lewis, Michael. *The Culture of Inequality*. Amherst: University of Massachussets Press, 1978.

Lim, Genny. *The Chinese American Experience.* San Francisco: National Conference of Chinese American Studies, 1980.

London, Jack. "Housekeeping in the Klondike." *Harper's Bazaar*, September 8, 1900.

———. "The Class Struggle." *Independent*, no. 5, November 1903, 2603–2610.

Loomis, Henry. "The Political Horizon." *Atlantic Monthly*, April 1900.

Lynch, Hollis. *The Black Urban Condition.* New York: Thomas Y. Crowell, 1973.

Maier, Charles."Democracy and Its Discontents: A Moral Crisis." *Foreign Affairs*, July–August 1994.

Mandle, Jay. *Not Slave, Not Free.* Durham, NC: Duke University Press, 1992.

Marable, Manning. "The Divided Mind of Black America: Race, Ideology and Politics in the post–Civil Rights Era." *Race and Class.* 19–32, 36, no.1 (July–September 1994).

Marcus, Robert D. *The Grand Old Party: Political Structure in the Gilded Age 1880–1896.* New York: Oxford University Press, 1971.

Mathews, William. "Men of Pluck." *Saturday Evening Post*, November 11, 1899.

May, Ernest. *Imperial Democracy: The Emergence of America as a Great Power.* New York: Harcourt Brace & World, 1961.

McChesney, Fred C., and William F. Shughart. *A Statistical Study of Antitrust Enforcement.* Chicago: University of Chicago, 1995.

McCullough, David G. *Truman.* New York: Simon and Schuster, 1992.

McEwen, Arthur. "The Trust as a Step in the March of Civilization." *Munsey's*, January 1900.

McGregor, Davianna Pomaika'i. *1898–1998: Rethinking the United States in Paradise.* Honolulu: American Friends Service Committee, 1999.

McKinley, William. William McKinley Papers, Library of Congress.

McWilliams, Carey. *Prejudice; Japanese Americans: Symbol of Racial Intolerance.* Boston: Little, Brown, 1944.

Meredith, Ellis. "The Feminine Factor." *Arena*, March 1900.

Merrill, Horace Samuel. *The Republican Command, 1897–1913.* Lexington: University of Kentucky Press, 1971.

Miller, Charles Grant. "The Trust Question: Its Development in America." *Arena*, January 1900.

Montgomery, David. *Workers Control in America: Studies in the History of Work, Technology, and Labor Struggles.* New York: Cambridge University Press, 1979.

Moody, J. Carroll, and Alice Kessler-Harris *Perspectives of American History: The Problem of Synthesis.* De Kalb: Northern Illinois University Press, 1989.

Morgan, H. Wayne. *Eugene V. Debs Socialist for President.* Syracuse: Syracuse University Press, 1962.

———. *William McKinley and His America.* Syracuse: Syracuse University Press, 1963.

Morris, Edmund. *The Rise of Theodore Roosevelt.* New York: Coward, McCann, and Geoghegan, 1979.

Nally, Edward C. "Why Young Men Fail." *Saturday Evening Post*, November 4, 1899.

Nelson, Daniel. *Managers and Workers: Origins of the New Factory System in the United States 1880–1920.* Madison: University of Wisconsin Press, 1975.

Nevins, Alan. *Grover Cleveland.* New York: Dodd and Mead, 1932.

Newby, Idus. *Jim Crow's Defense; Anti-Negro Thought in America, 1900–1930.* Baton Rouge: Louisiana State University Press, 1965.

———. *The Development of Segregationist Thought.* Homewood, IL: Dorsey Press, 1968.

Newman, Katherine. *Falling from Grace.* New York: Free Press, 1988.

Noble, David. *The End of American History.* Minneapolis: University of Minnesota Press, 1985.

Ogen, Robert C. "Getting and Keeping a Business Position." *Saturday Evening Post*, March 17, 1900.

O'Connor, Richard. *The Spirit Soldiers*. New York: G. P. Putnam and Sons, 1973.

O'Grady, Joseph. *How the Irish Became American*. New York: Twaiyne, 1973.

Omi, Michael, and Howard Winant. *Racial Formation in the United States*. New York, Routledge, 1994.

Painter, Nell Irvin. *Standing at Armageddon: The United States 1877–1919*. New York: W.W. Norton, 1987.

Parsons, Frank. "Remedies for Trust Abuses," *Arena*, December 1900, 869–872.

Paterson, Thomas G.. *Contesting Castro: The United States and the Triumph of the Cuban Revolution*. New York: Oxford University Press, 1994.

Patten, Simon. *The New Basis of Civilization*. Cambridge, MA: Belknap Press, 1968.

Peck, Harry Thurston. *Twenty Years of the Republic, 1885–1905*. New York: Dodd, Mead, 1924.

Pepper, Charles M. Literary Digest, 1900.

Perez, Louis A. *Cuba Between Two Empires, 1878–1902*. Pittsburgh: University of Pittsburgh Press, 1983.

———. *Cuba and the United States: Ties of Singular Intimacy*. Athens: University of Georgia Press, 1990.

Pessen, Edward. *Three Centuries of Social Mobility in America*. Lexington, MA: D.C. Heath, 1974.

Pew (Joseph) Papers, Series #15, Hagley Museum, Wilmington, Delaware.

Pizer, Douglas. *American Thought and Writing in the 1890s*. New York: Houghton Mifflin, 1994.

Polanyi, Karl. *The Great Transformation*. New York: Octagon, 1980.

Pollack, Norman. *Populist Response to Industrial America*. New York: W.W. Norton, 1962.

———. *The Populist Mind*. Indianapolis: Bobbs-Merrill, 1967.

Post, E.C. "Guam and Its Governor." *Munsey's*, April 1900.

Potter, Henry C. "Chinese Traits and Western Blunders." *Century*, October 1900.

Prather Jr., Leon. *We Have Taken a City*. Cranbury, NJ: Fairleigh Dickinson University Press, 1994.

Pratt, Julius. *Expansionists of 1898: The Acquisition of Hawaii and the Spanish Islands*. New York: Quadrangle Books, 1956.

Ramirez, Bruno. *When Workers Fight Back: The Politics of Industrial Relations in the Progressive Era, 1898–1916*. Westport, CT: Greenwood, Press, 1978.

Reed, Thomas. "Monopolies." *Saturday Evening Post*, February 10, 1900.

———. "Reform by Human Touch." *Atlantic Monthly*, November 1899.

Rensselaer, Mrs. Jorn K. "The Barons of New York Society." *Cosmopolitan*, August 1899.

Rhodes, James Ford. *The McKinley and Roosevelt Administrations, 1897–1909*. New York: Macmillan, 1922

Riccards, Michael. *The Ferocious Engine of Democracy: The American Presidency*. Lanham, MD: Madison Books, 1995.

Riis, Jacob. "The Battle with the Slum." *Atlantic Monthly*, May 1899.

———. "The Genesis of the Gang." *Atlantic Monthly*, September 1899.

Ringer, Benjamin. *"We the People" and Others: Duality and America's Treatment of Its Racial Minorities*. New York: Tavistock, 1983.

Ripley, E.A. "The Making of a Railroad Man." *Saturday Evening Post*, March 24, 1900.

Roediger, David. *Toward the Abolition of Whiteness*. New York: Verso, 1996.

Roosevelt, Theodore. Theodore Roosevelt Papers, Library of Congress.

Root, Elihu. *The Military and Colonial Policy of the United States*. New York: Addison, 1916.

Rosenberg, Emily. *Spreading the American Dream: American Economic and Cultural Expansion, 1890–1945.* New York: Hill and Wang, 1982.

Rosenfeld, Stephen. "Standing Watch on Imperium." *Washington Post*, July 16, 1999.

Rugoff, Milton. *The Gilded Age: Intimate Portraits from an Era of Extravagance and Change, 1880–1890.* New York: Holt, 1989.

Sangster, Margaret. "From a Woman's Viewpoint." *Collier's*, October 20, 1900.

Saxton, Alexander. *The Indispensable Enemy: Labor and the Anti-Chinese Movement in California.* Berkeley: University of California Press, 1971.

Schirmer, Daniel B. *Republic or Empire: American Resistance to the Philippine War.* Cambridge: Schenkman, 1972.

———. *The Philippines Reader: A History of Colonialism, Neocolonialism, Dictatorship and Resistance.* Boston: South End Press, 1987.

Schreiner, Olive. "The Woman Question." *Cosmopolitan*, October 1899.

Schreiner, Samuel A. Jr. *Henry Clay Frick: The Gospel of Greed.* New York: St. Martin's Press, 1995.

Schurz, Carl. "Peculiar Institutions." *Harper's Weekly*, December 18, 1898.

Selz, Harry. "How Trusts Affect Trade." *Saturday Evening Post*, April 21, 1900.

Shannon, David. *The Socialist Party in America.* New York: Macmillan, 1955.

Shaler, Nathaniel. "The Negro Since the Civil War." *Popular Science Monthly*, May–June 1900.

Shelton, Brenda K. *Reformers in Search of Yesterday: Buffalo in the 1890s.* Albany: State University of New York Press, 1976.

Sholty, John R. "Colored People in Baltimore, Maryland." *Catholic World*, June 1989, 519–529.

Shulman, Seth. *Owning the Future.* Boston: Houghton-Mifflin, 1999.

Simkins, Francis Butler. *Pitchfork Ben Tillman, South Carolinian.* Baton Rouge: Louisiana State University Press, 1944.

Sinkler, George. *The Racial Attitudes of American Presidents from Abraham Lincoln to Theodore Roosevelt.* Garden City, NY: Doubleday, 1971.

"The Skyscrapers of New York City" *Collier's*, December 1, 1900.

Sladen, Ellen Maury. *Washington Wife: Journal of Ellen Maury Sladen, 1897 to 1919.* New York: Harper and Row, 1962.

Slemons, James Samuel. "The Industrial Color-Line of the North." *Century*, July 1900.

Smock, Raymond W. *Booker T. Washington in Perspective.*

Spahr, Charles B. *America's Working People.* 1903.

———. *An Essay on The Present Distribution of Wealth.* New York: T.Y. Crowell & Co., 1896.

Spargo, John. *The Bitter Cry of the Children.* New York: Macmillan, 1906.

———. *America's Working People.* Chicago: Charles Kern, 1907.

———. *Capitalist and Laborer: Modern Socialism.* Chicago: Charles Kern, 1907.

Sproat, John G. *The Best Men: Liberal Reformers in the Gilded Age.* New York: Oxford University Press, 1968.

Stead, W.T. *The Americanization of the World, or the Trend of the Twentieth Century.* London: World, 1902.

Stewart, Jane A. "Service Reform in Boston." *Good Housekeeping*, September 1900.

Stewart, Robert. "Clubs and Club Life in New York." *Munsey's*, October 1899.

Storey, Morefield, and Maracial P. Lichauco. *The Conquest of the Philippines by the United States, 1898–1925.* New York: G.P. Putnam's Sons, 1926.

Strasser, Susan. *Satisfaction Guaranteed.* New York: Pantheon, 1989.

Stratton, John Roach. "Will Education Solve the Race Problem?" *North American Review*, June 1900.

Strong, Josiah. *The New Era of the Coming Kingdom*. Hicksville: Regina Press, 1975.
――――. *Expansion Under New World Conditions*. New York: Baker and Taylor, 1900.
Summit County Historical Society, *A Centennial History of Akron*, Akron: 1921.
Sumner, William Graham. *What Social Classes Owe Each Other*. 1883.
Tebbel, John. *From Rags to Riches: Horatio Alger and the American Dream*. New York: Macmillan, 1963.
Ten, Broek Jacobus: Edward M. Barnhart; and Floyd W. Matson. *Prejudice, War and the Constitution*. Berkeley: University of California Press, 1970.
Thatcher, Oliver S. "The Rise of Amateur Athletics in the Middle West." *Saturday Evening Post*, February 17, 1900.
Thernstrom, Steven. *The Other Bostonians: Poverty and Progress in the American Metropolis, 1880–1970*. Cambridge: Harvard University Press, 1973.
Thomas, Hugh. *Cuba: The Pursuit of Freedom*. New York: Harper and Row, 1971.
Thomas, William Hannibal. *The American Negro, What He Was, What He Is, and What He May Become*. New York: Macmillan, 1901.
Thompson, Bob. "Consumed." *Washington Post*, December 20, 1998.
Thompson, Holland. "Life in a Southern Milltown." *Political Science Quarterly*, March 1900.
Tillman, Benjamin. "The Race Question." *North American Review*, October 1900.
――――. "Bryan or McKinley: Causes of Southern Opposition to U.S. Imperialism." *North American Review*, September 1900.
Tolman, William Howe. "What More than Wages?" *Century*, December 1900.
Trachtenberg, Alan. *The Incorporation of America: Culture and Society in the Gilded Age*. New York: Hill and Wang, 1982.
Traxel, David. *1898: The Birth of the American Century*. New York: Knopf, 1998.
――――. *A Very Different Age*. New York: Knopf, 1998.
Traynor, W.J.H. "Policy and Power of the American Protective Association." *North American Review*, June 1896.
Turner, Frederick Jackson. "The Problem of the West." *Atlantic Monthly*, September 1896, 259–290.
Twain, Mark. "To the Person Sitting in the Dark." *North American Review*, February 1900.
United States. Census Office, *Twelfth Census of the U.S., 1900*. Washington, DC: Government Printing Office, 1901.
United States Commissioner of Education, *Report of the Commissioner of Education for the Year 1900–1901*. Washington DC: 1901.
U. S. Industrial Commission. Hearings Before the Industrial Commission. *Preliminary Report*. Washington, DC: Government Printing Office, 1900.
U.S. Industrial Commission, *Report of the Industrial Commission on Trusts, vol. II*. 1901.
U.S. Industrial Comission on Agriculture and Agricultural Labor. *Report no. 10*. Washington DC: U.S.Government, 1901.
Vanderlip, Frank A. "Our New Prosperity." *Saturday Evening Post*, November 25, 1899, 422.
Veblen, Thorstein. *The Theory of the Leisure Class*. New York: Viking Penguin, 1979.
Vreeland, Herbert. "Why Young Men Fail," *Saturday Evening Post*, October 1, 1899.
Ward, Lester. "Plutocracy and Paternalism," *The Forum*, November 1895.
Warner, Charles Dudley. "The Pursuit of Happiness," *Century*, December 1, 1900.
Washington, Booker T. "Signs of Progress Among the Negroes." *Century*, February 1900, 472–477.
――――. "Education Will Solve the Race Problem." *North American Review*, August 1900.
――――. "The Case of the Negro." *Atlantic Monthly*, November 1900.

Weibe, Robert H. *The Search for Order 1877–1920.* New York: Hill and Wang, 1967.

Welch Jr., Richard T. *Imperialists vs. Anti-imperialists: The Debate over Expansionism in the 1890's.* Itasca, IL: F.E. Peacock, 1972.

———. *Response to Imperialism: The United States and the Philippine-American War 1899–1902.* Chapel Hill: University of North Carolina Press, 1979.

Wells, H.G. *The Future in America.* New York: Scribners, 1906.

White, William Allen "Hanna." *McClure's,* November 1900, 60–62.

———. "Croker." *McClure's,* February 1901.

"Why Young Men Fail." *Saturday Evening Post,* October 1 and 28, November 18, 1899.

Williams, Herbert Pelham. "The Outlook in Cuba." *Atlantic Monthly,* n.d., 1899.

Williams, William A. *The Tragedy of American Diplomacy.* Cleveland: World, 1958.

———. *The Contours of American History.* Cleveland: World, 1961.

———. *Empire as a Way of Life.* New York: Oxford University Press, 1980.

Williamson, Joel. *The Crucible of Race; Black White Relations in the American South Since Emancipation.* New York: Oxford University Press, 1984.

Winant, Howard. *Racial Conditions: Politics, Theory, Comparisons.* Minneapolis: University of Minnesota Press, 1994.

Woodruff, Clinton Rogers. *Political Science Quarterly,* June 1900.

Woodward, C. Vann. *Tom Watson: Agrarian Rebel.* New York: Macmillan, 1938.

———. *The Origins of the New South.* Baton Rouge: Louisiana State University Press, 1951.

———. *The Strange Career of Jim Crow.* New York: Oxford Press, 1957.

———. *The Burden of Southern History.* Baton Rouge: Louisiana State University Press, 1993.

Wright, John L. "The Department Store in the East." *Forum,* August 1899.

Wrobel, David M. *The End of American Exceptionalism: Frontier Anxiety from the Old West to the New Deal.* Lawrence: University Press of Kansas, 1993.

Wyllie, Irving. *The Self-Made Man in America.* New Brunswick, NJ: Rutgers University Press, 1954.

Yergin, Daniel, and Joseph Stanislaw. *The Commanding Heights.* New York: Simon and Schuster, 1998.

Ziff, Larzer. *The American 1890s: Life and Times of a Lost Generation.* New York: Viking, 1966.

Index

Plessy v. *Ferguson*, 11, 114
Police Gazette, 25
Politics
  African-Americans and
    black leadership, 122
    Democratic Party, 112–14, 116, 126
    1900/2000 comparison, 187–88
    Populists, 113–14, 126, 130
    Redeemers, 112–14, 130
    Republican Party, 112, 114, 116, 126
  American dream and, 40–44
  corporate trusts and, 66–67, 69, 72–77
    Democratic Party, 67, 72, 73–74
    Progressives, 74–76
    Republican Party, 67, 72, 77
  corruption in, 40–44
  Democratic Party
    African-Americans and, 112–14, 116,
      126
    corporate trusts and, 67, 72, 73–74
    presidential elections, 12, 157, 158,
      166–67, 174, 175
    1900/2000 comparison, 178
  Populists
    African-Americans and, 113–14, 126,
      130
    American dream and, 29
    1890s, 8–9, 12, 197n.9
  Progressives, 74–76
  Redeemers, 112–14, 130
  Republican Party
    African-Americans and, 112, 114, 116,
      126
    corporate trusts, 67, 72, 77
    presidential elections, 158–60,
      163–66, 168–69, 172–73,
      175–76
  upper class participation, 59–60
  working class and, 86, 92
  See also Election, presidential (1896);
  Election,
presidential (1900); *specific names*
Populists
  African-Americans and, 113–14, 126, 130
  American dream and, 29
  1890s, 8–9, 197n.9
    presidential election (1896), 12, 158
Poverty
  class structure and, 51, 201n.4
    working class, 79, 87, 203n.5
  1900/2000 comparison, 183
    racism and, 188
Powell, Colin, 185
Price control, 63, 66–69

Proctor and Gamble, 84
Production expansion, 16, 198n.1
  overproduction, 63, 66
Progressives, 74–76
Puerto Rico, imperialism and, 13, 134
  civilizing mission, 137–38
  1900/2000 comparison, 190, 192
Pullman strike (1894), 10

Quaker Oats, 66
Quay, Matthew, 42, 60, 72

Race riots
  African-Americans, 126–29
  Northern region, 127–29
  Southern region, 126–27
Races of Empire, The (Ripley), 98
Racism
  Anglo-Saxonism, 97–98
  Asian-Americans, 105–8
    Chinese, 105–6
    immigration restrictions, 106, 108
    Japanese, 107–8
    1900/2000 comparison, 185, 186
  assimilation
    European Americans, 96, 99
    Native Americans, 102–3, 104–5
  Chinese Americans, 105–6
    immigration restrictions, 106
  as cultural norm, 94–98
    Anglo-Saxonism, 97–98
    genetic inferiority, 101–2, 103, 110–11
    imperialism and, 98
    Social Darwinism, 98
  1890s, 10–11
  European Americans, 96, 98–102
    assimilation, 96, 99
    Irish, 99–101
    restrictions on, 10–11, 96–97
    working class, 80–81, 84, 89, 97, 98–
      99
  genetic inferiority, 101–2, 103, 110–11
  government policy
    Chinese immigration, 106
    immigration restrictions, 10–11, 96–
      97, 106, 108
    Japanese immigration, 108
    Native American assimilation, 102–3
    Native American education, 103
    Native American reservations, 102–4,
      105
  immigration restrictions
    Chinese Americans, 106
    European Americans, 10–11, 96–97

About the Author

Noel Jacob Kent is professor of ethnic studies at the University of Hawaii at Manoa. His book *Hawaii: Islands Under the Influence* (1983) is recognized as one of the landmark works about Hawaii. He has also written widely about political economy and race relations in the United States. Kent lives in Honolulu with his wife and son.